Population History
OF
New York City

A NEW YORK STATE STUDY

Population History

OF

New York City

IRA ROSENWAIKE

SYRACUSE UNIVERSITY PRESS/1972

Library of Congress Cataloging in Publication Data

Rosenwaike, Ira, 1936-
  Population history of New York City.

  Bibliography: p.
  1. New York (City)—Population—History. I. Title.
  HB3527.N7R66   301.32'9'7471   75-39829
  ISBN 0-8156-2155-8

IRA ROSENWAIKE has been a statistician at the U.S. Bureau
of the Census and the National Center for Health Statistics,
Public Health Service, Department of Health, Education, and
Welfare. He is presently a biostatistician, Maryland
Department of Health and Mental Hygiene.

Manufactured in the United States of America

Contents

GLOSSARY xiii

PREFACE xv

1 THE COLONIAL CITY 1

The Founding   1
Religious and Racial Groups under the Dutch   4
The Settling of Manhattan's Neighbors   5
Population Growth in the English Colony   6
Religious and Racial Groups under the English   9
The Growth of Manhattan's Neighbors   12

2 THE AMERICAN CITY 14

The Revolutionary Period   14
The Nation's Largest City   15
Population Groups   19
Religious Groups   24
New York's Neighbors   28

3 THE "FOREIGN CITY" 33

Growth of the City, 1825-60   33
Components of Natural Increase   37
The Foreign Immigrant   38
The Irish   40
The Germans   43
The Negroes   44
Census Changes, 1845-60   45
Geographic Trends in Manhattan   48
Expansion of the Metropolitan Area   49
Religious Groups   52

4 THE WORLD'S SECOND CITY 55

Growth of Population and Area, 1860-1900   55
Natural Increase   60
Immigration and Emigration   62
Nativity and Parentage   71
Nonwhite Races   76
Ethnic Groups: Natural Increase   78
Ethnic Groups: Geographic Distribution   82
Religious Groups   85
Census Underenumeration   88

5 THE CITY OF FIVE BOROUGHS 90
   Population Growth, 1900-40   90
   Immigration   91
   Internal Migration   99
   Natural Increase   103
   Ethnic Groups   109
   Religious Groups   122

6 THE METROPOLITAN GIANT 131
   Population Growth, 1940-70   131
   Changes in Population Composition   132
   Internal Migration   143
   Natural Increase   150
   Religious Groups   151
   Nativity, Parentage, and Ethnic Origin   159
   The Metropolitan Area   168
   Conclusion   174

APPENDIXES 175
A Birth and Death Statistics, New York City, 1804-1969   175
B Age Distribution of Population by Race, Sex, Nativity, and
      Parentage, New York City, 1910-70   187
C Country of Origin of Foreign Stock, New York City,
      1890-1960   201

BIBLIOGRAPHY 207
   New York History   207
   New York Ethnic Group History and Sociology   208
   Government Statistical Sources   208
   Books   209
   Articles   213
   Census Sources   214

INDEX 217

List of Tables

1. Population of New York County and Kings County by Race, 1698-1771   8
2. Population Comparison of New York State and New York City with Pennsylvania and Philadelphia, 1790-1850   16
3. Population of New York City by Race and Annual Percentage Increase in Intercensal Period, 1786-1820   18
4. Population of Kings County by Town, 1790-1855   31
5. Population of Kings County and Richmond County by Race, 1790-1860   32
6. Population of New York City by Race and Increase in Intercensal Period, 1820-60   36
7. Alien Population, 1825-45, and Foreign-born Population, 1845, in New York City and Kings County   39
8. Deaths and Death Rates of the Foreign-born Population of New York City by Country of Birth, 1845 and 1850   41
9. Birthplace of the Population of New York City, 1845-60   42
10. Birthplace of the Negro Population of New York City, 1850 and 1860   45
11. Birthplace of the Population of Kings County, 1845 and 1850, and of Brooklyn, 1855 and 1860   51
12. Number of Churches and Usual Attendance, Religious Groups in New York City and Kings County, 1855   53
13. Population at 1890 Census Living in Counties Partially or Entirely Absorbed into Greater New York by 1898   58
14. Population Living within the Area Included in the Boroughs of Greater New York as Constituted under the 1898 Act of Consolidation, 1890 and 1900   58
15. Population of Kings County by Subdivision, 1860-90   59
16. Population of Selected Subdivisions of Queens County, 1860-90   60
17. Estimate of the Crude Birth Rate in New York City, Census Years 1880-1900   62
18. Fertility Ratios, White Population of the United States and New York City, 1880-1940   62
19. Population of New York City and Brooklyn, 1860-90, and of Greater New York, 1900, by Nativity   63
20. New York State-born Population of New York City by County of Birth and New York City-born Population of New York State by County of Residence, 1855 and 1875   65
21. New York State-born Population of Kings County by County of Birth and Kings County-born Population of New York State by County of Residence, 1855 and 1875   66
22. New York State-born Population Residing in New Jersey by County of Residence, 1850-80   66

23. Birthplace of the Population of New York City, 1865-90   67
24. Birthplace of the Population of Brooklyn, 1865-90   70
25. Population by Parentage, Color, and Nativity, New York City, 1870-90   72
26. Country of Origin of the Total Population of Foreign or Mixed Parentage, New York City, 1880, and of the White Population, 1890   73
27. Country of Origin of the Native-born Population of Foreign or Mixed Parentage, New York City, 1880, and of the Native-born White Population, 1890   74
28. Native-born Population of Foreign or Mixed Parentage by Country of Birth Distribution of Each Parent, New York City, 1880   76
29. Population of New York City, Kings County, and Richmond County by Race, 1865-90   77
30. Birthplace of the Nonwhite Population of New York City and Brooklyn, 1870 and 1890   78
31. Heads of Families by Color and of White Families by Nativity and Parentage, New York City, 1900; Proportion of United States Total in Each Group Residing in New York City   79
32. Differential Mortality by Country of Birth of Both Parents of Decedents, New York City, 1880-1900   80
33. Death Rates by Broad Age Groups, Population of Irish and German Parentage (According to Country of Birth of Mother), New York City and Brooklyn, 1890   81
34. Marriages Reported for Census Year 1865 by Type of Religious Ceremony, New York City and Kings County   86
35. Parentage of White Heads of Households for the United States by Size of Place, 1900   90
36. Foreign-born Population of New York City by Period of Immigration to the United States, Censuses of 1910-30   93
37. Foreign-born White Population by Period of Immigration to the United States, Principal Countries of Birth; United States and New York City, 1930 Census   94
38. Estimated Net Migration of the Foreign-born Population of New York City by County of Birth, 1900-10 and 1910-20   95
39. Estimated Net Migration of the Foreign-born Population of New York City, 1920-30; Comparison of Vital Statistics Method and Adjusted Census Migrant Method   97
40. Estimated Net Migration of the Foreign-born White Population of New York City by Country of Birth, 1930-40 and 1940-50   98
41. Estimated Net Migration of Native White Population of New York City by Age and Parentage, Census Intervals 1900-40   100
42. Percent of Native White Population of New York City of Foreign or Mixed Parentage by Age, 1890-1950   101
43. Native Population of New York City by State of Birth, 1900-40   102
44. White and Nonwhite Native Population of New York City by State of Birth, 1900 and 1940   103
45. Percent of Total and of Nonwhite Outmigrants (Persons Born in the State and Living in Other States) from Selected States Living in New York City, 1900-40   104
46. Number of Children Under 5 per 1,000 Women 20-44 Years of Age by Selected Characteristics, New York City, 1920   106

47. Crude and Age-adjusted Death Rates of the Foreign-born Population
    10 Years of Age and Over by Country of Birth and Sex, New York State,
    1910   107

48. Crude and Age-adjusted Death Rates by Race and by Selected Origins for
    the White Population, New York City, 1920   108

49. White and Nonwhite Population by Nativity and Parentage, New York City,
    1900, and New York City and Brooklyn Combined, 1890   110

50. Number of Children Under 10 Years Old in Families by Race, Nativity, and
    Parentage of Heads and by Country of Birth for Foreign-born White Heads,
    New York City, 1930   113

51. Estimate of White Population Under 10 Years Old by Generation Status,
    New York City, 1930   114

52. Native White Population with Father Foreign by Country of Birth of Father
    and Number with Mother Native Born, New York City, 1930 and 1940   115

53. Native White Population with Father Foreign by Country of Birth of Father
    and Nativity of Mother (Partly Estimated), New York City, 1900   118

54. Native White Population with Foreign Father by Nativity of Mother, New
    York City, 1900-40   119

55. Native White Population with Father Foreign by Age and Year of Birth
    Cohort and Number with Mother Native Born (Partly Estimated), New York
    City, 1920   120

56. Foreign-born Negro Population of the United States and New York City
    by Period of Immigration, Censuses of 1920 and 1930   121

57. Population of Puerto Rican Birth in the United States and New York City,
    1910-40   121

58. Estimated Percent Distribution by Religion of Total Population and Foreign
    Stock Population from Selected Countries of Origin, New York City, 1900   123

59. Estimated Percent Distribution by Religion of Total Youth Population
    (16-24 Years of Age) by Race and of Foreign Stock Youth Population from
    Selected Countries of Origin, New York City, 1935   125

60. Deaths of White New York City Residents Recorded in New York City,
    Selected Age Groups by Country of Birth and Denomination of Cemetery
    of Burial, 1940   126

61. Estimate of Foreign-born Jewish Population of New York City, 1940   128

62. Comparison of Percent Distribution by Age of Estimated Foreign-born
    Jewish Population and of Census Foreign-born Population Reporting
    Yiddish Mother Tongue, New York, 1940   128

63. Derivation of Estimate of Native-born and of Total Jewish Population
    25 Years of Age and Over, New York City, 1940   129

64. Population of the Boroughs of New York City by Race and Nativity,
    1900-70   133

65. Population of Selected Counties in Metropolitan New York by Race and
    Nativity, 1900-70   134

66. Net Migration of the White Population by Nativity and the Nonwhite
    Population of New York City, 1940-50 and 1950-60   136

67. Net Migration, 1950-60 and 1960-70, by Color: Selected Counties in
    Metropolitan New York   137

68. Persons of Puerto Rican Birth or Parentage by Borough of Residence,
    New York City, 1930, 1950-70   139

69. Race of the Population by Nativity, New York City, 1900-70   141

70. Native Population by Area of Birth and Color, New York City, 1940 and 1960   144

71. White and Nonwhite Native Population by Area of Birth, New York Standard Metropolitan Statistical Area, 1960   144

72. Migration Status, 1935-40, of the 1940 Population of New York City, 5 Years of Age and Older by Color and Nativity   146

73. Migration Status, 1955-60, of the 1960 Population of Metropolitan New York 5 Years of Age and Older by Color   147

74. Number of White Outmigrants 5 Years Old and Over, Principal States of Origin of White Inmigrants to New York Area, 1940 and 1960   148

75. Number of Nonwhite Outmigrants 5 Years Old and Over, Principal States of Origin of Nonwhite Inmigrants to New York Area, 1940 and 1960   148

76. Place of Destination of Outmigrants 5 Years Old and Over From New York Area, 1940 and 1960   149

77. Birth Rates and Fertility Rates by Color and Ethnic Group, New York City, 1950 and 1960   152

78. Birth Rates by Age of Mother for Color and Ethnic Groups in New York City and for Similar Groups Outside the City, 1960   153

79. Percent Distribution by Religion, Population of New York City by Color, 1952   153

80. Estimated Distribution of White Population of New York City by Age Group (1950 Census) and Religion   155

81. Percent Distribution of Deaths of Foreign-born White New York City Residents Recorded in New York City by Country of Birth and Sex According to Denomination of Cemetery of Burial, 1949-51   156

82. Percent Distribution of Deaths of White New York City Residents 25 Years of Age and Over, Recorded in New York City by Nativity, Age, and Sex According to Denomination of Cemetery of Burial, 1949-51   157

83. Percent Distribution of Deaths of Foreign-born White New York City Residents Recorded in New York City With Burial in a Jewish Cemetery by Sex, Age, and Country of Birth, 1949-51   158

84. Estimated Foreign-born Jewish Population by Age, Sex, and Country of Birth, New York City, 1950   159

85. Nativity and Parentage of the Foreign White Stock, New York City, 1900-60   161

86. Percent of Non-Puerto Rican Native White Population of New York City of Foreign or Mixed Parentage by Age, 1950 and 1960   162

87. Population of Italian Foreign Stock by Age Group Expressed as a Census Survival Cohort, New York City, 1930 and 1960   165

88. Cohorts of Native Whites of Foreign or Mixed Parentage, Selected Countries of Origin (of Parents), Aged 5-14 Years and 15-24 Years in 1930, Followed to 1960, New York City   166

89. Population of Italian Foreign Stock in New York SMSA by County of Residence, 1930 and 1960   167

90. Nativity and Parentage of Nonwhite Foreign Stock by Country of Origin, New York City, 1960   168

91. Labor Force Resident in Selected Counties Working in New York City, 1960   170

A-1. Recorded Deaths in New York City, 1804-1900, and in Brooklyn, 1866-1900   176

A-2. Death Rates in New York City and Brooklyn, 1866-1900   177
A-3. Birth and Death Rates in New York City, 1900-69   178
A-4. Recorded Births and Deaths by Color, New York City, 1910-40   179
A-5. Resident Births by Race and Nativity, New York City, 1940-67   180
A-6 Resident Deaths by Race and Nativity, New York City, 1940-67   181
A-7. Recorded Births by Birthplace of Mother, New York City, 1910-32   182
A-8. Recorded White Births by Birthplace of Mother, New York City, 1935-40   183
A-9. Recorded Deaths by Birthplace of Decedent, New York City, 1900-32   184
A-10. Recorded Deaths by Birthplace of Foreign-born White Decedents, New York City, 1935-48   185
A-11. Recorded Births and Deaths of Puerto Ricans by Color, New York City, 1950-69   185
B-1. Age by Race and Sex, New York City, 1910-70   188
B-2. Age and Sex of White Population by Nativity and Parentage, New York City, 1910-60   192
B-3. Age of Foreign White Stock by Nativity for Selected Countries of Origin, New York City, 1930, 1940, and 1960   195
B-4. Age by Color and Sex of Puerto Ricans (Persons of Puerto Rican Birth and Parentage), New York City, 1950 and 1960   197
B-5. Age and Sex of Puerto Ricans (Persons of Puerto Rican Birth and Parentage), New York City, 1970   198
B-6. Age and Sex of White Population Exclusive of Puerto Ricans, New York City, 1950 and 1960   199
C-1. White Population of Foreign or Mixed Parentage by Country of Origin, New York City, 1890 and 1900   202
C-2. Nativity and Parentage of Foreign White Stock by Country of Origin, New York City, 1910-40   203
C-3. Nativity and Parentage of Foreign White Stock by Country of Origin, New York City, 1950 and 1960   205
C-4. Nativity and Parentage of Foreign Stock by Country of Origin, New York City, 1970   206

Glossary

Age-adjusted Death Rate. The age-adjusted death rate is a summary figure which can provide a comparison of mortality among populations that is free of the effect of their age differences. It is the death rate that would have been observed if the age-specific rates for the given year, computed for specified age intervals, had prevailed in a population whose age distribution was the same as that of the standard population.

Age-specific Birth Rates. Also termed age-specific fertility rates, age-specific birth rates take account of the age and sex composition of the population. The denominator is the number of births to mothers in an age category (for instance 20-24 years), the numerator is the number of women of that age in the population. The rate is usually expressed per 1,000 population.

Birth Cohort. A birth cohort is a group of persons born in a specified year (or period of years) which serves to identify the group over time.

Birth Rate. More correctly termed the "annual crude live birth rate," the birth rate is computed by the following formula: number of live births to residents of a given geographic area during a given year/mid-year total population of the given geographic area in that year x 1,000.

Death Rate. More correctly termed the "annual crude death rate," the death rate is computed by the following formula: number of deaths to residents of a given geographic area during a given year/mid-year total population of the geographic area in that year x 1,000.

Migrant and Mover (census definitions). At the 1940 census "migrants" included those persons who in 1935 lived in a county (or quasi-county) different from the one in which they were living in 1940. A quasi-county was defined as a city of 100,000 or more or the balance of the county.

At the 1960 census "movers" referred to all persons whose residence in 1955 differed from that at the census date. A "migrant" was considered any person who moved into or from a specific area in the presentation of metropolitan area statistics and any person who moved to another state in the case of state of residence statistics.

Natural Increase Rate. The natural increase rate is derived simply by subtracting the crude death rate from the crude birth rate.

Net Migration. The estimate of net migration during an intercensal period is derived as a residual of the following formula: net migration = net change - births + deaths. As a residual value the net migration component reflects the net effect of errors in the data used, such as differences in enumeration completeness or accuracy in the two censuses, and incomplete registration of births or deaths.

Illustration: New York City's population was 7,455,000 on April 1, 1940, and 7,892,000 on April 1, 1950, a change of +437,000. Births during the intercensal period numbered 1,359,000 and deaths 811,000. Net migration was 437,000 - 1,359,000 + 811,000, or - 111,000.

In calculating the net migration of a population that is foreign born the equation becomes net migration = net change + deaths. (Births cannot occur since by definition all are born abroad.)

Illustration: The number of Italian-born persons in New York was 390,800 at the 1920 census and 440,200 at the 1930 census, a change of +49,400. Deaths of natives of Italy were estimated to number 47,500 in the intercensal period. Net migration was 49,400 + 47,500 or 96,900.

Net Inmigration. A positive net migration is termed net inmigration. This indicates more arrivals than departures in a particular area.

Net Outmigration. A negative net migration is termed net outmigration. This indicates more departures than arrivals in a particular area.

Preface

In 1653 a small settlement known as New Amsterdam, located at the southern tip of Manhattan Island, was granted legal status by Peter Stuyvesant, governor of New Netherland, as an incorporated city. Thus began the municipal history of the present City of New York—a city whose population has swelled over the centuries on an unparalleled scale, and a city whose successive inhabitants have come from an unprecedented number of racial and ethnic groups. New York's population grew because of the city's fine location, its ideal harbor, and a multitude of favorable economic factors. But these are only pointed out in passing in the following text, which is largely limited to reporting the population changes accompanying the physical expansion of the city.

Not only has New York City grown in size for three centuries, but each phase of its history has brought new elements into its citizenry. Sociologically New York has presented a pattern of invasion and succession on a mass scale. The settlers—chiefly English and Dutch—of the seventeenth and early eighteenth centuries had crystallized by the eve of the American Revolution almost into a new people with a common New World culture. This colonial stock emerged as the archetypal New Yorker, and as the nineteenth century brought its immigrant waves, it constituted the nucleus of the community. In the second third of the nineteenth century the successive failures of the potato crop in Ireland induced a quarter of the population to cross the Atlantic, and even though only a fraction of the emigrants settled in New York City, in numbers the New York Irish surpassed the old stock. When the movement from Ireland waned after the American Civil War, newcomers from Germany took their place. By the close of the nineteenth century natives of Germany and their children constituted the largest single nationality group in New York. But even as the tide from Germany ebbed, immigrants representing two other ethnic groups—Jews and Italians—poured into the city. By the end of the first quarter of the twentieth century these two groups ranked first and second respectively among the population mix of New York.

The tide from Europe diminished to a trickle after being beaten back by harshly restrictive legislation and worldwide depression. The city's demand for low-wage labor then had to be filled internally, and Negroes from America's South and Puerto Ricans from America's Caribbean possession entered in great numbers. The city's ethnic population composition shifted significantly after 1950, in part due to massive white outmigration to the suburbs, in part to continuing inmigration of blacks and Puerto Ricans. By the early 1960s the nonwhite and the Puerto Rican groups together constituted over one-fourth of all residents in the nation's largest city. Once again the typical New Yorker was changing. The present study of the statistical dimensions of three centuries of change, it is hoped, will enable greater understanding of this continuing process.

Although the primary focus here has generally been given to immigration from abroad, internal movement also has played a major role in changing the composition of New York City's population. State-of-birth statistics, available since the mid-nineteenth century, have been a useful tool in measuring internal migration. At the 1940 census, for the first time, persons were asked a question on place of residence five years prior to the census. It thus became possible to ascertain the place of origin of inmigrants to selected areas and the place of destination of outmigrants within a specific period of time. Comparing the number of migrants to and from New York in the same time interval, it became evident that (at least in the recent period) New York was contributing to the rest of the nation a larger stream of migrants than it was receiving.

There is reason to believe that the general pattern of population redistribution through mobility has been consistent for quite some time. The children and grandchildren of earlier generations of immigrants have tended to constitute the bulk of the outward movement. In the eighteenth century descendants of Dutch burghers who felt engulfed by English newcomers moved across the Hudson. In the nineteenth century the children of New Englanders who had settled in New York City were highly mobile; in the present century, the progeny of Southern and East European immigrants spread out across the nation. The continuous outmigration of native New Yorkers has meant that New York, to a considerable extent, has tended to remain heavily dependent on migrants from abroad for its population growth.

Among American cities probably none can match New York in the extent of census data available for analysis. Almost three centuries have passed since the first enumeration was made in the province of New York in 1686. (The earliest returns for New York City, unfortunately, have been lost.) In the ensuing eighty-five years the English provincial government made ten additional head counts. Since 1790, the federal government has conducted a census every ten years, as required by the United States Constitution. The earliest enumerations merely counted the number of people by sex, by color, by free or slave status, and—for males only—whether sixteen years of age and over or under that age. Gradually the method of census-taking altered and the scope of the census began to expand so that by 1850 detailed inquiries were made covering such variables as age, nativity, and occupation. Among numerous queries added in later years were those concerning place of birth of father and mother, year of immigration (of the foreign born), marital status, place of previous residence, education, and income. State censuses, required by the existing New York State Constitution, were inaugurated in 1825 and taken decennially until 1875. These also provide much valuable information, including some topics not available from the federal counts of the period.

The student of New York City's demography is fortunate, too, in having available data from one of the earliest vital registration systems established in the nation. Reliable detailed mortality statistics for the city date back to the first half of the nineteenth century, approximately a century before comparable information became available for the entire United States. On the other hand, reasonably complete registration of births was not accomplished until the early years of the twentieth century, so in this aspect of its statistical knowledge New York does not much precede most of the country.

Census figures and vital statistics make valuable contributions to the study of population change. In addition, demographers can derive other measures of change from such data. In one of the simpler methods of measuring migration—the so-called residual method—natural increase (the excess of births over deaths) is subtracted from the population change between two censuses to calculate net migration. This measure, interpreted as the difference between those who have moved into and out of an area during a specific period of time, can be subject to serious error—overstatement or understatement—produced by differential undercount between censuses.

It must also be mentioned that certain segments of any particular census may be subject to far more deficient reporting than the aggregate population figure. For example, based on information from the adjacent censuses, at the 1940 census the count of native whites classified as having foreign fathers or foreign mothers was seriously short. Thus census data invariably require close examination and careful interpretation if they are not to mislead.

Census figures, the framework for analysis, have been interpreted here in a manner that should enlighten and prove informative to the casual student of New York's population history and at the same time provide valuable documentation to the serious researcher. After the List of Tables is a Glossary which may aid those not entirely familiar with some of the technical terms used in demography. With a firm base of knowledge of population movement, sociologists, economists, planners, health professionals, and others should have a broader perspective for viewing the many related factors with which they are most familiar.

Population History
OF
New York City

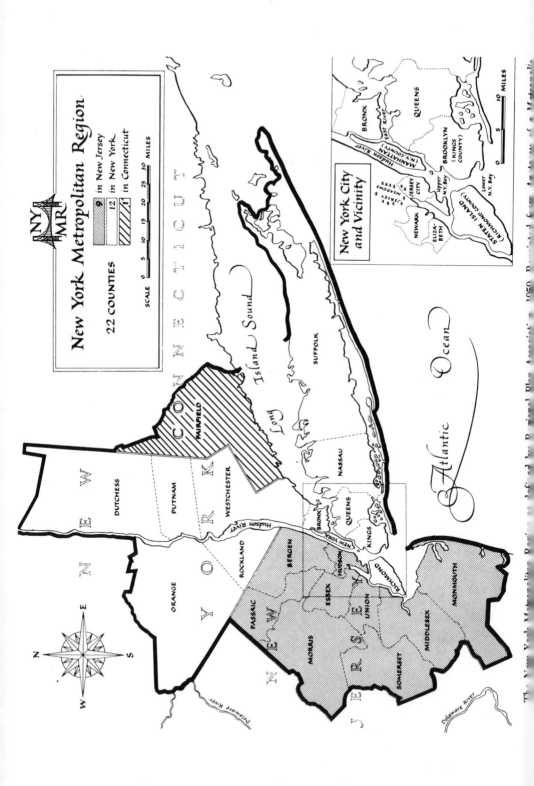

The New York Metropolitan Region as defined by Regional Plan Association in 1950. Reprinted from *Anatomy of a Metropolis*...

1 The Colonial City

The settlement founded in the 1620s by the Dutch West India Company on the southern tip of Manhattan Island developed from a trading post in the wilderness into an important seaport and center of commerce under English rule. After a century and a half of life as the capital of a colonial province, the city of New York contained about 25,000 residents. On the eve of the American Revolution it ranked second (behind Philadelphia) in population size among the colonial municipalities but was first in cosmopolitanism.

THE FOUNDING

Although Giovanni da Verazzano, an Italian navigator in the serivce of King Francis I of France, was the first European to leave a written record of his discoveries in the vicinity of New York City, it was the voyage of exploration of Henry Hudson eighty-five years later, in 1609, that led directly to white settlement in this part of the New World. Hudson, an English sea captain in the employ of the Dutch East India Company, sailed across the Atlantic with a crew of eighteen in the *Half Moon* and explored the North American coast from Newfoundland to the Chesapeake Bay. In a vain effort to find a northwest passage to the East Indies, Hudson entered what is now known as New York City and sailed up the great river that today bears his name to a point near present-day Albany before returning, disappointed, to Europe.

Upon Hudson's return to Amsterdam in 1610, a group of enterprising Dutch merchants sent a ship to the newly explored river to establish a profitable fur trade. Other voyages of exploration and trade soon followed. The Indians generally were friendly to the Europeans, and when in 1613 the ship of Captain Adriaen Block accidentally burned, he and his crew received help from the native inhabitants in securing food and shelter until they had built a new vessel. In 1614 a group of Dutch merchants who had sponsored Block's voyages, as well as those of other explorer-traders, received from the States General of the United Netherlands a monopoly of trade in the region from 40° to 45° north latitude, effective for four voyages, or three years. This area, lying between New France and Virginia, was given the name of New Netherland.

In 1621 the States General incorporated the Dutch West India Company which was given a monopoly of trade between Dutch ports and the west coast of Africa and all the coasts of America. The new company had the power to enter into treaties with the natives, to appoint governors and other administrators, and to promote colonization as well as trade.

In the spring of 1624 the Dutch West India Company sent over the ship *New Netherland,* under the command of Cornelis Jacobsen May, "with a command of thirty families, mostly Walloons, to plant a colony." The Walloons were French-speaking Belgians who had applied in 1622 for transportation to New Netherland as colonists. About eighteen families were brought to the present site of Albany where they constructed Fort Orange. Smaller groups were settled elsewhere.[1]

The establishment of a permanent colony began in earnest in 1625 and 1626 when the West India Company sent several ships to the Hudson, or North River (as distinguished from the Delaware or South River), carrying in addition to farm people, cattle, horses, sheep, and hogs, as well as "wagons, ploughs and all other implements of husbandry."[2] Peter Minuit, who was sent to New Netherland as Director General of the colony, bought Manhattan Island from the native Indians for sixty guilders. A report reaching Amsterdam in November 1626 indicated "the colony is now established on the Manhates, where a fort has been staked out by Master Kryn Frederycks, an engineer." Outside the fort thirty houses had been built. "In order to strengthen with people the colony near the Manhates" most of the families living at Fort Orange and at Fort Nassau (on the Delaware) were brought to this new settlement which was named New Amsterdam.[3]

The first published statement describing the population of the young colony appeared in the semi-annual register of news compiled by Nicolaes van Wassenaer, *Historisch Verhael,* dated October 1628. "The population consists of two hundred and seventy souls, including men, women and children. They remained as yet without the fort, in no fear, as the natives live peaceably with them. They are situate three leagues from the sea, on the river by us called Mauritius, by others, Rio de Montagne. These strangers for the most part occupy their farms."[4]

While fear of Indian attack discouraged many would-be colonists from cultivating the land, the opportunities for trade with the Indians

1. J. Franklin Jameson, ed., *Narratives of New Netherland 1609-1664* (1909; reissued New York: Barnes and Noble, 1959), p. 75   2. *Ibid.,* p. 82.   3. *Ibid.,* pp. 83-85. 4. *Ibid.,* p. 88.

induced many new pioneers to come to New Netherland; among these were English colonists from New England and Virginia. The first English settler to come to Manhattan was Thomas Hall, who deserted his master, George Holmes, after the latter's abortive attempt to take the Dutch fort on the Delaware in 1635.[5]

The second estimate of the population of the principal settlement of New Netherland comes from a descriptive account written by Father Isaac Jogues, a French missionary, after his visit in 1643. After describing Fort Amsterdam, with its garrison of sixty soldiers, he noted: "On the island of Manhate, and in its environs, there may well be four or five hundred men of different sects and nations: the Director General told me that there were men of eighteen different languages."[6] The Jesuit also reported on the Indian wars which took the lives of many settlers and impeded the progress of the colony.

Peter Stuyvesant, the last director general under the Dutch, was honest and capable, but he was also proud and tyrannical, and in 1649 eleven leaders of the community, reflecting popular discontent, asked the Dutch government to grant municipal government to New Amsterdam. It was not until 1653, however, that municipal government was allowed the town. New Amsterdam's population at this time has been estimated at seven or eight hundred inhabitants.[7] A survey made by Captain DeKoninck in 1656 indicated that the new municipality had one hundred and twenty houses and one thousand souls.[8]

The granting of municipal status to the fortified trading post on Manhattan Island occurred during the first of three wars fought between England and the Netherlands, strong commercial rivals, and seems to have been a concession made to soothe the dissatisfied colonists. Trade rivalry between the two European powers continued, and in 1664 the English king, Charles II, determined to annex the Dutch colony without waiting for a formal declaration of war. The region between the Connecticut and the Delaware was given to his brother James, duke of York, and to assure the gift the monarch sent Colonel Richard Nicholls and a fleet of four fully armed frigates to the Dutch colony. When the English forces appeared in the harbor, the citizenry of New Amsterdam, fearful of the destruction of their town, and still discontented with the administration of the Dutch West India Company, urged Stuyvesant to surrender. This he did on September 6, 1664, and all of New Netherland passed into English hands. The principal town, with a population "full fifteen hundred souls strong" was renamed New York. The inhabitants, burgher

5. *Ibid.*, pp. 290,375.   6. *Ibid.*, p. 259.   7. *Ibid.*, p. 291.

8. New York Secretary of State, *Census of the State of New York for 1855* (Albany, 1857), p. iii.

and farmer, were promised in the name of the king of England "free and peaceable possession of their property, unobstructed trade and navigation, not only to the King's dominions, but also to the Netherlands with their own ships and people."[9]

Religious and Racial Groups under the Dutch

The first settlers in New Amsterdam were members of the established church in the United Netherlands, the Reformed Church, but they were not all Dutch. When the first minister sent out from Amsterdam, the Reverend Jonas Jansen Michielse, arrived in Manhattan in 1628, he found Walloons and Frenchmen among the fifty communicants. Michielse reported that "the Walloons and French have no service on Sundays, otherwise than in the Dutch language, for those who understand no Dutch are very few."[10] Although the Dutch Reformed Church was the official religion of the new colony, other faiths soon came upon the scene. Father Jogues (1643) noted: "No religion is publicly exercised but the Calvinist, and orders are to admit none but Calvinists, but this is not observed; for besides the Calvinists there are in the colony Catholics, English Puritans, Lutherans, Anabaptists, here called Mnistes [Mennonites], etc."[11] The Reverend Johannes Megapolensis, minister of the Dutch Reformed Church in New Amsterdam from 1649 until his death in 1669, in a communication to the mother country dated 1655, reported: "we have here Papists, Mennonites and Lutherans among the Dutch; also many Puritans or Independents, and many atheists and various other servants of Baal among the English under this Government, who conceal themselves under the name of Christians." Megapolensis was particularly irritated by the appearance of Jews in the colony, declaring: "Some Jews came from Holland last summer in order to trade. Later some Jews came upon the same ship as DePolheymius [from Brazil]. . . . Some more have come from Holland this spring." He went on to request of "the Messrs. Directors, that these godless rascals, who are of no benefit to the country, but look at everything for their own profit, may be sent away from here." The West India Company, nevertheless, permitted the Jewish settlers to remain. In 1656 the ministry of the Dutch Reformed Church protested the arrival of a Lutheran pastor from Holland, Johann Ernst Gutwasser. The West India Company upheld Stuyvesant's decision to send him back to Holland in 1659; however, the Company would not permit the colonial

9. Jameson, *Narratives*, pp. 449, 452, 464.   10. *Ibid.*, p. 125.   11. *Ibid.*, p.260.

governor's order which forbade the Lutherans to worship in private homes to stand.[12]

Father Isaac Jogues, the French missionary, reported encountering only two Roman Catholics in New Amsterdam in 1643—a Portuguese woman and a young Irish man. Catholicism, however, found no foothold in New Amsterdam, although Father Simon Le Moyne, another French Jesuit, occasionally ministered to a few Catholic voyagers and sailors who were in port.[13]

Slavery was introduced into New Netherland in the first years of the colony, in 1625 or 1626. Probably the first written notice of the Negro population was that of the Reverend Michielse, who in a letter from Manhattan, declared in 1628: "the Angola slave women are thievish, lazy, and useless trash."[14] Included among the criticism of the administration expressed in a memorial written in 1649 by several of the leading colonists and submitted to the States General at the Hague was the attestation that "there are also various other negroes in this country, some of whom have been made free for their long service, but their children have remained slaves, though it is contrary to the laws of every people that any one born of a free Christian mother should be a slave and be compelled to remain in servitude." In 1660 the Reverend Henricus Selyns noted that Stuyvesant's Bowery, or farm, contained "forty negroes, from the region of the Negro Coast, besides the household families."[15] The first cargo of Negroes imported directly to New Amsterdam from Africa made its appearance in 1655.[16]

The Settling of Manhattan's Neighbors

The peopling of Manhattan's neighbors—Long Island on the opposite shore of the East River, Staten Island across New York Bay, New Jersey west of the Hudson River, and the mainland to the east of the Harlem River—commenced in earnest after 1630 when the West India Company, "the better to people their lands, and to bring their country to produce more abundantly, resolved to grant divers Privileges, Freedoms and Exemptions to all patroons, masters or individuals who should plant any

12. *Ibid.*, pp. 392-93.
13. Golda G. Stander, "Jesuit Educational Institutions in the City of New York," United States Catholic Historical Society, *Historical Records and Studies*, XXIV (1934), 213-14.
14. Jameson, *Narratives*, p. 129.   15. *Ibid.*, pp. 330, 407.
16. James Ford et al, *Slums and Housing* (Cambridge, Mass.: Harvard University Press, 1936), I, 26.

colonies and cattle in New Netherland."[17] Long Island, which according to an early document, "on account of its convenient bays and havens, and its good well situated lands is a crown of the province," attracted many buyers when the company for the first time permitted individuals to purchase property. In 1657 it was noted that "on Long Island there are seven villages belonging to this province, of which three, Breuckelen, Amersfoort and Midwout [Brooklyn, Flatlands and Flatbush], are inhabited by Dutch people.... The four other villages on Long Island, viz., Gravensand, Middelburgh, Vlissingen, and Heemstede [Gravesend, Newtown, Flushing, and Hempstead], are inhabited by Englishmen. The people of Gravensand are considered Mennonites.... At Vlissingen, they formerly had a Presbyterian minister ... but at present, many of them have become imbued with divers opinions.... At Middelburgh, alias Newtown, they are mostly Independents."[18]

When the first Dutch church on Long Island was established in 1654, the village of Midwout was selected for the site because of its central location among the Dutch villages. The first religious services in Breuckelen, in 1660, were held in a barn. The minister, Henricus Selyns, "found at Breuckelen one elder, two deacons, twenty-four members, thirty-one householders, and one hundred and thirty-four people."[19]

North of Manhattan only one village had been founded between the Hudson River and Long Island Sound by 1657, when two Dutch ministers wrote: "On the west shore of the East River, about one mile beyond Hellgate, as we call it, and opposite Flushing, is another English village, called Oostdorp [East Village, later Westchester], which was begun two years ago. The inhabitants of this place are also Puritans or Independents."[20]

The first colonists on Staten Island were sent by Dutch patroons, but their early settlements were destroyed by Indian attacks in the 1640s and 1650s. In 1664, when the Reverend Samuel Drisius was regularly traveling from Manhattan to Staten Island every two months to preach, the few settlers were French. According to Drisius, "the French on Staten Island would also like to have a preacher, but as they number only a few families, are very poor, and cannot contribute much to a preacher's salary, and as our support here is slow and small, there is not much hope, that they will receive the light."[21]

POPULATION GROWTH IN THE ENGLISH COLONY

Largely because of her geographical position, New York gradually developed from a Dutch fur trading post into one of the principal seaports

17. Jameson, *Narratives*, p. 89.   18. *Ibid.*, pp. 396-97.   19. *Ibid.*, p. 407.
20. *Ibid.*, p. 398.   21. *Ibid.*, p. 413.

of the English colonies. Trade was from the very outset the town's main-stay. In 1687 Governor Dongan reported that "New York and Albany live wholly upon trade with the Indians, England, and the West Indies."[22] About eighty years later, in the last years of English rule, a Londoner wrote: "The people of New York seem, to me, to be too infatuated with a foreign trade, ever to make any great progress in manufactures."[23]

From the start of life under an English governor until the closing years of the seventeenth century, New York ranked behind Boston as the largest town in the colonies. Philadelphia eventually passed New York in numbers and by 1760 replaced Boston as the foremost city in size in colonial America. By this date, New York too had passed Boston in population.[24]

One reason New York did not match Philadelphia's growth near the close of the seventeenth century was a comparative dwindling of immigration. The provincial governor of New York reported in 1687: "I believe for these 7 years past, there has not come over into this province twenty English Scotch or Irish familys. But on the contrary on Long Island the people encrease soe fast that they complain for want of land and many remove from thence into the neighboring province. But of French there have since my coming here several familys come both from St. Christophers & England & a great many more are expected as alsoe from Holland are come several Dutch familys."[25]

During the administration of Governor Thomas Dongan, who arrived in 1683, the province of New York was divided into twelve counties. New York County, comprising Manhattan and the small islands in the East River, was given boundaries similar to those of the modern political subdivision. Long Island was divided into three counties: Kings, Queens, and Suffolk. Staten Island became Richmond County, while the mainland of New York east of the Hudson River became Westchester County. At the request of the committee of trade in the province, Governor Dongan attempted the first census of the colony in 1686. Unfortunately, only scattered returns were preserved.[26]

The first census for which complete data for the province exist was that taken in 1698 by order of Governor Bellomont. Of the provincial population of 18,067, over one-fourth (4,937 persons) were resident in New York City and County.[27] The next official census, that ordered in 1703 by Governor Cornbury, found somewhat fewer in New York City and County: 4,375 or 4,436, according to different accounts.[28]

22. Edmund B. O'Callaghan, *The Documentary History of the State of New-York* (Albany: Weed, Parsons, 1849), I, 160.
23. Carl Bridenbaugh, *Cities in Revolt* (New York: Alfred A. Knopf, 1955), p. 271.
24. *Ibid.*, p. 5, and Carl Bridenbaugh, *Cities in the Wilderness* (New York: Alfred A. Knopf, 1955), p. 6.
25. O'Callaghan, *Documentary History*, p. 161.
26. *Census of the State of New York for 1855*, p. iv.   27. *Ibid.*   28. *Ibid.*

Responsibility for the reversal goes primarily to a yellow fever epidemic which devastated the city in 1702, claiming 570 lives.[29] Thus, more than one-tenth of the population was lost to this highly destructive disease. Ironically, the epidemic occurred just a few years after the Earl of Bellomont, then governor, had written: "I believe there is not a richer populace anywhere in the King's dominions than is in this town."[30]

The census ordered by Governor Hunter in 1712, after receiving a communication from the Lords of Trade inquiring into the affairs of the province, showed 5,840 residents in New York City. The returns from this count have been described as imperfect, "the people being deterred by a simple superstition and observation that the sickness followed upon the last numbering of the people."[31] Censuses were again conducted in 1723, 1731, 1737, 1746, 1749, 1756, and 1771, and the returns for New York County are shown in Table 1.

TABLE 1
Population of New York County and
Kings County by Race, 1698-1771

Census year	New York County			Kings County		
	Total	White	Negro	Total	White	Negro
1698	4,937	4,237	700	2,017	1,721	296
1703	4,375	3,745	630	1,912	1,569	343
1712	5,840	—	—	1,925	—	—
1723	7,248	5,886	1,362	2,218	1,774	444
1731	8,622	7,045	1,577	2,150	1,658	492
1737	10,664	8,945	1,719	2,348	1,784	564
1746	11,717	9,273	2,444	2,331	1,686	645
1749	13,294	10,926	2,368	2,283	1,500	783
1756	13,046	10,768	2,278	2,207	1,862	845
1771	21,863	18,726	3,137	3,623	2,461	1,162

Source: E. B. Greene and V. D. Harrington, American Population Before the Federal Census of 1790 (New York, 1932).

Of the several epidemics that visited the city during the mid-eighteenth century, the most significant occurred in 1731, when 549 persons (478 whites and 71 Negroes) were reported to have died of small-pox in a three-month period. This was approximately 6 percent of New York's population at the time.[32]

29. John Duffy, A History of Public Health in New York City; 1625-1866 (New York: Russell Sage Foundation, 1968), pp. 35-36.
30. Ford, Slums and Housing, p. 40.
31. Census of the State of New York for 1855, p. v.
32. Duffy, History of Public Health; p. 54; Bridenbaugh, Cities in the Wilderness, p. 400.

Despite the ravages of communicable disease the city's population doubled between 1712 and 1746, and after a spurt between 1746 and 1749 declined slightly, to 13,046 in 1756. The next decade and a half, however, witnessed an increase of almost nine thousand residents, an unprecedented gain. The province as a whole also experienced unparalleled growth between 1756 and 1771. The authorities assumed the reasons for this increase included "the high price of labor, and the abundance and cheapness of land fit for cultivation, which by increasing the means of subsistence, afforded strong additional incitements to early marriage."[33] New York's population continued to grow, and on the eve of the American Revolution a visitor observed: "There are computed between twenty-six and thirty thousand inhabitants in the city; in this number are, I believe included the slaves, who make at least a fifth part of the number."[34]

Religious and Racial Groups under the English

The first estimate of the national origins of New York's population while under English rule was that of Captain William Byrd, a visitor from Virginia who in 1685 reported the inhabitants to be "about six-eighths Dutch, the remainder French and English."[35] The religious diversity of the province of New York was attested to as early as 1678 when Governor Andros noted: "There are Religions of all sorts, one church of England, several Presbiterians & Independents, Quakers & Anabaptists of Severall sects, some Jews but presbiterians & Independents most numerous & Substantiall."[36]

A few years later, in 1687, Governor Dongan, in his report to the Committee on Trade in the Province of New York, described the religious situation in the provincial capital: "New York has first a Chaplain belonging to the Fort of the Church of England; secondly, a Dutch Calvinist; thirdly, a French Calvinist; fourthly, a Dutch Lutheran—Here be not many of the Church of England; few Roman Catholicks; abundance of Quaker's preachers, men and Women especially, Singing Quakers, Ranting Quakers; Sabbatarians; Anti-Sabbatarians; Some Anabaptists

33. *Census of the State of New York for 1855*, p. vii.
34. Patrick M'Robert, *A Tour through Part of the North Provinces of America*, cited in Bayrd Still, *Mirror for Gotham* (New York: New York University Press, 1956), p. 36.
35. William Byrd to "Bro. Dan'l," in *Historical Register and Literary Advertiser II*, cited in Still, *Mirror for Gotham*, p. 21.
36. O'Callaghan, *Documentary History*, p. 92.

some Independents some Jews; in short of all sorts of opinions there are some, and the most part of none at all."[37]

Dongan noted that "the most prevailing opinion is that of the Dutch Calvinists."[38] Charles Lodwich in 1692 wrote members of the Royal Society that "our chiefest unhappyness here is too great a mixture of Nations, and English ye least part."[39] The Reverend John Miller, describing New York City in 1695, prepared a table showing the religious distribution of the city's families to be as follows:[40]

Chapel in the fort	90
Dutch Calvinists	450
Dutch Lutheran	30
French	200
Jews Synagogue	20
Haarlem [Dutch Calvinist]	25
English [Anglican]	40
Dissenters	[no figure]

Mortality statistics indicating cemetery of burial gathered by the *New-York Gazette* in 1731, occasioned by the smallpox epidemic that year, provide what may serve as the best available means of estimating the religious distribution of the population at the time. Almost equal numbers among the 478 whites included in the weekly bills of mortality were buried in the cemetery of the Church of England (229) and in the Dutch Church (212). Presbyterian burials numbered 16, French Church burials, 15, and the burial grounds of the Lutheran Church, Quakers, Baptists, and Jews each had one or two.[41]

The eighteenth century saw the gradual decline of the Dutch way of life in New York in the face of a mounting tide of immigration from the British Isles. According to the noted historian, Dr. Marcus L. Hansen, by 1703 less than 50 percent of the eight hundred and eighteen heads of families in New York City were Dutch.[42] In the course of the following decades, as the city gradually lost its rural character, a constant outward migration to more agricultural land occurred among the Dutch community.[43] In 1744 Dr. Alexander Hamilton, a visitor from Annapolis,

37. *Ibid.*, p. 186.   38. *Ibid.*

39. Still, *Mirror for Gotham*, p. 21.

40. John Miller, *New York Considered and Improved . . . 1695* (London: Thomas Rodd, 1843), p. 11.

41. James H. Cassedy, *Demography in Early America* (Cambridge: Harvard University Press, 1969), p. 122.

42. Marcus L. Hansen, "The Minor Stocks in the American Population of 1790," *Annual Report of the American Historical Association for the Year 1931*, I, 364.   43. *Ibid.*, p. 370.

remarked that even though "Dutchmen" possessed the chief places of the government, their language and customs had begun "pretty much to wear out" and they threatened to die but for "a parcell of Dutch domines" who tried to preserve Dutch customs in the church schools.[44] A French visitor commented in 1765: "There are still two Churches in which religious worship is performed in [the Dutch] language but the number that talk it diminishes daily."[45]

As the city's population increased, new churches were added to the growing skyline. By 1774 New York contained sixteen houses of worship. Patrick M'Robert noted: "They have three English churches, three Presbyterian, two Dutch Lutheran, two Dutch Calvinists, all neat and well finished buildings, besides a French church, an Anabaptist, a Methodist, a Quaker meeting, a Moravian church, and a Jews synagogue."[46]

Noteworthy for its absence was a Catholic church. Catholic settlers (as distinct from transients) had first arrived in New York under the rule of Governor Andros, prominent among them being Lieutenant Anthony Brockholls, the governor's aide. The first mass was offered during the administration of the Irish-Catholic Governor, Thomas Dongan, who used a room in his house in the fort as a chapel after his arrival in New York in 1683.[47] Dongan's successors, however, persecuted the Catholic clergy, and they fled the colony. Governor Fletcher reported in 1696 that only nine Catholics remained in the city. A colonial statute of 1700 imposed life imprisonment on any Catholic priest found in the colony. This law ably served its purpose of keeping Catholics out of the province.[48]

The black population in New York City more than doubled between 1703 and 1723 (numerically the increase was from 630 to 1,362), a rate of growth considerably faster than that shown by the white residents. A shortage of labor appears to have been responsible for the importation between 1720 and 1726 of over eight hundred slaves, at high prices. After that date, however, indentured workers—whose passage across the Atlantic was paid by their servitude—and laborers from Ulster filled much of the need, and blacks came to be used primarily as household servants.[49] Between 1723 and 1771 the proportion of the city's population that was Negro fell from 18 percent to 14 percent. Through much of this period economic competition fostered hostile feeling between whites and Negroes,

44. Still, *Mirror for Gotham*, p. 22.   45. *Ibid.*

46. M'Robert, "A Tour," cited in Still, *Mirror for Gotham*, p. 34.

47. John Gilmary Shea, ed., *The Catholic Churches of New York City* (New York: L. G. Goulding and Co., 1878), pp. 23-24.   48. *Ibid.*

49. Bridenbaugh, *Cities in the Wilderness*, p. 409.

and mob action occurred in 1741. For participation in what was alleged to have been a conspiracy, thirty-one Negroes were executed.[50]

THE GROWTH OF MANHATTAN'S NEIGHBORS

The rate of population growth in Kings County, which early in the period of English rule had almost as many residents as Manhattan, was virtually the smallest in the colony of New York during the century before independence. In 1676 Kings County had 250 taxables compared with 303 in New York County; by 1698, however, Kings County's population of 2,017 was only two-fifths that of its neighbor. During the succeeding seventy-five years, a period in which New York County increased more than fourfold, Kings County did not quite double its population, which reached only 3,623 in 1771 (see Table 1).[51]

The first extant census of Kings County, that of 1698, shows that the population was then distributed among the six towns as follows: Brooklyn 509, Flatbush 476, Bushwick 301, New Utrecht 259, Flatland 256, Gravesend 215.[52] Only Gravesend had been settled by the English. The Dutch are estimated to have comprised some 1,500 of the total of 1,721 inhabitants.[53] During the late seventeenth and throughout the eighteenth century, slavery became increasingly important to the landowners of Kings County. In 1698 Negroes comprised 15 percent of the population; by 1737, 24 percent; and in 1771, fully 32 percent (see Table 1).

There was little to beckon newcomers to this slave society; hence far more rapid growth occurred in the non-Dutch portions of Long Island. Queens County increased in population from 3,565 in 1698 to 10,980 in 1771. Still more rapid was the growth in Westchester County, where the population climbed from only 1,063 in 1698 to 21,745 in 1771. An intermediate rate of increase during this period was shown by Richmond County which contained 727 persons in 1698 and 2,847 in 1771.[54] The population of Queens in 1695, according to the Reverend John Miller, was comprised of "300 or 400 English families, mostly Dissenters, and some Dutch." Westchester was largely English. Richmond had a more heterogeneous body of settlers at this time: Miller reported 40 English (Anglican), 44 Dutch, and 36 French families.[55]

---

50. Ford, *Slums and Housing*, p. 46.

51. Evarts B. Greene and Virginia D. Harrington, *American Population before the Federal Census of 1790* (New York: Columbia University Press, 1932), pp. 92—93, 102.

52. *Ibid.*, p. 93.

53. Hansen, "Minor Stocks," *AHA Annual Report*, p. 365.

54. Greene and Harrington, *American Population*, pp. 92, 102.

55. Miller, *New York Considered*, p. 11.

Although New York City grew faster than some of the nearby counties, its rate of growth did not keep pace with that of the province as a whole during the years of English dominion. Between 1698 and 1771 the population of the province multiplied almost tenfold while that of the city increased fourfold. Similarly, the share of the aggregate population of the thirteen English colonies living in the five largest urban places declined, falling from an estimated 9 percent in 1690 to approximately 4 percent in 1775.[56]

56. Greene and Harrington, *American Population*, pp. 6, 89, 91; Bridenbaugh, *Cities in the Wilderness*, p. 6; Bridenbaugh, *Cities in Revolt*, p. 216.

2 The American City

In the half century following the American Declaration of Independence New York City grew at a much faster rate (except during the Revolutionary War itself and during the period around the War of 1812) than it had during colonialism. The city, once its population had stabilized following the drastic shifts during and immediately after the Revolution, doubled and then redoubled in size within a very short span of years. During this era its population composition more closely resembled the ethnic mix of the United States as a whole than at any other time in its history. But, ironically, as New York began to burgeon it simultaneously commenced to diverge in character from the nation since the newcomers from abroad (principally Irish Catholics) were regarded as quite different from the archetypal Americans.

THE REVOLUTIONARY PERIOD

New York became an American city in 1775 when revolutionary committees took over the municipal government. Between 1775 and 1783 political and military events brought about the most radical fluctuations in population in the city's history. The actual dimensions of the population movements, however, are subject to conjecture.

According to one account, "nineteen twentieths at least of the inhabitants with their families & affects . . . left . . . between the latter part of the year 1775 & . . . June, 1776."[1] These emigrants included "rebels or persons in opposition to his Majesty's government," "those who feared the consequences of remaining in a besieged town," and loyalists who wished to avoid military duty. In addition there were included "some hundreds of persons who were taken up & rent into confinement, or on parole in different parts of the country by orders of the Generals, Provincial Congress, or Committees on account of their loyalty."[2]

Oscar T. Barck, leading historian of this period, did not believe the mass exodus was quite so complete. Of the original 25,000 residents just

---

1. Henry B. Dawson, ed., *New York City during the American Revolution* (New York: Mercantile Library Association, 1861), p. 149.   2. *Ibid.*, p. 150.

14

after the outbreak of war, Barck pointed out that "neutrals and those who successfully concealed their opinions must have numbered five thousand." He estimated that this number remained in the city when the British captured it in September 1776.[3]

The British military occupation of New York lasted seven years, a period in which the population of the city fluctuated continually due to "the movement of troops, the incoming and releasing of prisoners, and the ingress and egress of loyalists."[4] Immediately after the American forces were driven out, New York loyalists who had fled the city began returning. They were joined by others from neighboring parts of the country who preferred royal rule. By February 1777 the population increased to an estimated 12,000; by 1781 there were "probably about 25,000 civilians."[5] The city, which also had to house several thousand troops, suffered from a severe housing shortage because an extensive area had been destroyed by a great fire in 1776.

In 1783 New York again experienced a tremendous population turnover. Over 29,000 persons, including discharged soldiers and their families, sailed from New York City before the official evacuation November 25, 1783, the great bulk going to Canada.[6] Barck estimated that including the emigration prior to 1783, about 32,000 civilian loyalists left New York, "perhaps one-third of whom were originally New Yorkers."[7] The homecoming patriots began to enter the city in large numbers by the summer of 1783, and the influx accelerated in November. The population of the city at the date of the British evacuation has been put at 12,000.[8] A contemporary noted the Americans "took possession of a ruined city" with a "heterogeneous set of inhabitants, composed of almost ruined exiles, disbanded soldiery, mixed foreigners, disaffected Tories, and the refuse of a British army."[9]

THE NATION'S LARGEST CITY

After the British evacuated the city in November 1783, the citizenry faced the enormous problems of reconstruction. Urban areas that had been destroyed by fire were rebuilt, and overseas markets that had been lost during the war were regained. In 1784, New York, which had just recently become the capital of the new state of New York, became the

3. Oscar T. Barck, Jr., *New York City during the War for Independence* (New York: Columbia University Press, 1931), pp. 75-76.   4. *Ibid.*, p. 74.   5. *Ibid.*, p. 78.
6. *Ibid.*, p. 215.   7. *Ibid.*   8. *Ibid.*, p. 229.
9. *New York Packet*, December 16, 1784, cited in Sidney I. Pomerantz, *New York: An American City 1783-1803* (New York: Columbia University Press, 1938), p. 19.

temporary capital of the new republic. By 1788, New York once again was the profitable commercial center it had been prior to hostilities; it could thank both its excellent location and its enterprising businessmen. The city's population, which more than doubled between 1783 and 1786, then followed a more normal, though rapid, course.

Between 1790 and 1820 New York State almost tripled in population and in the process advanced from fifth largest state to first, truly becoming "the Empire State." New York City's proportionate population gain in this period matched, but did not exceed, that of the state. As indicated in Table 2, the portion of the state's residents in the principal city remained relatively stable at about 10 percent. Philadelphia, with its densely settled suburbs, was considered the largest city in the nation in 1790. It also similarly grew in proportion to the advance of its own state, and by 1820, when New York exceeded Pennsylvania, New York City surpassed in population the City of Brotherly Love.

TABLE 2
Population Comparison of New York State and New York City with Pennsylvania and Philadelphia, 1790-1850

Census year	Population				Percent of state population	
	New York State	New York City	Pennsylvania	Philadelphia	New York City	Philadelphia
1790	340,120	33,131	434,373	42,520	9.7	9.8
1800	589,051	60,489	602,365	69,403	10.3	11.5
1810	959,049	96,373	810,091	91,874	10.0	11.3
1820	1,372,812	123,706	1,049,458	112,772	9.0	10.7
1830	1,918,608	202,589	1,348,233	161,410	10.6	12.0
1840	2,428,921	312,710	1,724,033	220,423	12.9	12.8
1850	3,097,394	515,547	2,311,786	340,045	16.6	14.7

Source: J. D. B. De Bow, Statistical View of the United States (Washington, 1854).

Our knowledge of population trends in New York City during the period from the end of the Revolutionary War through 1825 comes from the censuses taken under three auspices: state, federal, and local. State censuses were conducted in 1786, 1814, and 1825. Federal counts were taken every ten years (beginning with the census of 1790) in accordance with the constitutional provision requiring the enumeration of the national population for the purpose of assigning congressional representatives. In 1805 a city census was taken by order of the Common Council of New York in order to obtain a return of "able and sufficient jurors."[10] The city

10. James Hardie, The Description of the City of New-York (New York: S. Marks, 1827), p. 129.

fathers felt the enumeration necessary in order to secure a portrait of the net effect of the dislocation caused by a recent epidemic of yellow fever. As a byproduct of the census, it was determined that 26,996 of the 75,770 enumerated persons had retired from the city during the epidemic.[11]

Repeated outbreaks of yellow fever, the most critical health problem on the urban scene, provided the impetus for the regular publication of official reports on health matters in American cities.[12] Following the epidemic of 1795 in New York the number of yellow fever deaths was placed at 732.[13] Three years later, when an epidemic again struck the city, the health committee estimated that 1,524 deaths had been caused by yellow fever. Including deaths of those who contracted the illness in New York but died outside the city, the total probably exceeded two thousand.[14] This was approximately 4 percent of the city's entire population at the time, a devastating level never matched by later epidemics. The records of the local health committee indicated there were 1,639 cases and 606 deaths during the yellow fever outbreak in 1803; the Board of Health reported 600 cases and 262 deaths resulted from the epidemic in September and October 1805.[15]

John Pintard, a civic leader who subsequently became city inspector, began collecting mortality statistics for New York City on his own initiative in 1802. He helped sponsor an ordinance in 1804 requiring physicians to complete statements on the cause of death of their patients and requiring sextons to submit weekly lists of interments to the city inspector's office. The city inspector was ordered to maintain a register of the names of decedents and to compile annual statistics.[16] From this order it was a simple step for the city inspector to compile annual statistics of the number of deaths in New York. Thus, New York became one of the first American cities with accurate knowledge of the year by year, decade by decade, fluctuations in its mortality rate.[17]

Table 3 indicates that the fears of a slump in the city's growth when New York ceased to be the capital of the United States in 1790, and again when the capital of New York State was transferred to Albany in 1796, did not materialize. The city gained about two thousand new residents annually in the last fifteen years of the eighteenth century, and over three thousand per year at the opening of the nineteenth century.

Natural increase, the excess of births over deaths, could hardly have been sufficient to produce such growth. It is apparent that during these

11. *Ibid.*, p. 130.
12. Cassedy, *Demography*, pp. 294-95.
13. Hardie, *Description*, p. 124.
14. Duffy, *History of Public Health*, p. 109.   15. *Ibid.*, pp. 111-13.
16. *Ibid.*, pp. 142-46.
17. Recorded deaths in New York City from 1804 through the close of the nineteenth century are shown in Appendix Tables A-1 and A-2.

years a substantial number of migrants came into the city. The two distinct components of population change, natural increase and migration, cannot be accurately ascertained if data pertaining to births and deaths are not available. (When the natural increase is known, net migration is represented by the residual element of the population change between two censuses.) While returns of deaths were tallied by 1804, it would be fully another century before accurate statistics of births were available.

TABLE 3

Population of New York City by Race and Annual Percentage Increase in Intercensal Period, 1786-1820

Census year	Total	White	Negro		Annual percentage increase in intercensal period
			Total	Slave	
1786	23,610	21,507	2,103	—	—
1790	33,131	29,661	3,470	2,369	8.8
1800	60,515	54,133	6,382	2,868	6.2
1805	75,770	71,762	4,008	2,048	4.6
1810	96,373	86,550	9,823	1,686	4.9
1814	95,519	86,328	9,191	—	−0.2
1816	,93,634	85,243	8,391	617	−1.0
1820	123,706	112,820	10,886	518	7.2

Source: New York Secretary of State, Census of the State of New York for 1865 (Albany, 1867).

New York City suffered a severe setback in 1807 with the passage of the Embargo Act which prevented foreign commerce. After the repeal of the act, trade revived, but the Nonintercourse Act (enacted to assure American neutrality in the conflicts between Napoleon and Great Britain) limited shipping. After the United States declared war against Great Britain in June 1812, a British fleet blockaded the harbor, forcing the port to close for more than a year. This brought near ruin to a large number of residents dependent upon trade for their livelihood.[18] When the state took a census of population in 1814, 95,519 persons were enumerated in New York City compared with 96,373 four years earlier. Since there is little doubt that the population at this time was experiencing a substantial natural increase, probably at least 2 percent per annum, it is evident (if we assume a reliable count) that the city had lost several thousand migrants in the interval from 1810 to 1814 in consequence of the economic crisis. When news of the peace treaty of Ghent reached New York early in 1815, the citizenry eagerly welcomed a new era.

18. Julius W. Pratt, "The War of 1812," *History of the State of New York*, ed. Alexander C. Flick (New York: Columbia University Press, 1934), V, 243-44.

A second enumeration of New York City by order of the Common Council was made in 1816, again in connection with the return of jurors. This enumeration showed only 93,634 residents, fewer than in 1814.[19] For the first time, an inquiry was made of citizenship. The city census showed 6,989 of the 85,243 white residents were aliens. Males among the alien population numbered 3,891; females, 3,098.[20]

Between 1816 and 1825 the population of New York leaped forward from 93,634 to 166,086, an increase of 77 percent. By the latter date, one observer, Karl Bernhard, duke of Saxe-Weimar Eisenach, remarked that the city appeared to be attracting "nearly the whole commerce of the country."[21] Actually the share of New York in the foreign commerce of the nation amounted to 29 percent in 1821, compared with 17 percent in 1791.[22]

POPULATION GROUPS

In the period between the two wars against the British, New York was more truly an American city, in the sense that the ethnic background of its population reflected the national composition, than in any other period in its history. In New York, as in the United States as a whole, persons of English background comprised the great majority. A visitor to the New York of 1794 observed: "Since the wealthier elements are English, the whole feeling and behavior of the town seems to be English."[23]

New York City's peculiarly distinctive population element at the beginning of independence was the Dutch, estimated by Hansen to number 5,000 in 1790, or about one-sixth of the total white population of 29,619.[24] At the beginning of the eighteenth century about one-half of the estimated 6,650 persons of Dutch descent in the province of New York lived in two counties—New York and Kings.[25] By 1790 the number of persons of Dutch stock had multiplied severalfold in New York, as well as in neighboring New Jersey. The Dutch in New York and Kings Counties, however, experienced heavy outmigration, and in consequence their number increased but

19. Published returns incorrectly gave a figure of 100,619. New York Secretary of State, *Census of the State of New York for 1865* (Albany: 1867), p. iv.   20. *Ibid.*

21. Still, *Mirror for Gotham*, p. 82.

22. Robert G. Albion, "Yankee Domination of New York Port, 1820-1865," *New England Quarterly*, V (October 1932), 683.

23. Kenneth Roberts and Anna M. Roberts, eds. and trans., *Moreau de St. Méry's American Journey* (Garden City, N.Y.: Doubleday, 1947), p. 156.

24. Hansen, "Minor Stocks," *AHA Annual Report, 1931*, p. 371.

25. "Report of Committee on Linguistic and National Stocks in the Population of the United States," *Annual Report of the American Historical Association for the Year 1931*, I, 120.

slightly. According to Hansen's estimate, these counties contained only about 12 percent of the 55,000 persons of Dutch origin in New York State in 1790.[26]

German settlement was stimulated by the American Revolution, since some of the German mercenaries who fought for the British opted to remain in the New World. In 1785 the German community in New York sought to incorporate a society "for encouraging emigration from Germany."[27] As individuals rather than as a community, however, Germans had been present from the earliest days of the settlement on Manhattan. Peter Minuit, director general of New Netherland, hailed from Wesel on the Rhine. Jacob Leisler, a native of Frankfurt, was another who reached New Amsterdam in the service of the Dutch West India Company.[28] The largest contingent of Germans to come to New York during the years of English rule were the Palatines, who arrived in 1710. Of more than two thousand Palatine immigrants who sailed over that year, only about thirty families or 150 persons remained in New York City, the bulk of the newcomers settling farther up the Hudson.[29] A number of German children, however, were apprenticed to residents of New York City. Among these was a youth, John Peter Zenger, who achieved fame for his fight for liberty of the press.[30]

At the end of the colonial period the German population in the colony of New York was quite small compared with that in Pennsylvania, for Philadelphia was the principal port of entry for Germans, and relatively few landed in New York. According to an estimate prepared by Howard F. Barker for the American Council of Learned Societies, the number of persons of German descent in New York State in 1790 was approximately 25,800, or 8.2 percent of the total white population.[31] The basis for this estimate was the frequency of appearance of thirty-two distinctive German name-groups among the list of household heads enumerated in the census of 1790. The number of Germans in subdivisions of the state was not estimated, but it may be assumed that roughly one-tenth, or between 2,000 and 2,500, were in New York City.[32]

Irish immigrants, like German, made their appearance on Manhattan, as individuals, during the Dutch administration. The first Irish immigrant

26. Hansen, "Minor Stocks," *AHA Annual Report, 1931*, p. 396.

27. Pomerantz, *New York: An American City*, p. 206.

28. Albert B. Faust, *The German Element in the United States* (Boston: Riverside Press, 1909), I, 10, 13.   29. *Ibid.*, p. 91.   30. *Ibid.*, p. 105.

31. Howard F. Barker, "National Stocks in the Population of the United States as Indicated by Surnames in the Census of 1790," *Annual Report of the American Historical Association for the Year 1931*, I, 304.

32. The basis for this estimate is the writer's count of 43 of the 466 identifiable German names—9 percent—from the list of 32 name groups (given in Barker, "National Stocks," pp. 289-90) as resident in New York City. The total number of households in the list for New York State was 487.

reportedly was a servant girl belonging to Isaac Allerton, English tobacco merchant, who in 1655 beat her for skylarking with a servant man.[33] Among the influx of immigrants to New York in the 1780s the Irish were particularly conspicuous. The many in need are said to have taxed the facilities of public and private agencies, including in 1784 the Friendly Sons of St. Patrick.[34]

The American Council of Learned Societies estimate of the Irish stock in the United States in 1790 (prepared by Howard F. Barker) is based on distinctive Irish names, and includes 25,400 in New York State, 8.1 percent of the white population.[35] Although the figure was not further broken down, it may be estimated that roughly one-fifth of this number, or approximately 5,000, lived in New York City.[36]

The Republican agitation in Ireland in the 1790s and the rebellion of 1798 led to considerable movement to America. President Timothy Dwight of Yale, who traveled throughout New York State in 1810-11, estimated Irish immigrants in New York City to be more numerous than those from other overseas areas. An indicator of the origin of New York's foreign-born population, which may or may not reflect the relative ranking of the various nationalities, is the annual report of the superintendent of the almshouse. According to the report for 1813, the largest group of immigrant paupers, 246, were born in Ireland. Those from England numbered 82; from Scotland, 37; Germany, 43; France, nine; Africa, nine; and the West Indies, eight.[37]

A disproportionate share of the Irish Catholic immigrants in New York during this period—the very beginning of industrialism—lived in abject poverty, frequently in overcrowded housing. The newcomers were especially subject to the catastrophic epidemics of infectious disease that were recurring events in New York as in other cities. A majority of the victims of the yellow fever epidemic in 1795 were members of the Catholic congregation; most were recent arrivals from Ireland. The Reverend O'Brien acknowledged that "on inquiry, I found the much greater part of them to be emigrants of that very summer, insomuch that out of four hundred and sixty-two of my congregation who sunk under the disorder, nineteen-twentieths were totally unknown to me."[38]

33. James W. Gerard, *The Impress of Nationalities upon the City of New York* (New York: Columbia Spectator, 1883), p. 28.

34. Pomerantz, *New York: An American City*, p. 203.

35. "Linguistic and National Stocks," *AHA Annual Report, 1931*, p. 124.

36. The writer located 496 of the 499 heads of households with names found to be representative of Irish ancestry in New York State (see Barker, "National Stocks"). Of these 93, or 19 percent, lived in New York City.

37. Timothy Dwight, *Travels in New-England and New-York* (London: W. Baynes and Son, 1823), III, 437.

38. Ford, *Slums and Housing*, pp. 63-64.

Probably the largest group to come to New York from abroad in the late eighteenth century, other than immigrants from the British Isles, was the French. The first migration in 1789, the year of the French Revolution, was augmented several years later by even larger numbers of the nobility and upper middle class. In addition, French refugees from Santo Domingo began to pour into New York, as well as to other cities on the Atlantic coast, in 1793. It has been estimated that as many as four thousand came from Santo Domingo.[39] If such a figure is not exaggerated, it must be assumed that many Frenchmen subsequently departed, for Dwight in 1810 placed the French near the bottom of the list of his "classes" of New York residents.[40]

The most important group settling in New York City in the three decades following the American Revolution were not Europeans but Americans, principally from New England. To contemporary observers, New Englanders were viewed as an element quite different from the original settlers of New York. Dwight observed that a great part of its rapid population increase could be attributed to migration from New England, and estimated that "from three-fifths to two-thirds of the inhabitants have originated from that country."[41] New York State, he noted, could ultimately be regarded as a colony of New England.

Although most of the New England contingent migrating to New York State settled upstate, New York City was by no means bypassed. Increasing numbers, particularly those from New England coastal towns, were attracted by the commercial opportunities available in the great port. The largest number came from Connecticut; others were from Rhode Island, Massachusetts, and Maine. The gradual infiltration from New England is reported to have become a "great rush" about 1800, and by 1820 "the Yankees had the situation well in hand."[42] "The same motive which lured farmers from the meager, stony areas of western New England to the richer fields of the Middle West was attracting other Yankees to the great commercial emporium of America."[43] The New Englanders in New York City were found to be "more conservative in character, more grave in temperament, and at the same time, more enterprising, and more persistent in action than the descendants of the Dutch and English settlers."[44]

Dwight, who prepared a list of the inhabitants of New York City on the eve of the War of 1812 "according to their supposed number" ranked

39. Pomerantz, *New York: An American City*, p. 204.
40. Dwight, *Travels*, p. 449.   41. *Ibid.*, p. 252.
42. Albion, "Yankee Domination," *New England Quarterly*, V (October 1932), 669.
43. *Ibid.*
44. Gerard, *The Impress of Nationalities*, p. 13.

the residents of New England origin first. His classes were as follows:[45]

1. immigrants from New England;
2. the original inhabitants, partly Dutch, partly English;
3. immigrants from other parts of this state, a considerable proportion of them from Long Island;
4. immigrants from Ireland;
5. immigrants from New-Jersey;
6. immigrants from Scotland;
7. immigrants from Germany;
8. immigrants from England;
9. immigrants from France;
10. immigrants from Holland;
11. Jews.

To these are to be added a few Swedes, Danes, Italians, Portuguese, Spaniards, and West Indians.

Dwight did not provide data on the actual size of the several classes. He did note, however, that two-thirds were "derived from different parts of the United States and from Europe."[46] This would mean that one-third fell into the class ranked second in size, "the original inhabitants." Accordingly, *more* than one-third would be estimated as of New England stock.

Like later observers, Dwight had difficulty in describing a "typical" New Yorker: "Among so many sorts of persons, you will easily believe it must be difficult, if not impossible, to find a common character; since the various immigrants themselves, and to some extent their children, will retain the features derived from their origin and their education."[47]

Dwight's failure to include the Negro population in his list of peoples is probably indicative of the low esteem in which this element was then held. Nevertheless, the quarter-century following the Revolutionary War was an extremely significant period for the Negroes in New York, for it was one in which a gradual movement toward emancipation of the slaves culminated in an act promising the eventual end of slavery. At the census of 1790, 1,115 of the 5,868 white families in New York City, 19 percent, were owners of slaves.[48] Most of the slaves were household servants since the number of families in Manhattan living on farms was comparatively small. Almost half of the slaveholding families, 553, owned only one slave; 479 owned two, three, or four slaves; 78 owned between five and nine slaves; only five families owned more than nine slaves.[49]

45. Dwight, *Travels*, p. 449.   46. *Ibid.*, p. 455.   47. *Ibid.*, p. 449.
48. U.S. Bureau of the Census, *A Century of Population Growth* (Washington, D.C.: U.S. Government Printing Office, 1909), p. 282.   49. *Ibid.*, p. 294.

Organized anti-slavery activity in New York commenced in 1785 when the Manumission Society was founded. Prominent among the membership, which included Governor George Clinton, Alexander Hamilton, and John Jay, were a number of Quakers. The Quakers, after due consideration, had found slavery inconsistent with their religious beliefs, and had by 1779 emancipated their slaves. Also in 1785 the state legislature passed an act prohibiting the importation of slaves for sale in the state. Three years later the sale of any slave brought into the state after June 1, 1785, was prohibited.[50]

In 1799, following a determined effort by the Manumission Society, the state legislature passed an act leading to gradual emancipation. It provided that male children born of a slave after July 4, 1799, should be free at the age of 28 and female children at the age of 25.[51] Table 3 indicates that with the passage of this act, the number of slaves in New York City began to decline. Within the decade 1800-10 the number fell from 2,868 to 1,686. In 1817 a new act of the state legislature ordered complete emancipation by 1827.[52] At the 1820 census only 518 slaves were counted in New York City.

Despite the decline of slavery, the Negro population in New York City grew proportionately about as rapidly as the white population during the period from 1786 to 1820, continuing to comprise about one-tenth of the total community. The increase apparently was due to an influx of free Negroes into the city. In the decade 1790-1800 the number of free Negroes more than tripled, climbing from 1,101 to 3,514. In consequence the proportion of free Negroes in the total Negro population climbed from 32 to 55 percent. An apparent decline in the number of Negroes between 1800 and 1805 (Table 3) was probably due to a defíciency in the 1805 enumeration, for the 1810 census showed more than double the number of Negroes enumerated in 1805. (Since the census was made to secure returns of jurors, there may have been less motive for an accurate count of Negroes.) A deficiency also appears evident in the 1816 count.

RELIGIOUS GROUPS

Visitors to New York after the American Revolution often remarked upon the great variety of religious groups in the city. Moreau de St. Mēry, for example, who came to the city in 1794, noted: "New York has 22 churches or houses of worship. Four are Presbyterian, three Dutch Reformed, three Episcopal, two German Lutheran, two Quaker, two

    50. Pomerantz, New York: An American City, p. 221.   51. Ibid., p. 223.
52. Ibid., p. 224.

Baptist, two Methodist, one French Protestant, one Moravian, one Roman Catholic, one Jewish synagogue."[53] It may be appropriate at this point to note briefly some background information concerning the faiths that were represented in New York at the close of the eighteenth century.

The Episcopal church, the established church of the colony, had received some support from public taxation prior to the Revolution. The church was disestablished during the war, and the New York State Constitution of 1777 guaranteed "the free exercise and enjoyment of religious profession and worship, without discrimination or preference ... to all mankind." When a state statute in 1784 provided for the incorporation of all religious bodies and repealed the colonial laws relating to the maintenance of the Anglican church, the congregation of the parish of Trinity Church became an American corporation. Trinity Church, the principal place of worship, which had been built in 1696 and destroyed in the great fire of 1776, was rebuilt after the Revolution and consecrated in 1790. Trinity's two chapels, St. George's (built 1759) and St. Paul's (built 1766), survived the Revolution. In the closing decade of the eighteenth century, two additional Episcopalian churches were founded, Christ Church (1793) and St. Mark's (1799).[54]

Protestant churches other than the Episcopalian were tolerated in New York in the colonial period, but only the Dutch Reformed Church had the special privilege of incorporation, with its right to hold property. The Dutch Reformed Church in New York acquired a new charter in 1784, replacing one granted by the British in the seventeenth century. The three prewar church edifices were rebuilt or repaired after the Revolution. Dutch Reformed congregations were also in existence in Greenwich Village and in the village of Harlem before the close of the eighteenth century.[55]

As early as 1706 a few New Englanders "who were Presbyterians in sentiment" met in private houses in New York City for purposes of worship.[56] The first Presbyterian church in New York City was founded in 1719, and by the eve of the Revolution, three places of worship existed. By 1794 a fourth had been founded, and at the turn of the century New York contained seven Presbyterian churches, more than the number for any other faith.[57]

The Baptists and the Methodists also gained many new affiliates in the federal period. The first Methodist church building in America was the home of the John Street congregation which was opened in 1768.

53. Roberts, *Moreau de St. Méry*, p. 149. Pomerantz, *New York: An American City*, p. 372 ff, indicated that a third Baptist church had been founded in 1791. The two German churches were Lutheran and Calvinist Reformed.

54. Pomerantz, *New York: An American City*, pp. 372-74.

55. *Ibid.*, p. 378; Hardie, *Description*, p. 168.

56. Jonathan Greenleaf, *A History of the Churches of All Denominations in the City of New York from the First Settlement to the Year 1846* (New York: E. French, 1846), p. 124.

57. Hardie, *Description*, p. 168; Pomerantz, *New York: An American City*, p. 378.

The earliest congregants were immigrants of the previous two years from Ireland; the first preacher was Philip Embury. By 1773 the church was reputed to have 180 members.[58] The earliest Baptist church in New York was organized in 1724, but proved to be short-lived. In 1762 John Gano became the pastor of a newly established church, which came to be known as the First Baptist Church, comprised of twenty-seven members who had been worshipping in private homes for about fifteen years. In 1770 a split occurred when fourteen members left to form the "Second Baptist Church in New York." Gano became a chaplain during the Revolution, and his congregation scattered. When he returned to New York in September 1784, only thirty-seven members of the prewar two hundred could be found for the rebuilding of the church.[59]

Persons of German descent formed the bulk of the membership of the Lutheran, German Reformed, and Moravian churches. Each of these faiths had founded congregations in New York prior to the War of Independence. The earliest known Lutheran church was a small stone building on Rector Street built in 1702 and destroyed in the fire of 1776 and not rebuilt. Services, originally in Dutch, were being conducted half in German and half in Dutch shortly before the war. The second Lutheran church, built in 1767 on William Street, absorbed the earlier congregation after the Revolution. Services were conducted in German.[60]

The Quakers, or Friends, had built their first place of worship in New York about 1706. After the Revolution congregations replaced the meeting houses. The influence of the Society of Friends in the city was out of all proportion to its numbers. In 1805 the number of Friends in New York was put at 160 families, or 820 persons.[61]

In 1728, the small congregation of Jews in New York, Shearith Israel, began building its own synagogue on Mill Street, after having worshipped in rented rooms for many years.[62] In 1773 Ezra Stiles reported that the Jewish congregation "consists of between thirty and forty families."[63] Growth was slow; as late as 1812, it was reported that there were but "fifty families of Jews in New York, which with a number of unmarried men, make from seventy to eighty subscribing members of the Congregation Shearith Israel."[64] It was not until 1818 that New York's only Jewish congregation erected a larger structure.[65]

58. Hardie, *Description*, pp. 165-66; Greenleaf, *History of the Churches*, p. 283.
59. Greenleaf, *History of the Churches*, pp. 222-30.   60. *Ibid.*, pp. 53-54.
61. Hardie, *Description*, p.163; Pomerantz, *New York: An American City*, p. 382.
62. Pomerantz, *New York: An American City*, p. 385.
63. *Collections of the Massachusetts Historical Society*, second series (1838), I, 150, from a manuscript describing the state of religious liberty in the Colony of New York found among the papers of Dr. Ezra Stiles, president of Yale.
64. Hannah Adams, *The History of the Jews from the Destruction of Jerusalem to the Nineteenth Century* (Boston: J. Eliot, Jr., 1812), II, 215.
65. Hyman B. Grinstein, *The Rise of the Jewish Community of New York 1654-1860* (Philadelphia: The Jewish Publication Society of America, 1945), p. 31.

While Jews had lacked some political privileges in the colonial era, the practice of their religion was tolerated. Roman Catholics, however, were unable to practice their religion, for Catholic clergy were barred from the province. By the state constitution of 1777 Catholics gained freedom of public worship. Nevertheless, state laws deprived Catholics from public office and Catholic aliens from citizenship. These laws were gradually removed. After the Revolution a small group of Catholics who had previously worshipped in secret began to pray in public under the Jesuit Father Farmer.[66] The Catholic population in New York City in 1785 has been estimated at two hundred.[67] In that year Dr. John Carroll noted: "the congregation at New York, begun by the venerable Mr. Farmer, of Philadelphia, he has now ceded to an Irish Capuchin resident there... He is not indeed so learned, or so good a preacher, as I could wish, which mortifies his congregation; as at New York, and most other places in America, the different sectaries have scarce any other test to judge of a clergyman than his talent for preaching, and our Irish congregations, such as New York, follow the same rule."[68]

In 1786 St. Peter's Church was opened as the first Catholic church in the city; the Catholic population increased with great vigor; by 1806 their number was placed at ten thousand.[69] In 1818 Dr. Connolly, Bishop of New York, reported: "At present there are here about sixteen thousand Catholics, mostly Irish."[70]

New churches were constructed with great speed after the Revolution, matching the march of population; by the close of the eighteenth century, the city had thirty-four places of worship. John Lambert noted in the first decade of the nineteenth century: "New York abounds with religious sects of various denominations; but the episcopalians and presbyterians seem to be the most numerous, at least they have more places of worship than any others. The quakers form but a small community in this city, and even that is decreasing; for the young people do not appear much inclined to follow up the strict ceremonials of their parents in point of dress and manners.... There are several rich and respectable families of Jews in New York; and as they have equal rights with every other citizen of the United States, they suffer under no invidious distinctions."[71]

At the turn of the century when the majority of the Negro population came to consist of free men, pressure mounted for the Negro congregants to worship in separate facilities. In 1800 the African Methodists erected their first edifice; by 1809 there were three. The Abyssinian Baptist

66. Pomerantz, New York: An American City, pp. 383-84.
67. John Francis Maguire, The Irish in America (New York: D. & J. Sadlier, 1869), p. 443.
68. Ibid., p. 357.
69. Pomerantz, New York: An American City, p. 385.
70. Maguire, The Irish in America, p. 370.
71. John Lambert, Travels through Canada and the United States of North America in the Years 1806, 1807, 1808, cited in Still, Mirror for Gotham, p. 73.

Church was founded in 1805 with the pastor and congregation "persons of color." St. Philip's, the first colored Episcopalian church, was built in 1819.[72] Lambert had noted in 1806-1807 that "negroes and people of colour in New York ... are mostly of the Methodist persuasion, and have a chapel or two of their own with preachers of their colour; though some attend other places of worship according to their inclination."[73]

According to contemporary sources the total number of churches in New York City increased from 55 to 99 between 1811 and 1825. The changes by denomination are shown below:[74]

	1811	1825
Presbyterian	12	22
Episcopalian	12	18
Baptist	8	14
Dutch Reformed	7	13
Methodist	7	13
Independent	—	4
Quaker	2	3
Roman Catholic	2	3
Lutheran	1	2
Universalist	1	2
Unitarian	—	2
Jewish	1	1
Moravian	1	1
German Calvinist	1	—
New Jerusalem	—	1
Total	55	99

NEW YORK'S NEIGHBORS

Of the counties surrounding New York City, Kings County changed the least during the eighteenth century. Its population of 4,495 in 1790 was little more than double its size nine decades earlier. The Dutch stock, numbering about 1,500 (approximately the same number as in 1698), were still the largest element of the population (comprising about one-half of the 3,021 whites).[75] Since the Dutch element in the New World benefited from a very favorable natural increase and had multiplied severalfold between the opening of the eighteenth century and 1790, the complete absence of growth in Kings County is indicative of a very heavy outmigration.

72. Hardie, *Description*, pp. 162, 166-67.
73. Lambert, *Travels*, cited in Still, *Mirror for Gotham*, p. 73.
74. Dwight, *Travels*, p. 431; Hardie, *Description*, p. 182.
75. Hansen, "Minor Stocks," *AHA Annual Report*, pp. 370, 396.

Kings County continued to experience only modest population growth in the quarter-century following the 1790 census. There were two reasons for this: the high price of land, which kept prospective settlers away; and the slave economy, which deterred immigrant laborers. The land was expensive, according to a contemporary account, "because the nearness of New York assures a market for all farm products, and because the Dutch families who form such a large part of the population refuse to sell their holdings."[76]

To one contemporary observer the inhabitants of Kings County seemed "almost entirely Dutch." Smyth, an Englishman, who visited Long Island during the Revolutionary War period found that "two-thirds of the inhabitants... especially on the west end, are of low Dutch extraction, and continue to make use of their customs and language in preference to English, which however they also understand.... There is no such thing as society amongst these people, at least for a Briton, for they and their constant companions the hogs and cattle appear to possess an equal share of sensibility and sentiment. Many of them however are opulent, and they all live well, or rather plentifully."[77]

In 1790, 61 percent of all families in Kings County were owners of slaves, the highest percentage of any county in New York State, and Negro slaves formed just under one-third of the entire population. Of the 333 slave-holding families, 67 owned a single slave, 129 owned two to four slaves, 112 five to nine slaves, and 25 between 10 and 19.[78]

With one exception the six towns comprising Kings County had in 1790 roughly twice the population they had contained in 1698. The exception was the town of Brooklyn, which had grown about threefold. A town in Kings County, it should be noted, in common with towns in other counties of New York State and in New England, was the designation for a minor civil division of a county, and not necessarily for a thickly settled area with urban characteristics. (Towns in New York State and New England correspond to townships in other states rather than places incorporated as towns or cities.)

In the town of Brooklyn a small village began to sprout near the point where the ferry connecting New York City with Long Island harbored. According to a French traveler, who visited in 1794: "Brooklyn has about one hundred houses, most of them only one story high... most are chiefly along the shore, or scattered without regular plan." The three churches of the village were described as "a Dutch Presbyterian, an Anglican Episcopal, a Methodist. Moreover, the Anabaptists meet in a building

76. Roberts, *Moreau de St. Méry*, p. 172.

77. J. F. D. Smyth, *A Tour in the United States of America* (London, 1784; reissued New York: Arno Press, 1968), II, 378-79.

78. U.S. Bureau of the Census, *A Century of Population Growth*, pp. 283, 293.

which is used as a school during the week."[79] The Dutch church, of course, dated from the seventeenth century. The Anglican church, St. Ann's Episcopal Church, which had been incorporated in 1787, stemmed from a congregation inaugurated during the Revolutionary War, when a Tory preacher conducted services for the British officers stationed in the area. Methodism had come to Brooklyn shortly after the Revolution by means of the missionary activity of enthusiastic young preachers. Unlike the Dutch and Anglican churches, which had been based along ethnic lines, the new church's appeal disregarded race and social standing. In 1800, one-third of the membership was colored. In 1819, however, most of the Negroes seceded and established a congregation of their own.[80]

New congregations came into being in the 1820s as the community expanded. Presbyterian families, primarily of English origin with a scattering of Scottish and Irish and a very few Dutch, erected a church building in 1822. One year later a Baptist church was organized, though it was not until 1826 that a small wooden structure was erected. The Roman Catholic Society of Brooklyn, made up largely of Irish families, worshipped in its own building in 1823.[81]

Even before the close of the eighteenth century commuting, at least during the summer months, from homes in Brooklyn to workplaces in Manhattan had begun. St. Méry (1794) noted that "just south of Brooklyn and overlooking the river is a small chain of hills on which are the country houses of many wealthy New Yorkers. Its proximity to New York leads New Yorkers to rent the houses and send their families there during the hot season. The men go to New York in the morning, and return to Brooklyn after the Stock Exchange closes."[82]

The location of Brooklyn at the terminus of the various roads branching from the ferry to the scattered settlements of Long Island had a decisive effect upon the course of its development into an urban center. Between 1790 and 1810, the population of the town of Brooklyn rose from 1,603 to 4,402 while Kings County's five other towns combined increased only from 2,892 to 3,901 (see Table 4). With the introduction of steam ferries in 1810, the crossing of the East River no longer posed a hazardous undertaking, and the development of Brooklyn as a bedroom community was greatly accelerated.[83] In 1816, in accordance with a local request, the state legislature gave the settlement by the Brooklyn ferry a village charter. The newly incorporated village, a square mile in area, had a population of about 4,000, most of whom lived in dwellings clustered near the ferries. The town of Brooklyn had a population of 7,175 at the 1820 census, of

79. Roberts, *Moreau de St. Méry,* p. 168.
80. Ralph Foster Weld, *Brooklyn Village* (New York: Columbia University Press, 1938), New York State Historical Association Series, VII, 57-71.   81. *Ibid.,* pp. 73-87.
82. Roberts, *Moreau de St. Méry,* p. 170.
83. Pomerantz, *New York: An American City,* p. 269.

whom 5,210 were in the village and 1,965 in the rural area. The state census of 1825 showed the town had 10,791 residents, including 8,800 in the village.[84]

TABLE 4
Population of Kings County by Town, 1790-1855

Town	1790	1800	1810	1820	1830	1840	1845	1850	1855
Kings, total	4,495	5,740	8,303	11,187	20,535	47,613	78,691	138,882	216,355
Brooklyn	1,603	2,378	4,402	7,175	15,394	36,233	59,574	96,838	205,250
Bushwick	540	656	798	930	1,620	1,295	1,857	3,739	‡
Flatbush	941	946	1,159	1,027	1,143	2,099	2,225	3,177	3,280
Flatlands	423	493	517	512	596	810	936	1,155	1,578
Gravesend	426	489	520	534	565	799	898	1,064	1,256
New Lots*									2,261
New Utrecht	562	778	907	1,009	1,217	1,283	1,863	2,129	2,730
Williamsburg†						5,094	11,338	30,780	‡

*Formed from Flatbush in 1852.   †Formed from Bushwick in 1839.
‡Annexed to Brooklyn in 1854.
Source: New York Secretary of State, Census of the State of New York for 1855 (Albany, 1857).

In contrast to Brooklyn, the other towns of Kings County experienced no aggregate increase in population between 1810 and 1825. Brooklyn's growth was tied to New York City's rise, and the close relationship between the two at this time was aptly expressed by James Fenimore Cooper when he reported Brooklyn to be "a flourishing village which has arisen within the last half dozen years from next to nothing; which from its position and connexion with the city, is in truth no more than a suburb differently governed; and which in itself contains about 10,000 souls."[85]

Unlike New York City, where the number of slaves fell by more than four-fifths in the first decades of the nineteenth century, the feeling for manumission was comparatively weak in Kings County, and the number of slaves declined only from 1,479 in 1800 to 879 in 1820. As a result, on the eve of emancipation in New York State, the number of slaves in Kings County was actually greater than in Manhattan. The bulk of the slaves were concentrated in the rural towns; Brooklyn contained 445 slaves in 1800 and 190 in 1820; the five rural towns held 1,034 in 1800 and 689 in 1820. Slaves formed less than 3 percent of the total population of Brooklyn in 1820, but still constituted 17 percent of the total in rural Kings County.[86]

84. Weld, *Brooklyn Village* pp. 25,274.
85. James Fenimore Cooper, *Notions of the Americans Picked up by a Traveling Bachelor* (Philadelphia: Carey, Lea, and Carey, 1828), I, 124.
86. *Census of the State of New York for 1855*, p. xi; U.S. Department of State, *Census for 1820* (Washington, 1821), p. 27.

On Staten Island (Richmond County), separated from Manhattan by five miles of sea, there was little change in the bucolic pattern during the first quarter of the nineteenth century, and slavery died hard. In 1820 there were still 532 slaves on the island, as compared with 675 in 1800. As only 78 free Negroes were enumerated in 1820, it would appear that the freedmen tended to emigrate (probably to New York City).[87] While Richmond County's total population grew modestly between 1790 and 1825, from 3,835 to 5,932, the Negro population declined from 886 to 507, or from 23 percent of all residents to less than 9 percent (see Table 5).

TABLE 5
Population of Kings County and Richmond County by Race, 1790-1860

Census year	Kings County			Richmond County		
	Total	White	Negro	Total	White	Negro
1790	4,495	3,017	1,478	3,835	2,949	886
1800	5,740	3,929	1,811	4,564	3,806	758
1810	8,303	6,450	1,853	5,347	4,636	711
1820	11,187	9,426	1,761	6,135	5,525	610
1825	14,679	13,137	1,542	5,932	5,425	507
1830	20,535	18,528	2,007	7,082	6,530	552
1835	32,057	30,128	1,929	7,691	7,265	426
1840	47,613	44,767	2,846	10,965	10,482	483
1845	78,691	75,745	2,946	13,673	13,197	476
1850	138,882	134,817	4,065	15,061	14,471	590
1855	216,355	211,875	4,480	21,389	20,799	590
1860	279,122	274,123	4,999	25,492	24,833	659

Source: New York Secretary of State, Census of the State of New York for 1875 (Albany, 1877).

With emancipation many of the freedmen from Long Island and Staten Island migrated to New York City. The influx of blacks, however, had very little effect on the population mix in the metropolis since concurrently a far greater tide was starting to stream into Manhattan from the ports of Europe. It was this flow that within a relatively short time came to transform New York into a city of foreign immigrants, a city in which the population of "American stock" would become a minority numerically, although an elite one.

87. *Census of the State of New York for 1855*, p. xi.

3 The "Foreign City"

In the first quarter of the nineteenth century, New York replaced Philadelphia as the largest city of the United States. In the second quarter of the century, not only did New York enhance its lead over its nearby rival, but it superseded Mexico City as the most populous city of the Western Hemisphere.[1] Within a decade after midcentury, on the eve of the Civil War, New York fully emerged as one of the great metropolitan centers of the world. In 1825 New York had contained 166,000 residents; across the East River the suburban village of Brooklyn held an additional 11,000. In 1860 the entire metropolitan area was home to more than one million persons, including 814,000 in New York City, and 267,000 in the city of Brooklyn.

New York's magnificent harbor not only provided it with an advantage over its rivals in the transatlantic trade, but was equally adaptable to coastwise commerce, and upon the completion of the Erie Canal in 1825, the city's communication with the interior of the nation was second to none. But the commercial eminence of New York must also be credited to its citizens, and among these the New England entrepreneurs tended to lead. "The Yankees," related the historian Robert Greenhalgh Albion, "captured New York Port about 1820 and dominated its activity at least until the Civil War. . . . The Yankees built and commanded most of the ships engaged in New York's ever-increasing commerce."[2]

Albion had described three representative types of New England immigrants in mercantile circles, in addition to shipbuilders and mariners. These included (1) businessmen who, having founded prosperous establishments in New England ports, came to New York to increase the scope of their activity; (2) representatives of large New England firms sent to New York to maintain and further commercial connections; and

---

1. Poinsett estimated the population of Mexico City in 1822 at between 150,000 and 160,000, as cited in *Encyclopedia Americana* (Philadelphia, 1835), VIII, 454. The Italian geographer, Adriano Balbi, placed the figure for 1828 at 180,000, *The American Almanac 1830* (Boston and New York, 1833), p. 147. New York City had 166,000 residents in 1825 and 202,000 by 1830.

2. Albion, "Yankee Domination," *New England Quarterly*, V (October 1932), 665.

(3) "the self-made-men, who worked up from the bottom."[3]

The New Yorkers whose ancestors had settled in the city in the colonial period, the Knickerbocker element, resented the New Englanders who "not only beat the old New Yorkers in the commercial game but . . . had the effrontery to boast about it."[4] They regarded with some dismay the establishment in 1805 of the New England Society in the City of New York. The Society included among its stated purposes the commemoration of the landing of the Pilgrim Fathers; membership was open to "any person being of full age, being a native, or the son of a native, of any of the New England States, and of fair character."[5]

The New Englanders, according to contemporaries, hardly needed a society to preserve their way of life. James Fenimore Cooper pointed out that "though somewhat softened, a good deal of that which is distinctive between the Puritans and their brethren of the other states is said to continue for a long period after their emigration. As the former generally go to those parts where they are tempted by interest in great numbers, it is probable that they communicate quite as much or, considering their active habits, perhaps more, than they receive."[6] Two decades later, in 1845, confirmation of the Yankee power of communication in the business life of New York is to be found in the remark that "the city borrows its institutions mainly from New England."[7]

James Fenimore Cooper, in a work of nonfiction written in 1827-28, descriptive of the United States in the mid-1820s, attributes to New York City a population that is one-third of New England background:

> The city of New York is composed of inhabitants from all the countries of Christendom. Beyond a doubt a very large majority, perhaps nine-tenths, are natives of the United States, but it is not probable that one-third who live here first saw the light on the island of Manhattan. It is computed that one in three are natives of New England, or are descendants of those who have emigrated from that portion of the country. To these must be added the successors of the Dutch, the English, the French, the Scotch and the Irish, and not a few who came in their proper persons from the countries occupied by these several nations. In the midst of such a melange of customs and people, it is exceedingly difficult to extract anything like a definite general character.[8]

By the second quarter of the nineteenth century, the old New Yorkers saw themselves a minority culture in the city of their birth. In 1835, in

---

3. *Ibid.*, p. 670.   4. *Ibid.*, p. 696.   5. *Ibid.*

6. Cooper, *Notions of the Americans*, p. 136.

7. *Hunt's Merchants Magazine*, XII, 519, cited in Albion "Yankee Domination," *New England Quarterly*, V (October 1932), 682.

8. Cooper, *Notions of the Americans*, p. 135.

what has been interpreted as a conscious effort to preserve its identity, the Knickerbocker element organized the St. Nicholas Society. To a contemporary diarist the new society represented "a sort of set off against St. Patrick's, St. George's and more particularly the New England."[9]

The New Englanders and the Knickerbockers constituted the governing classes of New York City on the eve of the Civil War. They ruled the metropolis politically, socially, and economically. But demographically, the native American stock had become a minority outnumbered by people of both Irish and German parentage. Thirty years of the "new" immigration from Europe had proved sufficient to give New York's anatomy a new appearance. In the period from 1830 to 1860, as in the three preceding decades, the bulk of the city's growth could be attributed to immigration. But in the period following the opening of the Erie Canal in 1825 the character of the immigrants to the city changed perceptibly, and consequently the ethnic stock of the community experienced a metamorphosis. The principal source from which New York drew its strength in the decades centering about the War of 1812 was the rugged coast of New England; in the decades prior to the Civil War the farms of Ireland and the villages of Germany were the chief sources of New York's newcomers.

Levasseur, secretary to Lafayette, who journeyed with the French general throughout America in 1824-25, noted that "of all the cities in the United States, New York is certainly the one in which society has lost most of the national character. The great number of foreigners which incessantly flow into it, is a continually operating cause."[10] The factors responsible for the flow of immigrants to New York tended to be cumulative. The construction of the Erie Canal called for laborers, and considerable numbers of workmen from Ireland responded. The overwhelming benefits of the Erie Canal which truly made New York the Empire State created greater demands for workers. Regular packet ships sailing from the British Isles to New York were instituted to meet the need. The increased convenience of the Atlantic voyage encouraged additional settlers. Shipbuilding flourished, and such new industries as the railroad and the clothing industry called for increasing numbers of new workers in the 1830s and 1840s. The federal census of 1830 enumerated 108,000 aliens in the United States, of whom almost half, some 52,000, were in New York State. New York City, with 17,773, had several times more alien residents than Philadelphia (4,184 in the city and county) and Boston (3,468).[11]

The march of population in New York from 1820 down to 1880 was measured by quinquennial enumerations; federal counts were made in the

9. Albion, "Yankee Domination," *New England Quarterly,* V (October 1932), 696. Quote from the diary of Philip Hove, February 14, 1835.

10. A. Levasseur, *Lafayette in America in 1824 and 1825; Or, Journal of a Voyage to the United States,* trans. John D. Godman (Philadelphia: Carey and Lea, 1829), I, 125.

11. U.S. Department of State, *Fifth Census, or Enumeration of the United States, 1830* (Washington, 1832), pp. 50, 51, 65, 163.

years ending in *zero* and state censuses, in accordance with the state constitutions of 1821 and 1846, in the years ending in *five*.[12] In 1845 the state census greatly enlarged its scope of demographic inquiry and within broad limits obtained, for the first time, data on place of birth. J. D. B. DeBow, superintendent of the United States census, called the 1845 enumeration "the most complete census of any state."[13] The federal enumeration of 1850 incorporated several of the demographic items of the New York State census and of the Boston census of 1845. Most noteworthy was the use of a single line to record the characteristics of each individual in a family. Previously only the name of the head of the family and the characteristics of the entire household had been recorded. As a result of this innovation, it was possible for the first time to secure detailed data by age, birthplace (individual countries and states), and occupation.

As New York's growth came to be a function of inmigration from abroad, population gains came to reflect the strength of the various streams of immigrants. Table 6 indicates that an unusually large increase compared with that of prior periods occurred in the number of white residents between the censuses 1845 and 1850. The gain of 143,000 amounted to more than twice any previous increment. Similarly, the number of immigrants who entered the United States in the half decade 1845-49, more than one million, was over twice the number reported in any earlier five-year span.

TABLE 6

Population of New York City by Race and Increase in Intercensal Period, 1820-6

| Census year | Population | | | Intercensal increase in period | | | |
| | | | | Number | | | Percent tota |
	Total	White	Negro	Total	White	Negro	annual increa
1820	123,706	112,820	10,886	—	—	—	—
1825	166,086	153,527	12,559	42,380	40,707	1,673	6.1
1830	202,589	188,613	13,976	36,503	35,086	1,417	4.0
1835	270,089	255,028	15,061	67,500	66,415	1,085	5.9
1840	312,710	296,352	16,358	42,621	41,324	1,297	2.5
1845	371,223	358,310	12,913	58,513	61,958	−3,445	3.5
1850	515,547	501,732	13,815	144,324	143,422	902	6.8
1855	629,904	618,064	11,840	114,357	116,332	−1,975	4.1
1860	813,669*	801,088	12,574	183,765	183,024	734	5.3

*Total includes 7 Indians.

Source: New York Secretary of State, Census of the State of New York for 1865 (Albany, 1867).

12. *Census of the State of New York for 1855,* p. xi.
13. J. D. B. De Bow, *Statistical View of the United States...A Compendium of the Seventh Census* (Washington: Nicholson, 1854), p. 26.

Components of Natural Increase

The rate of natural increase in New York City would seem to have declined in the second quarter of the nineteenth century as immigrants with high rates of mortality, living in increasingly squalid surroundings, came to constitute a major part of the population. From 1820 through 1846 a death rate as high as 30 per 1,000 residents occurred only in the years marked by cholera epidemics. These years were 1832, when 3,513 deaths from cholera pushed the city's death rate above 40 per 1,000; and 1834, when cholera claimed 971 lives. In contrast with the comparatively low death rates of this period (generally in the vicinity of 25 per 1,000), from 1847 through 1861 the death rate annually exceeded 30 per 1,000.[14] In 1849, when cholera accounted for 5,071 deaths, the crude death rate again surpassed 40 per 1,000. Cholera had the greatest impact among the foreign born; while 12 percent of the deaths of natives of the United States in 1849 were attributed to cholera, some 39 percent of all deaths among the foreign born were so assigned.[15] In 1851 and in 1854 (the latter year host to a cholera epidemic that took 2,509 victims) the mortality rate again surpassed 40 per 1,000.[16]

In their annual report for 1850, the city's health officials clearly recognized that the death rate had risen above the level for previous decades. It explained: "The tide of emigration . . . settling through New York . . . adds thousands to our bills of mortality. . . . [Mortality] has increased within the last ten years in a much greater ratio than the population. . . . We must take into consideration that within the last five years nearly 100,000 of our most healthy citizens (viz. of that class who live neatly and comfortably), since the ferries and avenues of access to our city have become so numerous and easy, have removed to Brooklyn, Williamsburgh, and other places adjacent, the heads of the families still doing business during the day in this city, whilst those least protected from disease always remain in our midst."[17]

Since accurate records of births were not kept, it is considerably more difficult to report trends in the birth rate during this period. One method often used when census data are believed to be reliable is an estimated reconstruction of the number of births from census age information. Only at the censuses of 1850 and 1860 were tallies made of the actual number of living children born within the previous year. In 1850 children under one year of age (14,807) were 2.87 percent of the population; in 1860 they were 3.01 percent (24,515).[18] These figures of children under one year of age represent survivors of births in the year preceding the census

14. New York City Board of Health, *Annual Report*, 1890, pp. 172, 178.
15. Computed from data in New York City Inspector, *Annual Report, 1849*, pp. 403, 503.
16. New York City Board of Health, *Annual Report, 1890*, pp. 172, 178
17. New York City Inspector, *Annual Report, 1850*, pp. 440, 442.
18. *Census of the State of New York for 1865*, p. 1 xiii.

date. To reconstruct an estimate of all births it would be necessary to add the number of infants born during the year who died prior to the census date. It may be assumed that in a complete enumeration the survivors would represent between 85 and 90 percent of the births.[19] Accordingly, increasing by 11 to 18 percent the number of persons under one year of age would give an approximation of the number of births in the previous year. An increase of 11 percent would indicate that birth rates for the two census years were within the range of 32 to 33 per 1,000 population; an increase of 18 percent gives a range of 34 to 35 per 1,000. These rates would naturally be too low if the census enumeration of small children was deficient.

The New York State enumerations in this period tried to ascertain through direct questioning the number of births in the year preceding the census date.[20] The tabulated numbers of births are not comparable to the federal census counts of children under one year of age, since infants who died prior to the census date are included. Returns of deaths gathered through census-taking invariably were substantially short of those obtained from the registration system. According to the statistics of births recorded by the state census, New York's birth rate ranged between 27.3 per 1,000 (1825) and 36.7 (1845). The returns of births undoubtedly failed to include many infants who did not survive to the census date. It seems likely that differences in the accuracy of census counts obscured the true pattern.

While the nature of the trend of the birth rate in the decades prior to the Civil War cannot be resolved, one fact does emerge: it is clear that in such years as 1849, 1851, and 1854, when the city's death rate exceeded 40 per 1,000, the number of deaths quite conceivably may have been greater than the number of births. And whether or not the death rate actually exceeded the birth rate in these years, it is evident that throughout the period after 1846 the natural increase of the population, as a result of higher death rates, was much reduced from the previous years.

THE FOREIGN IMMIGRANT

Although the state census of 1845 was the first to ascertain birthplace, the counts of 1825 and 1835 did inquire as to citizenship. Table 7 shows

19. These are approximations derived from model life tables which may be applicable to populations with expectations of life at birth between about 30 and 40 years. See United Nations Department of Economic and Social Affairs, *Methods for Population Projections by Sex and Age*, Population Studies No. 25 (New York: United Nations Publications, 1956), pp. 70, 76.

20. In the words of the 1855 census text: "All of the ... returns of births are much less than the true number." *Census of the State of New York for 1855*, p. xv.

the number of aliens enumerated at these counts, and for purposes of comparison, also indicates the total foreign-born population in 1845 for New York City and for Kings County. From the 1845 count it can be seen that not quite half of the foreign-born population in New York City were classified as unnaturalized. While this does not necessarily mean the same proportion applied in earlier years, it does not seem unreasonable to suggest that as early as 1825, when 11.3 percent of the city's residents were counted as aliens, as much as 20 percent of the population may have been of foreign birth.

TABLE 7

Alien Population, 1825-45, and Foreign-born Population, 1845, in New York City and Kings County

| Area | Alien population | | | Foreign-born population |
	1825	1835	1845	1845
New York City				
Number	18,826	27,669	60,946	134,656
Percent of total population	11.3	10.2	16.1	36.3
Kings County				
Number	850	3,414	13,998	26,405
Percent of total population	5.8	10.6	17.8	33.6

Source: New York Secretary of State, Census of the State of New York for 1855 (Albany, 1857).

The story of New York's population growth in the nineteenth century is inseparable from the saga of mass migration from Europe to the New World. Only eight thousand immigrants were reported to have arrived in the United States in the fiscal year ending September 30, 1820, the first for which statistics were published by the Department of State; but by 1860 some four million aliens had reached American shores.[21] The vast majority of the newcomers came from Ireland or Germany, "not because of national characteristics, but because they were the most numerous of those who experienced the profound economic and social changes in the first half of the nineteenth century."[22] In Ireland the bulk of the farm population had been reduced to rent-paying tenants and the great majority were cotters, or landless farmers or laborers. Population increased while agriculture degenerated, so that the only solution appeared to be emigration. After the passage of the Irish poor laws of 1838, the landlords

21. See E. P. Hutchinson, "Notes on Immigration Statistics of the United States," *Journal of the American Statistical Association,* LIII (December 1958), 963-1025.
22. Robert Ernst, *Immigrant Life in New York City, 1825-1863* (New York: Columbia University Press, 1949), p. 1.

stimulated the exodus, in part by mass evictions, in part by assistance in emigration. The appearance of the potato rot in 1845 led to conditions of starvation lasting for five years, that were virtually without parallel in the rest of Europe.[23] The Germans also left for America in mounting numbers because of deteriorating economic conditions. The failure of the revolution of 1848, however, eventually resulted in considerable movement abroad for political reasons. German Jews also participated in the exodus disproportionately, motivated by a desire to escape oppressive restrictions, as well as by economic and sometimes political considerations.[24]

The first immigration statistics of the Department of State, those of 1820, showed that passengers from Ireland outnumbered those from any other area, and this continued to be the case with the exception of only two years down through 1853.[25] In the succeeding years, until the Civil War caused a shift in the pattern, the principal immigrant group consisted of natives of the German states. The federal census of 1850 showed that of 2,245,000 foreign-born residents in the United States, 962,000 were natives of Ireland and 584,000 of Germany. At the 1860 census the 4,139,000 immigrants included 1,611,000 natives of Ireland and 1,276,000 from Germany.[26]

The 1845 census of New York State, which was the first to provide information on birthplace, gave only broad categories of origin. Of the 134,656 residents of New York City who were counted as born outside the United States, 96,581 were reported to be natives of Great Britain and British possessions (including Ireland, but not further broken down); 24,416 were from the German states; 3,710 from France; 3,277 from other European countries; and 508 from Mexico or South America. The remaining 6,164 presumably were of unreported nativity, a category which at subsequent censuses was included with the native population (see Table 9).[27]

THE IRISH

Although the number of natives of Ireland was not separately recorded in 1845, there can be no doubt that the Irish formed a majority of the city's foreign born. It is possible to arrive at a rough estimate of their number through the use of mortality statistics. Table 8 points out that in 1850 the

23. *Ibid.*, p. 5.
24. Grinstein, *The Rise of the Jewish Community*, p. 24; Ernst, *Immigrant Life*, p. 9.
25. U.S. Bureau of the Census, *Historical Statistics of the United States, Colonial Times to 1957* (Washington, D.C.: U.S. Government Printing Office, 1960), p. 57.   26. *Ibid.*, p. 66.
27. New York Secretary of State, *Census of the State of New York for 1845* (Albany, 1846), no paging.

crude death rate of natives of Ireland resident in New York City (about 25 per 1,000) was almost one-third higher than that among persons originating from England, Scotland, and Wales (about 19 per 1,000). If we assume that a similar relationship existed in 1845, then the total British rate of 18.8 per 1,000 could be reckoned to include a crude rate of 20.3 among the Irish and of 15.3 among the English, for a population of slightly over 68,000 natives of Ireland and slightly over 28,000 from other areas of British sovereignty. Hypothetically, supposing the Irish crude death rate did not differ in 1845 from the English, Scotch, or Welsh rate, the Irish population could be estimated at almost 74,000. This would certainly represent a maximum estimate, since it is likely that higher Irish mortality was present in 1845, as well as in 1850 and later years. Probably a figure of 70,000 is a close approximation of the number of natives of Ireland in New York City in 1845.

TABLE 8

Deaths and Death Rates of the Foreign-born Population of New York City by Country of Birth, 1845 and 1850

	1845		1850	
Place of birth	Number of deaths	Rate per 1,000 pop.	Number of deaths	Rate per 1,000 pop.
Total foreign	2,286	17.8	5,060	21.5
France	46	12.4	80	16.0
Germany	353	14.5	815	14.5
England, Scotland, Wales	399 ⎫		609	19.4
Ireland	1,384 ⎬ 18.8		3,382	25.3
Other British possessions	32 ⎭		48 ⎫ 18.2	
All other	72	19.0	126 ⎭	

Source: New York City Inspector, Annual Report of Deaths in the City and County of New York, 1845, 1850. Rates computed using data in Table 9.

By 1860 the Irish-born population in New York City had tripled to almost 204,000, about 13 percent of the total number from Erin then living in the United States. A contemporary observer was much depressed by the following fact:

> Notwithstanding the vast majority of those who emigrate Ireland to America have been exclusively engaged in the cultivation of the soil—as farmers, farm-servants, or outdoor laborers—so many of this class remain in cities and towns, for which they are not best suited; rather than go to the country, for which they are specially suited.... Irish emigrants of the peasant and labouring class were generally poor, and after defraying their first expenses on landing had but little left to enable them to push their way into the country in search

of such employment as was best suited to their knowledge and capacity; though had they known what was in store for too many of them they would have endured the severest privation and braved any hardship, in order to free themselves from the fatal spell in which the fascination of a city life has meshed the souls of so many of their race.[28]

TABLE 9
Birthplace of the Population of New York City, 1845-60

Place of birth	1845	1850	1855	1860
Total*	371,223	515,547	629,904	813,669
Native	236,567	279,814	307,444	429,952
Foreign	134,656	235,733	322,460	383,717
Native				
New York	194,916	234,843	262,156	379,034
New England	16,079	17,543	17,976	20,785
Connecticut	—	7,784	7,239	7,896
Massachusetts	—	5,587	6,205	7,638
Maine	—	1,432	1,380	1,663
Vermont	—	953	1,278	1,306
New Hampshire	—	826	1,001	1,170
Rhode Island	—	961	873	1,112
New Jersey		13,255	12,259	12,909
Pennsylvania	25,572	5,283	4,949	6,037
Other U.S.		6,828	6,381	9,066
At sea			103	88
Not stated	—	2,062	3,620	2,033
Foreign				
Ireland	96,581†	133,730	175,735	203,740
German states	24,416	56,141	97,572	118,292
Great Britain	†	31,331	32,135	37,187‡
England and Wales	—	23,671	23,648	27,977
Scotland	—	7,660	8,487	9,208
France	3,710	4,990	6,321	8,074
Brit. No. America	†	9,541	2,956	3,899
All other	3,785		7,751	12,525

*Population of "not stated" origin included with foreign in 1845 and with native in other years.

†Ireland plus Great Britain and British possessions combined.

‡Includes 2 with region not specified.

Source: New York Secretary of State, Census of the State of New York for 1845 (Albany, 1846); and Census of the State of New York for 1855 (Albany, 1857); also J. D. B. De Bow, Statistical View of the United States (Washington, 1854); U.S. Census Office, Population of the United States in 1860; Compiled from the Original Returns of the Eighth Census (Washington, 1864).

28. Maguire, *Irish in America*, pp. 214-15.

Lacking in both resources and skills the Irish peasant class in the cities had to take whatever jobs were available at the lowest levels of the labor market. With only their labor to offer they were disproportionately represented as unskilled laborers, construction workers, and household servants. Data on the occupations of the foreign born in New York, painstakingly tabulated by Ernst from the original manuscripts for the census of 1855, provide the statistical evidence. Almost 20 percent of the Irish immigrants who were gainfully employed in 1855 were described as laborers, compared with 3.5 percent of the immigrants from all other countries. Fully 26.4 percent of the Irish-born labor force was employed as domestic servants, as against 9.0 percent among all other immigrants.[29]

THE GERMANS

The German community in New York began to grow at a faster rate than the Irish in the years preceding the Civil War. In 1845 the number of natives of Germany—24,416—was only about one-third the number of Irish born. This figure more than doubled between 1845 and 1850, and had redoubled by 1860 to 118,292, equivalent to about 9 percent of all German immigrants in the nation. Among the Germans enumerated in New York at the 1860 census, 59,217 were attributed to specified countries among the still disunited German states and 59,075 to the category Germany, unspecified. A majority of those of stated origin came from three south German lands: Bavaria (18,576), Baden (9,136), and Wurttemberg (6,497). The remainder were natives of Prussia (12,842), Hesse (11,169), and Nassau (997).[30]

While the new immigrants, generally impoverished, had to take whatever housing was available, they tended eventually to congregate in neighborhoods where there were many others of their ethnic group. In one section of the city a visitor in the 1830s found an area where "one might suppose that a slice of Cork or Dublin had been transferred to America— houses, people, dirt, and all."[31] A majority of the German immigrants by 1860 were concentrated in Little Germany ("Deutschlandle"), a section of the city east of the Bowery, extending from Houston to Twelfth Street. Karl Theodor Griesinger, who lived in the United States in the 1850s, has given an· explanation of how this came about: "Naturally the Germans were not forced by the authorities, or by law, to settle in this specific area. It just happened. But the location was favorable because of its proximity

29. Derived from data in Ernst, *Immigrant Life,* p. 213.
30. U.S. Census Office, *Population of the United States in 1860; Compiled from the Original Returns of the Eighth Census* (Washington, 1864), p. 609.
31. Still, *Mirror for Gotham,* p. 89.

to the downtown business district where the Germans are employed. Moreover, the Germans like to live together; this permits them to speak their own language and live according to their customs. The cheapness of the apartments also prompted their concentration. As the first Germans came into *Kleindeutschland,* the Irish began to move and the Americans followed because they were ashamed to live among immigrants."[32]

Grinstein has described the Jewish population shifts prior to the Civil War. In 1818 a majority of the Jews lived on Pearl, Water, and lower Greenwich Streets. In the 1820s the principal area of residence shifted to what was later called "Midtown," an area east and west of Broadway from Houston Street to Pearl Street. In the 1850s the "Midtown" area was abandoned except by recent immigrants, the former residents moving "uptown," that is, above Eighth Street.[33]

THE NEGROES

The Negro community in New York City, despite the abolition of slavery in the Empire State, experienced no long-run population increase between 1825 and 1860. Census figures do indicate a gradual climb from 12,559 in 1825 to a peak of 16,358 in 1840, and then a return to the earlier level, 12,574, in 1860 (see Table 6). It was generally believed that the mortality among the Negro population in the city was so high that natural increase, unlike the situation in the South, did not result in growth. Whatever increases occurred were the effect of migration. Cooper, writing in the 1820s, declared: "I think it must be assumed as fact for our future reasoning, that the free blacks rather decrease than otherwise (always excepting the effects of manumission)."[34]

The available mortality statistics seem to indicate that deaths among the Negro population were so high they probably exceeded births. In 1825, for example, interment data reveal 875 deaths.[35] Even when allowance is made for including a small percentage of stillbirths, it would seem that the Negro death rate must have exceeded 60 per 1,000 that year. One likely indication that the natural increase of the Negro community was negative was the actual decline in the number reported as born in New York State between the censuses of 1850 and 1860 (see Table 10).

Migration of Negroes depended to a large extent upon the opportunities for employment. These became considerably reduced after 1840 when

32. *Ibid.,* p. 161.
33. Grinstein, *Rise of the Jewish Community,* pp. 31-33.
34. Cooper, *Notions of the Americans,* p. 288.
35. Hardie, *Description,* p. 161.

Negroes had to compete for the available jobs with overwhelming numbers of Irish newcomers. Cooper, in the 1820s, found "the scarcity of domestics and the large proportion of families who keep servants induce thousands of free people of colour to resort [to New York] for employment. A great many are also hired as the labourers on board of vessels."[36] In the 1850s British observers found the colored residents competing for their jobs as house servants, barbers, and coachmen with the Irish.[37] According to a report based on the 1855 census returns, the bulk of the Negro labor force had the following occupations: domestic servants (1,025), laborers (536), waiters (499), and laundresses (366).[38]

TABLE 10
Birthplace of the Negro Population of New York City, 1850 and 1860

Place of birth	1850	1860
Total	13,815	12,574
Native	13,201	12,160
Foreign	614*	414
Native		
New York	8,356	7,868
New Jersey	1,480	1,166
Maryland	750	799
Pennsylvania	682	651
Virginia	878	532
All other	1,055	1,144
Foreign		
West Indies	147	207
All other	467*	207

*Includes nativity not stated.
Source: J. D. B. De Bow, Statistical View of the United States (Washington, 1854); U.S. Census Office, Population of the United States in 1860 (Washington, 1864).

CENSUS CHANGES, 1845-60

Table 9, which shows the birthplace of New York City residents at the four enumerations from 1845 through 1860, indicates some striking peculiarities in the growth of the native population. A gain of about 43,000 is recorded between 1845 and 1850, followed by an increase of only 28,000 between 1850 and 1855, and of over 122,000 between 1855 and 1860. It is pertinent to explore whether these changes do represent real

36. Cooper, Notions of the Americans, p. 284.
37. Still, Mirror for Gotham, p. 131.
38. Ernst, Immigrant Life, p. 213.

fluctuations in growth or are products of various types of defects in enumeration.[39]

Six possible explanations for the statistical patterns may be mentioned:

1. There may have been an overcount of foreign born. Some writers have suggested that there may have been considerable reporting of the American-born children of immigrants as foreign born. If this is to provide the explanation for the changes recorded for the 1850s, one would have to assume that this overenumeration of foreign born and underenumeration of native born occurred in 1855, but was not particularly substantial at other censuses. If, for example, thirty thousand persons were incorrectly reported as foreign born in 1855 and can be transferred to the native category, the trend of growth in the native population of 1845-50 would show no dip in the 1850s.

2. The whole population in the 1855 census may have been underenumerated relative to other censuses. If one assumes that all components of the population were underenumerated in 1855, an increment in the native-born population to account for the missing element could raise the total to a level in line with expectations based on the trend for 1845-50. Also, at least a partial explanation would be provided for the apparent losses shown in the number of persons born in nearby states such as New Jersey, Pennsylvania, and Connecticut between 1850 and 1855, and the uniform gains of 1855-60 (see Table 9).

3. A shift may have occurred in the interstate migration stream in the five-year periods. State-of-birth statistics, which are frequently used to measure migration, are limited in that they merely show survivors of all preceding movement from one state to another area. A native of New Jersey, for example, may have arrived in New York one year or fifty years before the date of a particular census. If data for a city from two successive censuses are available, a rough estimate of the net migration during the time interval among a given state-of-birth group (but not necessarily persons coming directly from that state since migrants may have lived in states other than their native state prior to their most recent migration) can be attempted if adequate allowance for deaths occurring during the time interval among the migrant group resident in the city is made. State-of-birth statistics show relatively small differences during the period 1845-60 in the number of American-born residents of New York City who were born outside New York State. The number of U.S. natives born outside the Empire State changed by less than two thousand between 1845 and 1850, and between 1850 and 1855. The increase of about six thousand

---

39. A useful discussion of inaccuracies in population counts may be found in A. J. Jaffe, *Handbook of Statistical Methods for Demographers* (Washington, D.C.: U.S. Government Printing Office, 1951), Chap. IV, Evaluating and Correcting Census Returns.

between 1855 and 1860 can account for only a very minor part of the large growth in the number of native born.

4. A shift may have occurred in the intrastate migration stream in the five-year periods. Examining the data for New York State natives alone indicates an increase of about 40,000 between 1845 and 1850, of 27,000 between 1850 and 1855, and 117,000 between 1855 and 1860 (see Table 9). There is no evidence that the very substantial gain of the latter period could have occurred from an influx of upstate residents. In the early 1850s, J. D. B. De Bow, superintendent of the United States census, had included among suggestions made as a "result of eighteen months familiarity with the returns an outline for the next decennial census, which may possibly afford some aid also to those who are engaged in framing the forms for State and city enumerations" a query that would "denote whether the party was born in the town, city, or county of his residence, or in another part of the same State."[40] The New York State census authorities asked the county of birth of residents in 1855, but, unfortunately, the federal census never followed suit. The successive New York State censuses, therefore, provide a rough picture of intrastate movement over time. Since the 1865 census showed that the aggregate number of persons living in New York City who were born in New York State outside New York County was then smaller than it had been in 1855, one can assume that the inflow from within the state was not especially significant.

The movement from New York City to other parts of the state, principally the adjacent counties, was much greater in extent between 1845 and 1860 than was the reverse traffic. A sharp drop in the strong outflow of native New Yorkers from Manhattan could be suggested as one explanation of the sharp rise in the recorded native-born population between 1855 and 1860, but there is no evidence that the heavy movement of New York natives (and foreign born as well) to Brooklyn and other environs subsided in the late 1850s from the level of earlier years.

5. A change in fertility may have effected a large increase in the native population. While the birth rate of the U.S. population is generally believed to have declined gradually prior to the Civil War, one need not assume that this was also the case in New York City, whose largely foreign-born adult population of 1860 was quite dissimilar to its largely native-born adult population of 1825.[41] Although statistics of births, as has been noted, are lacking, ratios of young children to women of child-bearing age can be obtained from census tabulations. Birth ratios, representing the number of children under five years of age per 1,000 females aged 15-49, are as follows: 1850 census, 422; 1855 census, 439; 1860

40. De Bow, *Statistical View*, p. 14.
41. See, for example, J. Potter, "The Growth of Population in America, 1700-1860," *Population in History*, ed. D. V. Glass and D.E.C. Eversley (Chicago: Aldine Publishing Co., 1965), p. 672 ff.

census, 490. If the statistics can be accepted, an increase in the fertility rate occurred between 1855 and 1860.

6. The population at the 1860 census may have been overenumerated. This explanation was seriously offered in 1865 when the state census showed a drop in population in New York County and in several other counties in the state from the count five years earlier.[42]

GEOGRAPHIC TRENDS IN MANHATTAN

By the 1830s it was becoming increasingly evident that New York's growing command of business and its advantageous location with respect to securing abundant supplies of water, fuel, and food would lead eventually to a completely urban Manhattan.[43] Yet as late as 1837 a writer could declare that "not more than a sixth part of the island of Manhattan is compactly covered with houses, stores, and paved streets. The rest is occupied with farms and gardens; though the limits of the city comprise the whole island; and the farmers and gardeners of the upper five-sixths are included in one of the wards of the city, are subject to the same municipal privileges as their more crowded neighbors, who walk on paved streets, and are surrounded with all the bustle of city life."[44]

By the 1840 census the "rural" ward, the city's Twelfth Ward, had lost additional territory to the urbanized city. It then embraced all of the island north of 40th Street. With a population of 11,652 the Twelfth Ward could boast of less than 4 percent of New York's population, but almost 90 percent of the total number of persons engaged in agriculture: 2,488 of 2,773.[45]

The railroad saw to it that northern Manhattan did not remain agricultural. By 1860 several lines of trains were carrying downtown Manhattan's workers to their homes in uptown sections. Almost all of the vast increase in population in metropolitan New York took place outside the boundaries of the earliest settled part of Manhattan, that area below Canal Street, where a large majority of the city-dwellers resided in 1825. Examination of the population trends in three principal sections of Manhattan prior to the Civil War indicates that the march uptown became a flood in the 1830s, as the area below Canal Street was steadily converted to business and commercial use. In the 1850s the population living between Canal Street and 14th Street reached a stable level, and the tide moved

42. Ernst, *Immigrant Life*, p. 185.
43. *The American Annual Cyclopaedia and Register of Important Events of the Year 1861* (New York: Appleton, 1862) p. 525.
44. Asa Green, *A Glance at New York*, cited in Warner S. Tryon, ed., *A Mirror for Americans* (Chicago: University of Chicago Press, 1952), I, 168.
45. U.S. Department of State, *Sixth Census or Enumeration of the Inhabitants of the United States* (Washington, 1841), p. 115.

farther north; the 1860 census found a majority of Manhattan's residents living above 14th Street.[46]

EXPANSION OF THE METROPOLITAN AREA

It also became clear in the early decades of the nineteenth century that the metropolitan character of New York was not limited to Manhattan. As lower Manhattan was being transformed into an area where business predominated, and as new immigrants were pouring into the available housing, increasing numbers of the city's residents moved east and west of the crowded wards—over the East and Hudson Rivers to new homes from which they could easily commute by ferry to the core area. Charles Mackay, a British visitor, indicated the metropolitan extent of New York in the late 1850s when he described the city as "the Queen of the Western World, with New Jersey on the one side, and Brooklyn on the other. The three form but one city in fact though differing in name like London and Westminster."[47]

Rapid ferry service made commuting across the East River a mass affair. By the early 1830s it was evident that the village streets in Brooklyn were expanding into the countryside. Real estate speculators hastened the division of farms outside the village limits into city lots.[48] Leaders of the town and village of Brooklyn embraced the idea of union, and in 1834 Brooklyn attained city government when the village and the balance of the town were united as a single municipality. The new city had 24,310 residents at the 1835 enumeration, of whom 18,977 were in the five wards which had comprised the former village. This was 58 percent more than the population five years earlier, in 1830, when the town of Brooklyn held 15,396 persons, including 12,403 in the village.[49]

The rapid rate of population growth resulted from the impact of the same economic forces that were enlarging New York: the advantages of the new canal system, and the impressive development of domestic commerce. As transportation facilities improved and as a supply of laborers became available, manufacturing establishments on an ever-growing scale

46. The percentage of the city's population living above 14th Street in selected years was: 1835, 9; 1840, 15; 1850, 22; 1855, 43; and 1860, 52. *American Annual Cyclopaedia 1861*, p. 526.
47. Charles Mackay, *Life and Liberty in America: Or Sketches of a Tour in the United States and Canada in 1857-58* (London: Harper and Brothers, 1859), I, 11.
48. Weld, *Brooklyn Village*, p. 47.   49. *Ibid.*, p. 25.

came into being in Brooklyn. According to a leading historian of the village period, these were even more of a factor bringing about population growth than "the influx of New York businessmen looking for convenient suburban residences."[50]

Table 4 shows the population growth in the subdivisions of Kings County prior to the Civil War. Between 1835 and 1850 the population of the city of Brooklyn soared from less than 25,000 to almost 97,000, becoming the seventh largest city in the nation. In 1855 under the Act of Consolidation, Brooklyn absorbed the city of Williamsburgh and the town of Bushwick.[51] Williamsburgh, formerly part of Bushwick, had grown very rapidly as a result of the immigrant influx of the 1840s. Its population grew sixfold between 1840 and 1850, increasing from 5,094 to 30,780. Williamsburgh was incorporated as the second city in Kings County in 1851. The consolidated city of Brooklyn had a population of 205,250, according to the state census of 1855, of whom 48,367 lived within the area formerly the city of Williamsburgh, and 8,109 in former Bushwick.[52] At the 1860 census Brooklyn, with 266,661 inhabitants, was the third largest city in the United States.

The newcomers to Kings County in the generation preceding the Civil War were of similar origin to those in the metropolis across the East River. At the 1845 census the bulk of the Kings County population reported as born outside the United States—22,342 of 26,405—came from Great Britain and British possessions. Presumably, a very large majority were from Ireland. Immigrants from the German States numbered 2,229. At the 1860 census the foreign-born population of the city of Brooklyn numbered 104,589, of whom 56,710 were from Ireland, 23,993 the German States, and 17,947 Great Britain (see Table 11). Like New York City, Brooklyn showed a surprisingly small increment in its foreign-born population between the 1855 and 1860 censuses, and a very substantial gain in its native-born group. In 1855 the native population of 109,376 included 45,586 born in Kings County, 29,340 in New York City, 13,099 in other parts of New York State, and 10,489 in New England. Details on the place of birth of the native population of 162,072 were not available for 1860.

The Negro population in Kings County, unlike that in New York City, experienced continuous, if gradual, growth between 1825 and 1860. Numbering 1,542 the former year, the low for any point in the nineteenth century, the community rose to 4,999 at the latter date (see Table 5). Despite this gain the Negro proportion of the county's total population fell from over 10 percent to only 1.8 percent.

---

50. *Ibid.*, p. 26.
51. Edward H. Hall, *A Volume Commemorating the Creation of the Second City of the World* (New York: New York Republic Press, 1898), p. 15.
52. *Census of the State of New York for 1855*, p. xxii.

TABLE 11
Birthplace of the Population of Kings County, 1845 and 1850, and of Brooklyn, 1855 and 1860

Place of birth	1845	1850	1855	1860
Total*	78,691	138,882	205,250	266,661
Native	52,286	82,681	109,376	162,072
Foreign	26,405	56,201	95,874	104,589
Native				
New York	42,818	—	88,025	—
New England	4,891	—	10,489†	—
New Jersey		—	4,921	—
Pennsylvania		—	1,961	—
Other U.S.	4,577	—	3,130	—
At sea		—	41	—
Not stated	—	—	809	—
Foreign				
Ireland	22,342‡	—	56,753	56,710
German states	2,229	—	19,119	23,993
Great Britain	‡	—	15,647	17,947
England and Wales	—	—	12,949	15,162
Scotland	—	—	2,598	2,785
France	322	—	1,005	1,346
Brit. No. America	‡	—	1,628	1,673
All other	307	—	1,722	2,920

*Population of "not stated" origin included with foreign in 1845 and with native in other years.

†Includes Connecticut, 3,890; Massachusetts, 3,751; Maine, 1,062; Rhode Island, 688; Vermont, 580; New Hampshire, 518.

‡Ireland plus Great Britain and British possessions combined.

Source: Same as Table 8.

The over-all population surge in Kings County between 1825 and 1860—from 14,679 to 279,122—placed this area far in the lead among the growing counties on the various shorelines facing New York City. Richmond County (Staten Island) saw its population climb from 5,932 in 1825 to 25,492 in 1860, while the western towns of Queens County (Newtown, Flushing, and Jamaica) also jumped fourfold in this period—from 7,204 to 30,429.[53]

As a result of the consolidation of 1855 at the state census that year, only 11,105 persons in Kings County (of 216,355) were living outside the boundaries of the city of Brooklyn, in contrast to more than 40,000 at the 1850 count. The rural towns in Kings County were Flatbush, New Utrecht, Gravesend, Flatlands, and New Lots, the latter having been formed from part of Flatbush in 1852.[54]

53. New York City Department of Health, *Annual Report of the Board of Health for...* *1904*, pp. 888-89.   54. *Ibid.*, pp. 878-79.

During the 1840s southern Westchester County began to feel the population push emanating from New York City. Much of this growth took place in the town of West Farms, which was formed from a part of the town of Westchester in 1846. Between 1850 and 1855 this new town grew from 4,436 to 12,436. By the 1860 census the town of Morrisania, with 9,245 residents, had been created from West Farms. Morrisania and West Farms, together containing 16,343 of Westchester County's 1860 population of 99,497, accounted for almost 12,000 of the county gain of about 41,000 during the 1850-60 decade.[55]

RELIGIOUS GROUPS

Until 1825 New York was overwhelmingly a Protestant city, containing only two Roman Catholic churches and one Jewish synagogue. In the second quarter of the nineteenth century the increasing immigration from Europe added ever greater numbers of Catholics, and on a much smaller scale, of Jews, to a city which would eventually have three major religious faiths. The statistics of the number of churches gathered at the state and federal censuses after 1840 are of minimal value. First, they are incomplete, excluding the congregations meeting in halls and rented quarters. Second, they completely ignore the different ratios of population per church among the religious groups. Published statistics of church members suffer from these same defects as well as from conceptual factors.

Probably the most informative data published on religion were the figures on usual attendance secured at the 1855 state census. These are shown in Table 12. "Attendance" is an indicator of size that is more comparable among religious groups than number of church edifices, seating capacity of edifices, or membership. But the attendance statistics also were incomplete, for included were only those congregations with church edifices. The state census authorities acknowledged "this inquiry did not extend to societies worshipping in school-houses, or other places of secular use."[56]

The figures of Jewish attendance probably are especially low since several Jewish congregations meeting in halls were not included. The principal value of the query, however, was that it brought out the fact that 24 Roman Catholic churches had nearly as large a usual attendance as 218 Protestant places of worship.

The growth of the Catholic population closely paralleled the influx of Irish immigrants. In 1830, according to an estimate of Bishop John Dubois,

55. *Ibid.*, p. 776; *Census of the State of New York for 1855*, p. xxx.
56. *Census of the State of New York for 1855*, p. 1 xi.

TABLE 12

Number of Churches and Usual Attendance, Religious Groups in New York City and Kings County, 1855

	Number of churches				Usual attendance			
	New York	Kings County			New York	Kings County		
Religious groups	City	Total	Brooklyn	Balance	City	Total	Brooklyn	Balance
Total	252	149	127	22	222,550	83,215	79,375	3,840
Protestant	218	131	111	20	118,225	46,455	43,115	3,340
Roman Catholic	24	17	15	2	100,500	36,690	36,190	500
Jewish	10	1	1	—	3,825	70	70	—

Source: New York Secretary of State, Census of the State of New York for 1855 (Albany, 1857).

the city had 35,000 Catholics.[57] The Irish Catholic population was estimated variously at 30,000 and 40,000 in 1834.[58] The total Catholic population was given as at least 50,000.[59] The German Catholic community was only a minute fraction of the total, numbering perhaps a thousand in 1832, and it did not have its own congregation until 1834. By the start of the Civil War the number of German Catholic churches had increased to seven.[60]

One indication of the magnitude of the Catholic population in the city comes from interment statistics of the city inspector. In the late 1830s burials (including stillbirths) in New York were tabulated by denomination of cemetery. The data for 1839, for instance, show that 32 percent of all interments (2,543 of 8,732) took place in Roman Catholic cemeteries.[61] Since about 19 percent of all burials were in Potter's Field, it is likely that somewhat in excess of 32 percent of all decedents were of Catholic origin, perhaps as many as 40 percent. At the same time it is logical to assume that the death rate among the Roman Catholic population, largely newcomers in particularly impoverished circumstances, was higher than among the non-Catholic population. If one concludes that the actual proportion of Catholics in the population was between 25 and 30 percent in 1839, then they comprised between 75,000 and 90,000 of the approximately 300,000 residents. By 1852 the Catholic population was being estimated at 200,000.[62]

57. Maguire, *Irish in America*, p. 423.
58. *Weekly Register and Catholic Diary*, February 1, 1834, cited in Ernst, *Immigrant Life*, p. 136.
59. Maguire, *Irish in America*, p. 423.
60. Ernst, *Immigrant Life*, pp. 136, 271.
61. New York City Inspector, *Annual Report, 1839*, p. 505.
62. Maguire, *Irish in America*, p. 443.

The Jewish population was estimated by Harby at 950 in 1826.[63] Grinstein, making use of seating lists of the three Jewish congregations, estimated that the total had grown to 2,000 in 1836.[64] Immigration surged after 1836, principally from Germany. In 1846 the community was placed at 12,000; by 1850 at 16,000.[65] In 1856 the population was placed at 30,000, and in 1859 the Jewish Board of Deputies estimated 40,000.[66]

The data compiled at the 1855 census also showed that in Brooklyn, as well as in New York City, the usual attendance at a relatively small number of Roman Catholic churches (15) was almost as great as at a relatively large number of Protestant churches (111). In both cities Catholics comprised about 45 percent of those estimated to be regular worshippers (see Table 12). The first Jewish religious society meeting held in Brooklyn reportedly took place in 1848 when it was necessary, in order to have the required ten males over thirteen years of age, "to import some from New York."[67]

63. Isaac Harby's "Discourse on the Jewish Synagogue" to S. Gilman in *North American Review* (July 1826), cited in Charles P. Daly, *The Settlement of the Jews in North America* (New York: P. Cowen, 1893), p. 75.

64. Grinstein, *Rise of the Jewish Community*, p. 470.   65. *Ibid.*

66. *Ibid.*, pp. 470-71.

67. Samuel P. Abelow, *History of Brooklyn Jewry* (New York: Scheba Publishing Co., 1937), p. 14.

4 The World's Second City

GROWTH OF POPULATION AND AREA, 1860-1900

The urbanized region of New York, as has been noted, spread beyond the boundaries of the island of Manhattan very shortly after the introduction of the steam ferry. By the Civil War era New York City had become the nucleus of a metropolitan area containing a host of cities, villages, and unincorporated suburban communities linked by a nexus of rapid-transit ferry and rail lines. This metropolitan region had multiplied in size from one to four million residents when the nineteenth century ended. By 1890, despite a doubling of its population over the previous quarter-century, Manhattan had only about one-half of the urban region's population. In 1898, by virtue of a vast consolidation of territory, New York City became very nearly coextensive with its urban region in New York State. All the suburbs in New Jersey, however, and some in Westchester County still remained outside the greater city's limits. Greater New York emerged as the second largest city on the globe, behind only London in population.

New York City almost certainly lost population between 1860 and 1865, though the decline probably was not so great as was indicated by the 1865 census. When the results of the New York State census for 1865 were published, so widespread were the adverse comments on the many declines reported since the 1860 tally that a county-by-county investigation was conducted by census officials.[1] Some decline in New York City is plausible because components of growth, natural increase (when the thousands of New Yorkers who lost their lives while in the service are included), and net migration probably were negative quantities between 1860 and 1865. The birth rate must have fallen even more sharply in New York City than in the nation as a whole because proportionately more men were absent, serving in the Union forces.[2] Migration from Europe fell drastically during the war years, so newcomers probably did not fully replace the older residents who continued to depart for Brooklyn, New Jersey, or other areas.

1. For some comments on census inaccuracy see Ernst, *Immigrant Life*, p. 185.
2. One estimate indicates that the equivalent of more than 20 percent of New York State's male population (of all ages) served during the Civil War and that 53,114 lives were lost. Milledge L. Bonham, Jr., "New York and the Civil War," *History of the State of New York,* ed. Alexander C. Flick (New York: Columbia University Press, 1935), VII, 125.

Commentators remarked that many of the troops had not yet returned to New York when the state census was taken in June 1865, and that even though the war had ended many men of draft age attempted to avoid being counted—associating the census takers with conscription officers despite the fact that these officials had been deliberately titled "enumerators" rather than "marshals" as at prior censuses. According to the New York Secretary of State, "suspicions still lingered in the minds of the ignorant, in densely settled localities, and many could not believe but that some scheme of military service lay concealed beneath these inquiries. This jealousy led to embarrassments and short returns in many cases."[3]

It seems most logical to conclude that the 1865 census did understate the city's population. If there is circumstantial evidence that the 1855 state count was too low, there is still more reason to conclude the 1865 count, "taken under peculiar difficulties occasioned by the late war," was incomplete.[4] The 1865 census returned 726,000 in New York City, down some 86,000 from the 1860 count, but a conjecture may be ventured that the actual figure was perhaps between 780,000 and 800,000.

The resumption of large-scale immigration from Germany and Ireland was largely responsible for the growth of the New York City population to 942,000 in 1870. The physical expansion of the city began on a comparatively small scale on January 1, 1874, when a portion of southern Westchester County, the towns of Morrisania, West Farms, and Kingsbridge were annexed by New York. The 1875 state census showed 36,194 persons in this territory which then constituted the Twenty-third and Twenty-fourth Wards of the city.[5] Of the total increase of almost 100,000 reported for New York City between the 1870 federal census and the 1875 state census, over one-third resulted from the annexation.

Growth in the "annexed district" was not as immediate as had been anticipated. Following the 1880 enumeration, which reported 41,626 persons in the two new wards,[6] the Census Office noted:

> It is often not known or not remembered that a large part of the adjacent county of Westchester has recently been brought within the corporate limits. This added country, with the exception of the villages of Morrisania, Fordham, and West Farms, is an almost purely country district, with hill and dale, upland and meadow, forest and open. . . . This portion of the city, where sometimes scarcely a hundred inhabitants can be counted to the square mile [contrasts with] some of the crowded wards of the older part of the city [where] more than 220,000

3. *Census of the State of New York for 1865*, Preface by Francis C. Barlow (no page number).   4. *Ibid.*

5. New York Secretary of State, *Census of the State of New York for 1875* (Albany, 1877), pp. 21, 381.

6. *Annual Report of the Board of Health for 1904*, p. 776.

human beings reside within the area of one square mile, besides thousands of others who come to them to attend to their daily avocation.[7]

In the 1880s two new migration streams, Jews from Eastern Europe and Italians from southern Europe, gathered momentum. Combined with the continuing inflow from Central Europe and the British Isles, the force of the tide pushed the total population of the city up by more than 300,000 to 1,515,000. This gain, however, could not compare with that of almost 600,000 by Chicago, which with 1,100,000 residents, superseded Philadelphia as the second largest American city at the 1890 census.[8] The city fathers of New York needed little imagination to see that unless New York's boundaries could expand beyond the confines of New York County, their domain would soon lose its long-held rank as the first city to the Midwestern metropolis.

In 1890 the state legislature created a commission "to inquire into the expediency of consolidating the various municipalities in the State of New York occupying the several islands in the harbor of New York," presided over by Andrew H. Green, a prominent civic leader, who as early as 1868 had focused attention on the desirability of bringing the City of New York, Kings, and Richmond Counties and the suburban parts of Westchester and Queens under one common municipal government.[9] Bills prepared as a result of the commission's unanimous recommendation of consolidation were introduced into the legislature in 1891 and in 1892 but without success. A referendum, not binding in character, was held in 1894 in greater New York on the issue of consolidation. New York, Kings, Queens, and Richmond counties voted for annexation; Westchester County towns split. In 1895 southern Westchester (the towns of Eastchester, Pelham, and Westchester, and the villages of Wakefield and Williamsbridge) was annexed to New York City.[10]

It was not until 1897 that a charter describing the terms of the political consolidation of New York City and its neighboring counties became law, with the new city coming into being on January 1, 1898. Greater New York was made up of five distinct boroughs: Manhattan, Brooklyn (Kings County), Queens (Queens County), Richmond (Staten Island), and the Bronx (comprised of the territory ceded by Westchester County in 1874 and 1895). The Borough of Queens included only the western part of pre-1898 Queens County: Long Island City, Newtown, Flushing, and Jamaica towns, and part of the town of Hempstead. The eastern sector of the county—the towns of Oyster Bay, North Hempstead, and most of

7. U.S. Census Office, *Report on the Social Statistics of Cities, Part I* (Washington, D.C.: U.S. Government Printing Office, 1886), p. 568.

8. U.S. Census Office, *Population of the United States at the Eleventh Census, Part I* (Washington, 1895), p. 1 xvii.

9. Hall, *Second City of the World*, p. 34.   10. *Ibid.*, pp. 75-77, 99 ff.

Hempstead—withdrew to form a new political subdivision known as Nassau County.[11]

The two great cities of New York and Brooklyn had a combined population of 2,321,644 in 1890, while the entire area which was to form the enlarged City of New York in 1898 then contained 2,507,414 residents. Tables 13 and 14 show the populations of the areas comprising greater New York, by designation before and after consolidation, according to the 1890 census, and the population by boroughs at the 1900 enumeration as well.

TABLE 13
Population at 1890 Census Living in Counties Partially or Entirely Absorbed into Greater New York by 1898

County	Total population in 1890 boundaries	Boundaries in 1898		
		New York City	Nassau County	Westchester County
New York	1,515,301*	1,515,301	—	—
Kings	838,547†	838,547	—	—
Queens	128,059	87,050	41,009	—
Richmond	51,693	51,693	—	—
Westchester	146,772	14,823	—	131,949
Total	2,680,372	2,507,414	41,009	131,949

*Coextensive with New York City.   †Of which 806,343 in city of Brooklyn.

Source: Derived from data in New York City Department of Health, Annual Report of the Board of Health for 1904, and U.S. Bureau of the Census, U.S. Census of Population: 1950, Vol. II, Part I (Washington, 1953).

TABLE 14
Population Living within the Area Included in the Boroughs of Greater New York as Constituted under the 1898 Act of Consolidation, 1890 and 1900

Borough	1890	1900
Total	2,507,414	3,437,202
Manhattan	1,441,216	1,850,093
Bronx	88,908	200,507
Brooklyn	838,547	1,166,582
Queens	87,050	152,999
Richmond	51,693	67,021

Source: U.S. Bureau of the Census, U.S. Census of Population: 1950, Vol. II, Part 1 (Washington, 1953).

11. For background on the history of consolidation see Harold C. Syrett, *The City of Brooklyn, 1865-1898* (New York: Columbia University Press, 1944).

One early indication of the influence of New York City upon its neighboring counties was the "usual place of employment" question asked at the state census of 1865. This was the first attempt to secure statistics of commuting. The great majority of all commuters to New York City—19,756—were residents of Kings County. Residents of Westchester County in 1865 who worked in New York numbered 1,757; of Richmond, 794; of Queens, 756; of Suffolk, 218; and of Rockland, 121.[12] Since the census covered only New York State residents, those commuters who resided in New Jersey were not enumerated.

The commuting streams grew larger each year and accelerated after the opening of the Brooklyn Bridge in 1884. By the time of its merger with New York, Brooklyn had annexed all of the suburban towns in Kings County, so that its boundaries were coextensive with the county limits. The town of New Lots, which had been formed from Flatbush in 1852, was absorbed into Brooklyn in 1886. Flatbush, New Utrecht, and Gravesend became wards of the city in 1894, and the last remaining town, Flatlands, was annexed in 1896.[13] Table 15 traces the population growth of the Kings County towns prior to their absorption.

TABLE 15
Population of Kings County by Subdivision, 1860-90

Area	1860	1865	1870	1875	1880	1890
Total	279,122	311,090	419,921	509,154	599,495	838,547
Brooklyn	266,661	296,378	396,099	482,493	566,663	806,343
Flatbush	3,471	2,778	6,309	6,940	7,634	12,338
Flatlands	1,652	1,904	2,286	2,651	3,127	4,075
Gravesend	1,286	1,627	2,131	2,180	3,674	6,937
New Lots	3,271	5,009	9,800	11,047	13,655	*
New Utrecht	2,781	3,394	3,296	3,843	4,742	8,854

* Annexed to Brooklyn in 1886
Source: New York City Department of Health, Annual Report of the Board of Health for . . . 1904.

Growth in Queens County after the Civil War was most rapid in the areas closest to New York City. Table 16 shows the population change between 1860 and 1890 in those political jurisdictions entirely consolidated into greater New York in 1898. Long Island City, the only city in the county, was formed in 1870 from part of Newtown. Its population advanced from 15,587 in 1875 to 30,506 in 1890.[14] According to an account written at the time of the creation of Greater New York, Long Island City

---

12. *Census of the State of New York for 1865*, p. lxxvi.
13. *Annual Report of the Board of Health for 1904*, p. 877.   14. *Ibid.*, pp. 888-89.

TABLE 16
Population of Selected Subdivisions of Queens County, 1860-90

Area	1860	1865	1870	1875	1880	1890
Total	30,249	31,481	42,669	50,541	52,927	82,299
Flushing	10,189	10,813	14,650	15,357	15,906	19,803
Jamaica	6,515	6,777	7,745	8,983	10,088	14,441
Long Island City*	—	—	—	15,587	17,129	30,506
Newtown	13,725	13,891	20,274	10,614	9,804	17,549

*Long Island City formed in 1870 from Newtown.

Source: New York City Department of Health, Annual Report of the Board of Health for . . . 1904.

"consisted of three communities—Astoria, Ravenswood and Hunter's Point—so distinct and separate that in common parlance their connection with each other was generally ignored, and they were referred to by their former names. Astoria, forming the eastern shore of the famous Hell Gate, contains many charming residences and old buildings. Ravenswood lies between Astoria and Hunter's Point, and is composed almost entirely of suburban residences. Hunter's Point is a great oil refining depot, with factories extending for more than a mile along the river front."[15]

Richmond County, a collection of small towns and villages, grew less rapidly than Queens, but managed to double its population between 1860 and 1890, from 25,492 to 51,693.[16]

NATURAL INCREASE

The natural increase of the population of New York during the last four decades of the nineteenth century must be estimated in part inasmuch as statistics of births, though gradually becoming more complete, remained inadequate until after the turn of the century. Only mortality data can be provided with relative certainty.

Even though epidemic pinnacles of the magnitude of those of the 1850s—crude death rates in excess of 35 per 1,000 population—did not occur during or after the Civil War, the general level of mortality remained high and did not begin to fall markedly until the last decade of the nineteenth century. The average crude death rates for the three-year periods around each decennial census were as follows[17]: 1859-61, 29.5; 1869-71, 28.0; 1879-81, 27.3; 1889-91, 27.2; and 1899-1901, 20.1.

15. Hall, *Second City of the World*, p. 16.
16. *Annual Report of the Board of Health for 1904*, pp. 888-89.
17. Computed from data in *ibid.*

Birth statistics for the United States were totally lacking during the nineteenth century; in fact, for only a small number of areas did the birth registration system yield data deemed reliable at the close of the century. New York was not among them. Demographers have had to rely on decennial census data to estimate in retrospect national birth rates, and the various methods employed have yielded different results. The birth rate of the white population of the United States in 1860, for example, has recently been estimated at 41.8 per 1,000 by Coale and Zelnik,[18] and between 37.7 and 42.1 by Yasuba.[19] The two principal problems encountered when census returns of children are used to estimate the number of births in the year (or specified number of years) preceding the census are supplying appropriate estimates of mortality for the birth cohort (group of individuals born in a specific period) up to the census date and correcting for inaccuracies in the census count, especially underenumeration. An undercount at one census is frequently evinced when the successive decennial enumeration shows substantially more "survivors" than expected among the original cohort. For the United States as a whole, the native population age x at a given census represents approximately the survivors of the native population at age x-10 at the preceding enumeration. For a particular city, however, this is not the case because of the effect of migration, and it is therefore vastly more difficult to attempt to estimate underenumeration for New York than for the United States.

To provide plausible estimates of the birth rate in New York City, a relatively simple method has been employed: the assumption that the ratios of the estimated crude white birth rates for the nation (in this case, the Coale-Zelnik estimates) to the percentage of the census white population under one year of age were the same for New York City in 1880, 1890, and 1900.[20] The necessary calculations are shown in Table 17. On the basis of this series of estimated birth rates (which may be regarded as illustrative rather than definitive), New York's population is seen as having a crude rate below the national level in 1880, a rate similar to the national average in 1890, and a slightly higher rate in 1900. This change did not come about because the fertility of the city women shifted vis-á-vis the nation's, but as a result of mass immigration's addition of a disproportionately large number of women in the childbearing age brackets to the city population. Table 18 shows that fertility, as expressed by the ratio of children to the city's women 20 to 44 years of age, continued to

18. Ansley J. Coale and Melvin Zelnik, *New Estimates of Fertility and Population in the United States* (Princeton: Princeton University Press, 1963), p. 24.

19. Yasukichi Yasuba, *Birth Rate of the White Population in the United States, 1800-1860: An Economic Study*, the Johns Hopkins University Studies in Historical and Political Science, Series LXXIX, No. 2 (Baltimore: Johns Hopkins Press, 1962), p. 99.

20. The published reports for the 1870 census did not classify the population of New York City by age.

remain below the national level, but that the proportion these women constituted of the total population rose.

TABLE 17
Estimate of the Crude Birth Rate in New York City, Census Years 1880-1900

Census year	(1) Percent of U.S. white pop. under 1 year	(2) Est. U.S. white birth rate per 1,000 pop. (Coale-Zelnik)	(3) Ratio (2) x (1)	(4) Percent of New York City pop. under 1 year	(5) Est. New York City birth rate per 1,000 (3) x (4)
1880	2.81	33.6	11.96	2.59*	31.0
1890	2.47	31.2	12.63	2.46*	31.1
1900	2.49	28.5	11.46	2.52	28.9

*White population.
Source: Computed from data in U.S. Census Office, Report on the Mortality and Vital Statistics of the United States, Tenth Census, Part 2 (Washington, 1886); Population of the United States at the Eleventh Census, Part 2 (Washington, 1897); Twelfth Census of the United States, Taken in the Year 1900; Population, Vol. I, Part 2 (Washington, 1902); and Ansley J. Coale and Melvin Zelnik, New Estimates of Fertility and Population in the United States (Princeton, 1963).

TABLE 18
Fertility Ratios, White Population of the United States and New York City, 1880-1940

Census year	Ratio of children under 5 years per 1,000 women 20-44 years		Women 20-44 years as percent of total population	
	United States	New York City	United States	New York City
1880	754.0	535.6	17.7	21.8
1890	666.7	481.4	18.0	22.7
1900	644.3	520.0	18.4	22.2
1910	609.3	484.5	18.7	22.1
1920	581.3	456.8	18.8	22.0
1930	485.5	342.6	18.9	22.5
1940	400.0	253.6	19.5	22.8

Source: Derived from U.S. Bureau of the Census data.

IMMIGRATION AND EMIGRATION

Despite the fact that only estimates of the natural increase, and therefore of the remaining increase, that due to migration, can be ventured for periods of time in the nineteenth century, it is clear that even as early as the decade 1860-70 the city of New York depended entirely upon the foreign inflow for its net inmigration. Although native American migrants, of course, also settled in New York, the hinterland of the United States did not make a net contribution to the city's growth because the native-born population who left New York exceeded in number those who entered. This pattern continued into the twentieth century.

Table 19 indicates that the foreign-born population of the city increased by 35,000 between 1860 and 1870. Deaths among the foreign-born residents in this period approximated 75,000, indicating that the net migration of the foreign born was about 113,000. Since the total increase in New York's population was only 129,000 in this decade, it is obvious, as the natural increase undoubtedly was well above 16,000, that a substantial outmigration took place among the native population.

TABLE 19
Population of New York City and Brooklyn, 1860-90, and of Greater New York, 1900, by Nativity

City and year	Population			Increase since preceding census		
	Total	Native	Foreign	Total	Native	Foreign
New York City and Brooklyn						
1860	1,080,330	592,024	488,306	—	—	—
1870	1,338,391	774,579	563,812	258,061	182,555	75,506
1880	1,772,962	1,116,598	656,364	434,571*	342,019	92,552
1890	2,321,644	1,420,001	901,643	548,682†	303,403	245,279
1900	3,437,202	2,167,122	1,270,080	1,115,558‡	747,121	368,437
New York City						
1860	813,669	429,952	383,717	—	—	—
1870	942,292	523,198	419,094	128,623	93,246	35,377
1880	1,206,299	727,629	478,670	264,007*	204,431	59,376
1890	2,515,301	875,358	639,943	309,002	147,729	161,273
Brooklyn						
1860	266,661	162,072	104,589	—	—	—
1870	396,099	251,381	144,718	129,438	89,309	40,129
1880	566,663	388,969	177,694	170,564	137,588	32,976
1890	806,343	544,643	261,700	239,680†	155,674	84,006

*Includes increase due to annexation in 1874 of Westchester County towns of Morrisania and West Farms (population in 1870: 28,981) and Kingsbridge (est. pop. in 1870: 2,216).

†Includes increase due to annexation in 1886 of Kings County town of New Lots (population in 1880: 13,655).

‡Includes areas in Kings, Queens, Richmond, and Westchester Counties consolidated with New York or Brooklyn after 1890 (population in 1890: 185,770).

Source: U.S. Census Office, Population of the United States in 1860; Compiled from the Original Returns of the Eighth Census (Washington, 1864); Population of the United States at the Eleventh Census, Part 1 (Washington, 1895); Twelfth Census of the United States Taken in the Year 1900; Population, Vol. I., Part 1 (Washington, 1902).

In what direction did the emigrants from New York City go? Since federal census queries on the place of birth of the native population have not provided more detail than state of birth, the natives of New York City who moved out of the Empire State cannot be distinguished from other natives of New York State in national censuses. Intrastate migration of New York City natives can, however, be ascertained from data secured at the New York State censuses of 1855, 1865, and 1875 which tallied county of birth. At every census the number of natives of the city living outside their home town was greater than the number of natives of the balance of the state residing in New York City. The obvious explanation is the strong movement of New York City natives to the neighboring suburban counties of Kings, Queens, Richmond, and Westchester. However, even when net migration to these counties is excluded, it appears that New York City natives who moved upstate outnumbered, by a slight amount, the upstate natives who came in. The net loss upstate was small in 1855 (592 of the 35,008 statewide net loss) but sizable in 1875 (14,620 of 90,222).

The net gain or loss through intercounty movement shown in Table 20 represents the difference at the census date between the total number of surviving native persons who had moved out of the specified county to New York City since birth and the total number of surviving natives of New York City who moved into the specified county since birth. Statistics of county of birth do not indicate the number who have moved from one place to another during any given period of time; however, by examining place of birth data for successive censuses a general outline of the direction and scope of migration streams can be sketched. From Table 20 it will be seen that as of 1855 New York City had experienced a net gain from such Hudson River Valley counties as Albany, Dutchess, and Orange. The inmigration from these counties then apparently dwindled, and by 1875, when the number of natives of these three counties living in New York City was considerably smaller than it had been two decades earlier, New York City had experienced a net loss to this area. The apparent reduction in New York City's net loss to Westchester between 1855 and 1875 resulted from the fact that the city's annexation of part of Westchester County in 1874 made many Westchesterites who were natives of New York City residents of their native city once again. At the same time many natives of Westchester living in the annexed area became residents of New York.

Brooklyn was the place of settlement of the largest number of New York City natives who left Manhattan, but this migration can, in an important sense, be regarded as an internal shift within the metropolitan region. Between 1855 and 1875 the number of natives of New York City living in Kings County more than doubled, climbing from 30,000 to 69,000. Kings County also experienced net inmigration from all of the nearby counties (see Table 21). By consolidating place of birth data for New York and Kings counties a more meaningful picture of the migration streams within New York State to and from its principal urban agglomeration can be obtained. The combined statistics for the two metropolitan counties indicate a small net gain (2,195) from the balance of the state in 1855 and a moderate loss to upstate (17,974) in 1875.

TABLE 20

New York State-born Population of New York City by County of Birth and New York City-born Population of New York State by County of Residence, 1855 and 1875

County	Resident of New York City by county of birth in New York State		Native of New York City by county of residence in New York State		Net gain or loss to New York City through intra-state migration	
	1855	1875	1855	1875	1855	1875
Total	262,156	535,547*	297,164	627,024	−35,008	−91,477
New York City	232,155	497,572	232,155	497,572	—	—
Balance of State	30,001	37,975	65,009	129,452	−35,008	−90,222
Kings	2,556	5,651	30,101	69,621	−27,545	−63,970
Westchester	4,825	11,084	8,600	12,122	− 3,775	− 1,038
Queens	1,616	2,123	3,368	9,656	− 1,752	− 7,533
Richmond	753	888	2,097	3,949	− 1,344	− 3,061
Rockland	1,029	712	1,173	2,991	− 144	− 2,279
Suffolk	1,248	724	1,654	2,750	− 406	− 2,026
Albany	2,158	2,320	1,157	2,588	+ 1,001	− 268
Orange	3,176	2,174	1,517	2,346	+ 1,659	− 172
Dutchess	2,753	1,944	1,318	2,269	+ 1,435	− 325
All other	9,687	10,355	14,024	21,160	− 5,137	−10,805

*Excludes 1,255 persons for whom county of birth in New York State was not reported.
Source: New York Secretary of State, Census of the State of New York for 1855 (Albany, 1857); and Census of the State of New York for 1875 (Albany, 1877).

While direct evidence is thus available that the New York-Brooklyn complex lost more native sons than it gained from upstate, a statement that outmigration to other states also exceeded inmigration is more conjectural. The most obvious case can be made for migration to New Jersey, which absorbed a flood of natives of New York State between 1850 and 1880, the great majority in the northeastern counties nearest New York City. Table 22 shows that the natives of New York State living in New Jersey increased in number from 20,561 in 1850 to 94,692 in 1880. At the latter date more than one-third were in Hudson County, many probably commuting to jobs in New York City, and over one-sixth in Essex County. It is reasonable to assume that the great bulk from the Empire State, perhaps 80 to 90 percent, were from New York City or Brooklyn.

Hence by 1880 there were probably not less than 75,000 natives of New York City and Brooklyn living in New Jersey, compared with about 28,000 natives of New Jersey resident in the two cities.

TABLE 21
New York State-born Population of Kings County by County of Birth and Kings County-born Population of New York State by County of Residence, 1855 and 1875

County	Resident of Kings County by county of birth in New York State		Native of Kings County by county of residence in New York State		Net gain or loss to Kings County through intra- state migration	
	1855	1875	1855	1875	1855	1875
Total	94,122	286,448*	56,919	214,200	+37,203	+72,248
Kings County	50,005	196,774	50,055	196,774	—	—
New York City	30,101	69,621	2,556	5,651	+27,545	+63,970
Balance of State	14,016	20,053	4,358	11,775	+ 9,658	+ 8,278
Queens	3,172	4,539	1,163	3,836	+ 2,009	+ 703
Westchester	1,276	1,936	557	1,154	+ 719	+ 782
Suffolk	1,393	1,746	463	1,346	+ 930	+ 400
Albany	1,054	1,525	120	310	+ 934	+ 1,215
Orange	1,056	1,383	171	491	+ 885	+ 892
Dutchess	877	1,046	211	322	+ 666	+ 724
Richmond	345	861	201	578	+ 144	+ 283
All other	4,843	7,017	1,472	3,738	+ 3,391	+ 3,279

*Excludes 5,031 persons for whom county of birth in New York State was not reported.
Source: New York Secretary of State, Census of the State of New York for 1855 (Albany, 1857); and Census of the State of New York for 1875 (Albany, 1877).

TABLE 22
New York State-born Population Residing in New Jersey by County of Residence, 1850-80

County	1850	1860	1870	1880
State total	20,561	38,540	74,750	94,692
Hudson	—	—	26,651	35,202
Essex	—	—	13,296	16,977
Union	—	—	6,294	8,763
Passaic	—	—	4,455	6,944
Bergen	—	—	5,502	6,560
All other	—	—	18,552	20,286

Source: J. D. B. De Bow, Statistical View of the United States (Washington, 1854); U.S. Census Office, Population of the United States in 1860 (Washington, 1864); Ninth Census, Vol. I (Washington, 1872): Statistics of the Population of the United States at the Tenth Census (Washington, 1883).

New York City, it has been noted, depended upon Europe for its net migratory gain. The increments in the number of foreign born from census to census (Table 23) tell only part of the tale of the mass movement from abroad. The net in-migration of the foreign contingent can be calculated by adding to the intercensal gain in the immigrant population the number of foreign born who died in the city during the same decade. Between 1880 and 1890 the foreign population of New York City increased from 478,670 to 639,943, a gain of 161,000. By adding to this figure the approximately 133,000 foreign-born decedents of the decade, one attains

TABLE 23

Birthplace of the Population of New York City, 1865-90

Place of birth	1865	1870	1875	1880	1890
Total	726,386	942,292	1,041,886	1,206,299	1,515,301
Native	412,909	523,198	595,843	727,629	875,358
Foreign	313,477	419,094	446,043	478,670	639,943
Native					
New York	364,667	484,109	536,802	647,299	740,787
Other U.S.	42,170	39,089	58,843	80,330	93,685
New Jersey	9,741	8,061	12,463	17,937	19,651
Pennsylvania	5,499	5,099	7,584	11,055	12,694
Massachusetts	7,190	5,995	8,245	10;589	10,601
Virginia	1,439	2,073	4,136	5,696	8,875
Connecticut	6,262	5,140	7,020	8,726	8,207
All other	12,039	12,721	19,395	26,347	33,657
State not reported	6,072*	—	198	—	40,886
Foreign					
Germany	109,004	151,216	165,021	163,482	210,723
Ireland	161,334	201,999	199,084	198,595	190,418
Russia	307	1,151	2,099	4,551	48,790
Great Britain	26,888	32,595	35,247	39,340	48,306
Italy	955	2,794	6,507	12,223	39,951
Austria	427	2,737	2,678	4,743	27,193
Hungary	—	521	867	4,101	12,222
France	5,805	8,265	9,432	9,910	10,535
Canada	3,505	4,419	4,985	7,004	8,398
Bohemia	—	1,487	3,133	8,093	8,099
Sweden	501	1,558	1,870	3,194	7,069
Poland	1,285	2,393	5,809	9,020	6,759
Switzerland	843	2,178	2,244	4,545	4,953
Norway	156	372	527	893	1,575
Denmark	359	682	798	1,096	1,495
All other	2,108	4,727	5,742	7,880	13,487

*Includes 5,535 persons of unknown nativity.

Source: New York Secretary of State, Census of the State of New York for 1865 (Albany, 1867); and Census of the State of New York for 1875 (Albany, 1877). U.S. Census Office, Ninth Census, Vol. I (Washington, 1872); Statistics of the Population of the United States at the Tenth Census (Washington, 1883); Population of the United States at the Eleventh Census, Part 1 (Washington, 1895).

an estimated net foreign inmigration of 294,000. Ireland and Germany, the principal overseas sources of New York's population during the preceding half-century, continued to send their sons and daughters. Although the number of Irish-born in New York City declined by 8,000 between 1880 and 1890—from 198,595 to 190,418—when the estimated 63,000 natives of Ireland who died in New York during the decade are considered, it is seen that a net inmigration of about 55,000 occurred. From Germany the net inflow was substantially larger in this decade, about 86,000; sufficient to increase the German-born residents from 163,482 to 210,723. This compares with a net inflow of about 32,000 from Italy and somewhere near 45,000 from Russia.

In the last decade of the nineteenth century, Germany and Ireland were eclipsed by Russia and Italy as the leading countries of origin of New York's newcomers. This shift came about in part because the movement from the former countries slackened, in part because the tide from the latter countries greatly increased in strength. The decline in migration to the United States from the German Empire became particularly marked following major improvements in the German economic picture; the recorded number of German immigrants entering the United States dropped steadily from 251,000 in fiscal 1882 to 17,000 in fiscal 1898. The Irish decline was also substantial, but more gradual.

Two distinct but parallel movements of population across the Atlantic, from Russia and from Italy, first became significant in the 1880s. As early as 1850, 708 natives of Italy were enumerated as residents of New York City, and by 1860 the figure had doubled, reaching 1,504. Between 1870 and 1880 the number increased more than fourfold, rising from 2,704 to 12,223. The earliest Italian immigrants who, according to one observer, were predominately in "the itinerent class—ragpickers, organ grinders and the like" were eventually overwhelmed by another class— "the stable element."[21] The members of this class, who were recruited from the ranks of the more industrious peasantry, "whom only extreme poverty induced to break the bonds attaching them to their native land," generally began their careers in America as unskilled day laborers. A third class of Italian immigrants also came into being in this period; men who made up a "great army of barbers, boot blacks, fruiterers and shoemakers." These newcomers generally had been engaged in commercial occupations in cities and small towns in the home country. The new immigrants were frequently single men or men who had left their families in Italy. After a few years, if the immigrant decided to settle permanently in America, he either married or brought over his family.[22]

21. Kate H. Claghorn, "The Foreign Immigrant in New York City," *Reports of the Industrial Commission on Immigration* (Washington, D.C.: U.S. Government Printing Office, 1901), XV, 473.   22. *Ibid.*

The immigration from Russia was largely part (the major part to be sure) of the great influx of East European Jews to America. The statistical progress of this movement is more difficult to chart than the Italian migration, for instance, because of the appearance of "Poland" as a separate country of origin in American censuses of the nineteenth century. Poland had ceased to exist as an independent nation after the Napoleonic Wars, its territory divided among Russia, Prussia, and Austria. Those who reported Poland as their country of birth came from one of these nations. It should be realized that prior to 1890 it is likely that many, if not most, Jews who came from the Russian Empire reported "Poland" as their birthplace. While it is useful for some purposes to combine the census figures of natives of Russia and Poland, it must be noted that the latter classification also includes some German and Austrian nationals. The number of persons living in New York City who were returned as native of Russia rose from 116 in 1855 to 467 in 1860; 1,151 in 1870; and 4,551 in 1880. The number reported as born in Poland increased from 1,200 in 1855 to 1,586 in 1860; 2,393 in 1870; and 9,020 in 1880.

Jewish immigration from Eastern Europe began to take shape in the 1870s following the Polish famine of 1869, the Odessa pogrom of 1871, and above all, "emigration fever" in the Lithuanian provinces. The movement accelerated sharply after the tsarist May Laws of 1881, whose prohibitory features drove Jews from the Russian countryside. The Jews in Galicia, in Austria's Polish province, though possessing more political liberties than their co-religionists in Russia, suffered from the same economic impoverishment. Migration to America, especially to New York, began to appeal to increasing numbers by the 1880s as a means of escape from the competition of a choked economy.[23] The total number of Austrian born in New York City (exclusive of those reported from "Bohemia" or "Poland") soared from 4,743 in 1880 to 27,193 in 1890. The great bulk of these were Jews from Galicia.

Before the Jewish movement from Galicia took on mass dimensions the most sizable group emigrating from Austria-Hungary to New York had consisted of Czechs. By 1870 natives of Bohemia, though an Austrian crownland and not an independent country, were separately recorded in the American census. Between 1870 and 1880 the population born in Bohemia resident in New York City climbed from 1,487 to 8,093, but reflecting the truncated migration stream of the 1880s, the number rose only to 8,099 in 1890.

The growth of the foreign-born population in Brooklyn in the decades after the Civil War followed a pattern similar to that in its sister city. The natives of Ireland constituted the largest immigrant group until after the 1880 census when, as in New York City, the greater strength of the tide

23. Moses Rischin, *The Promised City: New York's Jews, 1870-1914* (Cambridge, Mass.: Harvard University Press, 1962), p. 20 ff.

from Central Europe pushed the German born into first place by 1890. The British were relatively more numerous in Brooklyn than in New York City, accounting for some 13 percent of the immigrant population in the former city in 1890, as against less than 8 percent in the latter. By 1890 the Italians and the Russian Jews had strong footholds in Brooklyn, but these groups were considerably less well represented proportionately than they were in Manhattan. Scandinavians, however, favored Brooklyn over its neighbor. The 1890 census found about 16,000 natives of Sweden, Norway, and Denmark in Brooklyn, compared with 10,000 in New York City (see Table 24).

TABLE 24
Birthplace of the Population of Brooklyn, 1865-90

Place of birth	1865	1870	1875	1880	1890
Total	296,378	396,099	482,493	566,663	806,343
Native	188,527	251,381	313,633	388,969	544,643
Foreign	107,851	144,718	168,860	177,694	261,700
Native					
New York	158,966	219,774	275,427	344,324	466,810
Other U.S.	28,451	31,607	38,206	44,645	56,624
New Jersey	6,175	6,009	8,328	9,941	13,765
Pennsylvania	2,976	3,294	3,988	5,410	7,340
Massachusetts	5,224	5,711	6,157	6,743	7,489
Connecticut	4,593	5,264	6,051	7,003	6,616
Virginia	1,000	1,420 }	13,682	{ 2,315	3,413
All other	8,483	9,909 }		{ 13,233	18,001
State not reported	1,110*	—		—	21,209
Foreign					
Germany	26,467	36,771	53,359	55,339	94,798
Ireland	57,143	73,985	78,880	78,814	84,738
Great Britain	18,034	23,490	24,924	25,477	34,512
Italy	112	225	—	1,188	9,563
Sweden	287	1,105	—	2,848	9,325
Canada	2,190	2,806	—	4,363	5,897
Norway	199	301	—	874	4,873
Russia	62	73	—	209	3,397
France	1,135	1,894	—	1,936	2,402
Poland	72	209	—	501	1,887
Denmark	173	384	—	814	1,839
Austria	106	321	—	628	1,493
Switzerland	242	667	—	969	1,402
Hungary	—	70	—	81	663
Bohemia	—	91	—	130	143
All other	1,629	2,326	11,697	3,523	4,768

*Includes 887 persons of unknown nativity.
Source: Same as Table 23.

Between 1860 and 1890 the foreign-born population fell proportionately, from 47 percent of New York City's residents to 42 percent. The proportion in the total population, however, is generally not so meaningful as the percentage in the adult population. It must be realized that throughout the second half of the nineteenth century (and well into the twentieth) undoubtedly a substantial majority of the city's adults were immigrants. The earliest census to reveal this directly was that of 1875, when age was first tabulated by nativity. Although about 43 percent of the white population of all ages was of foreign birth, among persons twenty years of age and over almost 68 percent were foreign born. In Brooklyn the 1875 census returns showed about 35 percent of the total white population was of foreign birth, but almost 58 percent of all persons twenty years of age and over were immigrants.[24]

In 1890 some 60 percent of the white population of New York City twenty years of age and over were of foreign birth, as were 49 percent of the same age group in Brooklyn.[25] It is logical to assume, therefore, that most of the children born in the New York area in the latter part of the nineteenth century were the children of immigrant parents.

Nativity and Parentage

At the 1870 census, for the first time, a question on parentage was asked. This reflected the desire to know not only the number of first-generation Americans (immigrants) but the number of second-generation Americans (children of immigrants) as well. The inquiry was of the most simple kind, merely asking of each person whether or not his father or his mother was of foreign birth. In New York City almost 83 percent of the population (781,745 persons) had at least one foreign-born parent. The vast majority (745,729 persons) had two foreign-born parents, while 23,829 had only foreign-born fathers and 12,187 had foreign-born mothers. Just 17 percent of the city's population (160,547 persons) were the children of two American-born parents (see Table 25).

At the 1880 census the scope of the parentage question was extended to ask the specific country of birth of each parent. The tabulations showing the country of origin by parentage were further broken down to distinguish the native from the foreign born. Although these detailed classifications were published for populations of states, New York was the only city

---

24. Computed from data in *Census of the State of New York for 1875,* pp. 118-19, 178-79.

25. Computed from data in U.S. Census Office: *Report on Vital and Social Statistics in the United States at the Eleventh Census, Part 2* (Washington, 1896), pp. 338-39, 348-49.

so treated. The list of countries of origin became more inclusive at the 1890 census. Table 25 shows for the population of New York City parentage by color and nativity at the censuses of 1870 to 1890. Census practice established the tradition of including persons of mixed parentage (those with one foreign-born and one native-born parent) with the population of foreign parentage. This treatment should be kept in mind when comparisons of the growth of the native and foreign parentage groups are made.

TABLE 25
Population by Parentage, Color, and Nativity, New York City, 1870-90

Census year, color, and nativity	Total	Native parentage	Foreign or mixed parentage			
			Total	Foreign parentage	Father foreign	Mother foreign
Total, 1890	1,515,301	296,083	1,219,218	N.A.	N.A.	N.A.
White	1,489,627	274,164	1,215,463	1,104,728	76,920	33,815
Native born	852,641	270,487	582,154	473,642	75,631	32,881
Foreign born	636,986	3,677	633,309	631,086	1,289	934
Nonwhite	25,674	21,919	3,755	N.A.	N.A.	N.A.
Native born	22,717	N.A.	N.A.	N.A.	N.A.	N.A.
Foreign born	2,957	N.A.	N.A.	N.A.	N.A.	N.A.
Total, 1880	1,206,289	240,330	965,969	895,848	48,063	22,058
Native born	727,629	239,898	487,731	418,349	47,656	21,726
Foreign born	478,670	432	478,238	477,499	407	332
Total, 1870	942,292	160,547	781,745	745,729	23,829	12,187

N.A. = Not available.
Source: U.S. Census Office, Ninth Census, Vol. I (Washington, 1872); Statistics of the Population of the United States at the Tenth Census (Washington, 1883): Population of the United States at the Eleventh Census, Part 1 (Washington, 1895).

In 1870, in the absence of nativity data cross-classified with parentage, it may be assumed that virtually all of the 419,000 foreign born were of foreign or mixed parentage. Accordingly, the foreign born then constituted almost 54 percent of the 782,000 persons of foreign or mixed parentage. At the 1880 census, when an exact count was made, the foreign born comprised just over and the native born just under 50 percent of the 966,000 persons of foreign origin. By 1890, however, the foreign born were again somewhat more numerous than the second-generation Americans.

Table 26 shows the population of foreign and mixed parentage coming from each of the countries of origin for which such information was tabulated in 1880 and 1890. In 1880 natives of Ireland and their children

TABLE 26

Country of Origin of the Total Population of Foreign or Mixed Parentage, New York City, 1880, and of the White Population, 1890

Year and country of origin	Total all foreign and mixed parentage	Foreign parentage Total	Both parents from same foreign country	Mixed foreign parentage*	Mixed parentage Father foreign	Mother foreign
Total (white), 1890	1,215,463	1,104,728	1,058,248	46,480	76,920	33,815
Germany	435,544	396,214	386,546	9,668	31,563	7,767
Ireland	417,757	377,745	369,912	7,833	24,305	15,707
Great Britain	86,374	68,602	56,505	12,097	11,491	6,281
Scandinavia	14,587	13,793	12,316	1,477	588	205
Canada	10,957	7,256	5,695	1,561	2,106	1,595
Russia	72,284	71,257	67,967	3,290	840	187
Italy	55,757	54,867	54,074	793	778	112
France	18,480	16,176	13,288	2,888	1,707	597
Hungary	15,936	15,619	14,969	650	236	81
Bohemia	12,341	12,175	11,868	307	100	66
All other	75,446	71,024	65,108	5,916	3,206	1,216
Total, 1880	965,969	895,848	862,339	33,509	48,063	22,058
Germany	360,961	339,560	331,589	7,971	17,175	3,956
Ireland	423,159	395,758	388,920	6,838	16,210	11,191
Great Britain	73,035	59,155	50,528	8,621	9,075	4,805
Scandinavia	5,625	5,353	4,771	582	223	49
Canada	7,371	5,786	4,439	1,347	1,487	1,098
All other	95,088	90,236	82,092	8,144	3,893	959

*By country of birth of father.

Source: U.S. Census Office, Statistics of the Population of the United States at the Tenth Census (Washington, 1883); and Population of the United States at the Eleventh Census, Part 1 (Washington, 1895).

formed 44 percent of the total, those from Germany and their children, 37 percent. Ten years later the Irish proportion had declined to 35 percent, the Germans, now first, to 36 percent. By 1880, when such a tabulation was first made, there were more second-generation than first-generation persons of Irish, German, and British origin living in New York City. This was also true in 1890, but this enumeration showed relatively small numbers of second-generation Americans among those originating from countries where emigration had just recently assumed mass proportions. The numbers of American-born children of Russian and Italian background were only about two-fifths the size of the immigrant populations from these two countries. In Table 27 the native population of foreign and of mixed parentage is shown by country of origin according to the 1880 and the 1890 census tabulations.

To what extent did the immigrant population intermarry with the native population? Intermarriage has frequently been viewed as representing assimilation. The only direct answer provided by nineteenth-century data was that from the 1875 enumeration. The state census disclosed that 115,296 or 66 percent of New York City's 174,174 married couples consisted of foreign-born husbands and wives; 37,601 or 22 percent of native-born husbands and wives; and 21,267 or 12 percent, of couples where one spouse was foreign born and one native born. About 11 percent of all foreign-born husbands (14,480 of 129,976) were living with native-born wives, and about 5 percent of the total number of foreign-born wives (6,597 of 121,893) were married to American-born husbands.[26] The higher proportion of intermarriage among foreign men than women probably reflects the excess of single men over single women among emigrants from Europe. It is likely that many, if not most, instances of generation inter-marriage were not ethnic intermarriage—for example, a male Irish immigrant of the 1870s married to an American-born daughter of Irish immigrants of the 1830s or 1840s.

One means of estimating the degree of intergeneration marriage at subsequent periods is by inference, based on census information relating to native-born persons of foreign or mixed parentage. At the 1880 census,

TABLE 27

Country of Origin of the Native-born Population of Foreign or Mixed Parentage, New York City, 1880, and of the Native-born White Population, 1890

Country of origin	1890			1880			
	Foreign parentage*	Mixed parentage		Foreign parentage		Mixed parenta	
	Both parents from same foreign country	Father foreign	Mother foreign	Both parents from same foreign country	Mixed foreign parentage†	Father foreign	Mo for
Total	435,321	75,631	32,881	388,172	30,177	47,656	21,
Germany	177,174	31,217	7,586	160,992	7,485	17,119	3,
Ireland	176,176	24,024	15,512	184,990	5,869	16,137	11,
Great Britain	17,593	11,238	6,144	17,921	7,521	8,958	4,
Scandinavia	2,300	580	199	874	543	220	
Canada	1,511	1,981	1,481	987	1,150	1,431	1,
Russia	18,373	808	134				
Italy	14,068	752	103				
France	3,501	1,658	577	22,408	7,609	3,791	
Hungary	3,372	220	27				
Bohemia	4,060	99	64				
Other	17,193	3,054	1,054				

*For the mixed foreign parentage group, which totalled 38,321, information was not available by cou of origin.

†By country of birth of father.

Source: Same as Table 26.

26. Census of the State of New York for 1875, p. 229.

for example, 10.2 percent of New York's native-born population whose fathers were of foreign birth had mothers who were of American birth (47,656 of 466,005). This is in remarkably close agreement to the 1875 census count already noted, showing that 11.3 percent of the city's foreign-born husbands had native-born wives. Similarly, the 1880 census indicated that 4.9 percent of all native Americans who had foreign-born mothers had American-born fathers (21,726 of 440,055), while the 1875 census had indicated 5.4 percent of all foreign-born wives were married to native-born men. Intergeneration marriage apparently increased during the 1880s; at the 1890 enumeration 13.8 percent of all native whites who reported a father of foreign birth specified a mother of American birth (75,631 of 549,273), and 6.5 percent of native white persons with foreign-born mothers had American-born fathers (32,881 of 506,523).[27]

The immigrant population intermarried not only with native Americans, of course, but also among themselves, one nationality with another. Unfortunately, only the census of 1880 provided data (by showing country of birth of father cross-classified by country of birth of mother) for New York City that could adequately reveal this phenomenon. At later censuses cross-classifications by country of birth were shown only for states or for the country as a whole. Hence it is necessary to dwell on the 1880 material, though it provides a picture that is applicable only to one stage of the migration period.

Table 28 indicates that 4.1 percent of the native whites in 1880 who reported a father of German birth, 2.8 percent of those who reported a father of Irish birth, and 21.9 percent of those who reported a father of British birth specified a mother of another foreign nationality. In general, a similar proportional distribution was to be found when tabulation is made of the percentage having mothers from each place of birth who had fathers originating from other areas; however, it is of interest that Irish women were considerably more likely to marry other foreign nationals than were Irish men.

Cross-classification of the age of the population with parentage did not commence until 1890. Interesting evidence was then provided that the proportional distribution by parentage of the births for a given period quite closely resembled the nativity distribution of married couples (or more broadly, of the adult population) at the same time. From the data secured in New York City in 1890 it could be observed that among native white persons aged fifteen to nineteen years (survivors of the cohort of births in 1870-75) 21.8 percent were of native parentage (having two native-born parents); in Brooklyn the comparable figure was 31.0 percent.[28] Paralleling this closely was the fact that according to the state

27. Based on data in Table 25.

28. Computed from data in *Report on Vital and Social Statistics, Eleventh Census, Part II*, pp. 338-39, 348-49. See also Table 42.

census of 1875, 21.6 percent of New York City's married couples consisted of two native-born persons, as did 31.8 percent of Brooklyn couples.[29]

TABLE 28
Native-born Population of Foreign or Mixed Parentage by Country of Birth Distribution of Each Parent, New York City, 1880

Foreign-born parent by nativity of other parent	Total	Country of birth of foreign-born parent			
		Ireland	Germany	Great Britain	All other
Foreign-born father, number	466,005	206,996	185,596	34,400	39,013
Birthplace of mother (percent) Total	100.0	100.0	100.0	100.0	100.0
United States	10.2	7.8	9.2	26.0	13.9
Foreign born	89.8	92.2	90.8	74.0	86.1
Same country as father	—	89.4	86.7	52.1	—
Other country	—	2.8	4.1	21.9	—
Foreign-born mother, number	440,075	207,486	171,193	29,197	32,199
Birthplace of father (percent) Total	100.0	100.0	100.0	100.0	100.0
United States	4.9	5.4	2.3	16.2	6.1
Foreign born	95.1	94.6	97.7	83.8	93.9
Same country as mother	—	89.2	94.0	61.4	—
Other country	—	5.4	3.7	22.4	—

Source: U.S. Census Office, Statistics of the Population of the United States at the Tenth Census (June 1, 1880) (Washington, 1883).

NONWHITE RACES

New York City's Negro community, which was some three thousand smaller in 1870 than it had been at its 1840 peak, began to expand during the 1870s. By 1880 it numbered 19,663; up by 6,591, or fully 50 percent from the figure returned at the census a decade earlier. Growth was less rapid in the 1880s; nevertheless, a gain of 3,938 pushed the city's total to 23,601. Brooklyn's Negro population doubled between 1870 and 1890, rising from 4,957 to 10,287. Between 1890 and 1900 the community made its greatest gain of the century; the 1900 census enumerated 60,666 Negroes in the greater city, equivalent to 1.8 percent of the total population (see Table 29).

29. Census of the State of New York for 1875, pp. 228-29.

TABLE 29

Population of New York City, Kings County, and Richmond County
by Race, 1865-90

Area and race	1865	1870	1875	1880	1890
New York City					
Total	726,386	942,292	1,041,886	1,206,299	1,515,301
White	716,443	929,199	1,026,632	1,185,843	1,489,627
Negro	9,943	13,072	15,036	19,663	23,601
Other races	—	21	218	793	2,073
Kings County					
Total	311,090	419,921	509,154	599,495	838,547
White	306,229	414,254	502,160	590,201	826,555
Negro	4,861	5,653	6,979	9,153	11,307
Other races	—	14	15	141	685
Richmond County					
Total	28,209	33,029	35,196	38,991	51,693
White	27,566	32,242	34,325	38,054	50,712
Negro	643	787	870	932	964
Other races	—	—	1	5	17

Source: New York Secretary of State, Census of the State of New York for 1875
(Albany, 1877); and U.S. Census Office, Population of the United States at the Eleventh
Census, Part 1 (Washington, 1895).

Probably all of the Negro increase resulted from immigration. An extremely high death rate prevented real gain from occurring through natural increase. As a contemporary observer reported: "While there undoubtedly exists an important movement of the negroes to the north, directed in the main to the cities, negro mortality is here so high on account of climatic and other conditions, that in most of the great cities it prevents the negro race gaining upon the whites, or even holding its own."[30]

Data by birthplace show that in the face of the sizable growth in the Negro population in New York City between 1870 and 1890 the nonwhite population reported as born in New York State (almost entirely Negro) increased by less than one thousand (see Table 30). Brooklyn showed a larger gain in New York-born Negroes, probably due to some extent to migration from Manhattan of part of the older community. The number resident in New York City and Brooklyn combined who were born in the United States outside of New York increased by about 12,000 in this period, of which 7,000 was contributed by natives of Virginia and about 2,000 by natives of North and South Carolina. That a major change was occurring in the character of the metropolitan Negro population can be seen by the fact that whereas in 1870, 65 percent of the nonwhite population in New

30. Adna F. Weber, The Growth of Cities in the Nineteenth Century (1899; reprinted Ithaca, N.Y.: Cornell University Press, 1963), p. 312.

York and Brooklyn were born in New York State, by 1900 the corresponding percentage in Greater New York was no more than 35.

TABLE 30
Birthplace of the Nonwhite Population of New York City and Brooklyn, 1870 and 1890

Place of birth	New York City and Brooklyn*		New York City		Brooklyn	
	1870	1890	1870	1890	1870	1890
Total	18,050	36,620	13,093	25,674	4,957	10,946
Native	17,415	32,688	12,645	22,717	4,770	9,971
New York	11,728	14,296	8,763	9,056	2,965	5,240
Other U.S.	5,675	17,621	3,875	13,109	1,800	4,512
Virginia	1,444	8,451	940	6,533	504	1,918
North Carolina	367	1,656	116	844	251	812
Maryland	965	1,538	765	1,216	200	322
New Jersey	849	1,201	616	859	233	342
South Carolina	251	814	133	595	118	219
Pennsylvania	680	781	533	609	147	172
All other	1,119	3,180	772	2,453	347	727
State not reported	12	771	7	552	5	219
Foreign	635	3,932	448	2,957	187	975

*Includes in 1870: 18,016 Negro, 34 other nonwhite; in 1890: 33,888 Negro, 2,732 other nonwhite.

Source: U.S. Census Office, Ninth Census, Vol. I (Washington, 1872); and Population of the United States at the Eleventh Census, Part 1 (Washington, 1895) (computed).

New York City's Chinese population, according to the census takers, increased from 12 in 1870 to 1,970 in 1890, while in Brooklyn the Chinese rose from 7 to 528 in this period. By 1900 the greater city had a Chinese community of 6,321, living mostly in Chinatown in the Lower East Side of Manhattan. An unusual characteristic of this immigrant community was its sex distribution; there were at least thirty times as many males as females.[31]

ETHNIC GROUPS: NATURAL INCREASE

Although the ethnic composition of New York City's population changed substantially between 1860 and 1900, the over-all shifts were much less marked than were those of either the preceding or succeeding

31. There were only 183 females in New York City in 1900 enumerated among the combined total for Chinese, Japanese, and Indians. U.S. Census Office, *Twelfth Census of the United States: 1900*, Vol. II *Population*, Part 2 (Washington, 1902), p. 138; U.S. Bureau of the Census, *Thirteenth Census of the United States Taken in the Year 1910* (Washington, 1913), I, 226.

forty-year period. In 1900, as in 1860, it could be said that the majority of the city's population was of Irish or German descent. At the 1900 enumeration a unique tabulation was prepared which showed household heads according to nativity, parentage, and country of origin. Some 28 percent of all white heads of families were reported as having German-born parents, while 22 percent had Irish-born parents. This is clearly a reversal from the order in 1860 and reflects not only the strength of the migration stream from Germany in the last quarter of the century, but probably the higher rate of natural increase of the German population as well. Just 16 percent of the white family heads in New York City in 1900 had two American-born parents (see Table 31).

TABLE 31

Heads of Families by Color and of White Families by Nativity and Parentage, New York City, 1900; Proportion of United States Total in Each Group Residing in New York City

Color, nativity, and parentage	Heads of families	Percent of U.S. total in New York City
Total	722,670	4.5
White	707,843	5.0
Nonwhite	14,827	0.8
White by nativity		
Native	265,936	2.6
Foreign born	441,907	11.5
White by parentage*		
Germany	195,335	9.9
Ireland	157,486	12.6
United States†	113,565	1.4
Russia	46,998	36.7
Great Britain	46,059	5.5
Italy	44,958	31.7
Austria-Hungary‡	36,983	19.3
Scandinavia	15,048	3.4
Poland	10,364	8.5
Canada§	5,088	1.4
Other countries	19,830	5.9
Mixed foreign parentage	16,129	7.1

*Country of birth of parents. †Includes persons of unknown parentage.
‡Includes Bohemia. §Includes Newfoundland.
Source: Derived from data in U.S. Census Office, Twelfth Census of the United States Taken in the Year 1900; Population, Vol. I Part 2 (Washington, 1902).

From 1880 on, when the decennial census first broke out parentage by country of origin, comparisons of the rate of mortality of the population of German parentage and those of Irish parentage can be made. Mortality data by parentage were never entirely complete; in 1880, for example, about five percent of all decedents were of "unknown" parentage; in 1900, about 10 percent. The deficiency, however, may not by itself favor any particular nationality group. In Table 32 the deaths of the "unknown" groups are distributed proportionately to the known, and death rates for each parentage group are computed based on the adjusted numbers.

TABLE 32
Differential Mortality by Country of Birth of Both Parents of Decedents, New York City, 1880-1900

Country of origin	Population (in thousands)			Deaths			Adjusted crude death ra		
	1880	1890	1900	1880	1890	1900	1880	1890	190
Total	1,206.3	1,515.3	3,437.2	31,937	40,103	70,872	26.5	26.5	20.
Decedents of unknown parentage	—	—	—	1,420	2,652	7,296	—	—	—
Germany	331.6	386.5	658.9	6,918	7,280	10,662	21.8	20.2	18.
Ireland	388.9	369.9	595.3	10,235	10,996	15,158	27.5	31.8	28.
Great Britain	50.5	56.5	121.6	1,021	1,295	2,068	21.2	24.5	19.
Russia		68.0	288.6†		973	3,121†		15.3	12.
Italy		54.1	214.8		2,117	4,852		41.9	25.
Austria-Hungary	91.3		177.2	2,383		2,373	27.3		14
Scandinavia		127.0‡	63.2		2,858	1,123		24.1	19
Other foreign			92.5			1,444			17
United States	240.3	296.1	793.2	6,028	7,253	14,873	26.2	26.2	20.
Mixed parentage	103.6	157.2	431.9	3,932	4,679	7,902	39.7	31.9	20

*Per 1,000 population. Rates adjusted to account for decedents of unknown parentage by distributing unknowns in proportion to the known deaths for each parentage group.

†Includes "Poland."

‡Includes all 3,800 nonwhites of foreign parentage, country of origin not available but assumed to be "other foreign."

Source: Derived from U.S. Census Office data and numbers of deaths given in New York City Department of Health Annual Reports of the Board of Health for . . . 1880, 1890, 1900.

　　Table 32, which indicates mortality for the census years 1880, 1890, and 1900, shows that the crude death rate among the Irish community was somewhat above the general rate in 1880, while the crude rate among persons of German parentage was somewhat below the average. These differences had become more marked by 1890 when the Irish rate was more than one and one half times the German rate. This was also the case in 1900.

　　These crude death rates, of course, fail to take into account possible differences in the age composition of the population subgroups. Dr. Billings of the United States Census Office noted after the 1880 census that it was "very desirable that in the statistics of the living population the principal races should be distinguished" and commented: "What is wanted is the number of living population of Irish or German descent, with distinction of sex and age."[32] At the 1890 census, when new techniques of data processing permitted the tabulation of the population by sex and age according to country of origin, age-specific death rates were secured. The 1890 census age details by country of origin of parents as well as a special set of mortality tabulations for the census year were based on country of birth of mother. The special mortality data—deaths in the year ending May 31, 1890 (the day before the census)—were statistics prepared by the United States Census Office from registered deaths reported to the local registration authorities. The official report noted: "It is impossible to properly distribute those with unknown birthplaces of mothers among the several races . . . and hence, the rates . . . are probably somewhat below the truth for foreign and the native born of foreign parents."[33]

Detailed age-specific death rates of ethnic groups thus are deficient to an unknown extent. In an effort to attempt some meaningful comparison of age-specific death rates for major groups while allowing for the limitations of the mortality statistics, a practicable compromise is seen in the use of the rates produced for three broad age categories. Table 33 compares death rates by age for the Irish and German population of New York City and Brooklyn. The data give evidence that the inordinately high mortality of the Irish population was not due to age composition. Death rates for the Irish at each age group were higher than for the German population. The Census Office found that death rates for New York City and Brooklyn in the census year ending May 31, 1890, were higher than those for most other large American cities (only Newark's rate was higher than that for New York). In explanation Dr. Billings declared: "The heavy death rate

TABLE 33

Death Rates* by Broad Age Groups, Population of Irish and German Parentage (According to Country of Birth of Mother), New York City and Brooklyn, 1890

Age	New York City Country of origin		Brooklyn Country of origin	
	Ireland	Germany	Ireland	Germany
Total, all ages	32.2	22.1	27.8	21.6
Under 15 years	43.3	36.9	38.7	36.4
15-44 years	19.6	10.6	16.0	9.5
45 years and over	61.1	39.2	52.3	36.7

*Per 1,000 population.
Source: U.S. Census Office, Vital Statistics of New York City and Brooklyn Covering a Period of Six Years Ending May 31, 1890 (Washington, 1894).

32. U.S. Census Office, *Report on the Mortality and Vital Statistics of the United States as Returned at the Tenth Census*, Part 2 (Washington, 1886), p. clviii.
33. U.S. Census Office *Vital Statistics of New York City and Brooklyn, Eleventh Census: 1890* (Washington, 1894) p. 18.

both in New York City and in Brooklyn was largely due to the excessive death rate among the children of Irish mothers."[34]

In distinct contrast to the Irish, the East European Jews, comparative newcomers that they were, had lower than average mortality. A contemporary writer observed that "the Jews, already accustomed to city life have withstood the physical influences of the tenements most remarkably, keeping the death rate down most perceptibly in wards where they predominate."[35] The population identified in 1890 as having Russian and Polish mothers were shown in the age-specific tabulations to have death rates that were "very low between 15-45, and at the other groups of age also lower than that of almost every race." The Census Office report further remarked that "these people were nearly all of the Jewish race," and concluded this phenomenon "shows that poverty does not necessarily produce a high death rate."[36] In the Lower East Side area of Jewish concentration (Wards Seven, Ten, and Thirteen) the death rate in 1890 among persons having Russian- or Polish-born mothers was only 16.7 per 1,000 population, compared with a rate of 36.0 among persons with Irish mothers.[37]

Unfortunately, data to show the relative birth rates for the ethnic components of New York's population in the nineteenth century are largely unavailable. About all that can be achieved is the preparation of selected fertility ratios based upon census statistics of the number of children under five years of age. The 1890 census is of especial value in this respect since it was the first to provide age according to nativity of mother. The 1890 returns for the white population of New York City indicated there were 390 children under five years of age with native mothers per 1,000 native females at ages 20-44 years, and 559 children of foreign-born mothers under five years of age per 1,000 foreign-born women aged 20-44 years.[38] The much higher fertility ratio shown for the foreign women probably reflects to some extent the higher proportion married. It also should be noted that about 30 percent of the children of native-born mothers had fathers who were foreign born.

ETHNIC GROUPS: GEOGRAPHIC DISTRIBUTION

New York's ethnic communities were also in varying degrees geographic communities. The reasons for this development were economic, social, and religious. New immigrants, with little means, had to settle in

34. *Ibid.*

35. Claghorn, "Foreign Immigrant in New York City," *Industrial Commission on Immigration,* XV, 478.

36. *Vital Statistics of New York City and Brooklyn*, p. 18.   37. *Ibid.*, pp. 66-67.

38. Computed from data in *Report on Vital and Social Statistics, Eleventh Census,* Part II, pp. 348-49.

areas where rentals were cheapest, and these tended to be areas of older tenements, usually near the center of the city. But if the new immigrants were Jewish, for example, they tended to settle not in a tenement area where Italians were concentrated, but in one where the elements of Jewish religious and social organization existed. Americans of earlier immigrant stock, on the other hand, chose not to remain in a neighborhood once its ethnic character changed, and moved to town houses, or apartment houses, depending upon their economic level, in areas farther from the city's core.

At the 1890 census detailed statistics were produced for the first time which showed the ethnic distribution of the population by city wards. The Irish were revealed to be the least concentrated of all major groups. Handlin has pointed out this to some extent reflected the fact that many were household servants.[39] Persons having mothers born in Ireland constituted 26 percent of New York City's total population, and at least 10 percent of the total population in all but two of the twenty-four wards. In Brooklyn, where 24 percent of the population had Irish mothers, only two of twenty-six wards did not have populations that were at least 10 percent Irish. In Manhattan the only neighborhoods of marked Irish character were the once densely settled, but by 1890 thinly populated, wards below Canal Street—the "central business district." In five of these six wards over 40 percent of the population was of Irish background. However, these wards housed only 6 percent of New York City's Irish. The bulk lived uptown and in Brooklyn neighborhoods where their influence was noticeable but not predominant.[40]

The Germans were also spread throughout the metropolitan area, but still were somewhat more concentrated than the Irish. Forming 27 and 24 percent, respectively, of the populations of New York City and Brooklyn (according to the country of birth of mother criterion used by the Census Bureau), they accounted for at least 10 percent of the residents in all but one of the wards in the former city and all but eight of those in the latter. In Manhattan the heavy concentration of Germans in the East Side area south of 14th Street—Wards Eleven and Seventeen—had existed for several decades. These two wards, which were the only areas where Germans predominated, had 23 percent of New York's population of German descent in 1890. Germans were more concentrated in Brooklyn where two wards, the Sixteenth (Williamsburg) and the Eighteenth (Bushwick) held over 35 percent of the city's total.[41]

Italians and East European Jews, most of whom had arrived in the New World within the decade preceding the census, were much more "ghettoized" than were older immigrant groups. Wards Six, Eight, and

39. Oscar Handlin, *The Newcomers* (Cambridge, Mass.: Harvard University Press, 1959), p. 33.

40. *Vital Statistics of New York City and Brooklyn*, pp. 234-37, 242-45.   41. *Ibid.*

Fourteen centering around Canal Street were the area of residence of 52 percent of New York's Italian population (28,150 of 54,334).[42] As early as 1864 a report on New York's housing had mentioned an Italian population in the Sixth Ward, an area then heavily settled by the Irish, who comprised 74 percent of its foreign population.[43] From this base the Italians had by 1880 expanded to the north, moving into the Fourteenth Ward, which was then spoken of as "New Italy."[44] The Italians exhibited a tendency to residential segregation by province of origin. One observer commented: "In their colonies they gather in provincial groups. For instance, in the Mulberry Bend district are to be found Neapolitans and Calabrians mostly; in Baxter Street, near the Five Points, is a colony of Genoese: in Elizabeth Street between Houston and Spring, a colony of Sicilians. The quarter west of Broadway in the Eighth and Fifteenth Wards is made up mainly of North Italians who have been longer in New York and are rather more prosperous than the others, although some Neapolitans have come into Sullivan and Thompson Streets to work in the flower and feather trades. In "Little Italy," 110th to 115th Street, South Italians predominate. In 69th Street near the Hudson River, a small group of Tyrolese and Austrian Italians."[45]

The East European Jews were still more concentrated geographically. In 1890 almost 75 percent of New York's residents with mothers born in Russia and Poland, nearly all of them Jews, lived in three wards on the Lower East Side—Wards Seven, Ten, and Thirteen (59,961 of 80,235).[46] The Tenth Ward, which had once been an area of German settlement, had by the 1880s become known as the "Jewish quarter."[47] In 1890 a majority of this ward's population were of Russian or Polish parentage (30,476 of 57,596 persons). Persons of German descent numbered 14,402, and those whites who had two American-born parents numbered only 1,992, a minority of less than 4 percent.[48]

Other immigrant groups that exhibited intensely concentrated settlement were natives of Bohemia (a crownland of Austria-Hungary but separately reported by the American census) and of Hungary. Of the Bohemians in New York in 1890 about 65 percent (7,944 of 12,287) were in the Nineteenth Ward, an area on the Upper East Side embracing Yorkville; of the Hungarians, 50 percent (7,708 of 15,555) were in the Eleventh Ward.[49]

Whites of native parentage, the "old-stock Americans" were numerically the third largest among New York's several minority groups. However, as the most affluent, they were the principal residents of the

42. *Ibid.*

43. Claghorn, "Foreign Immigrant in New York City," *Industrial Commission on Immigration*, XV, 457.   44. *Ibid.*, p. 473.   45. *Ibid.*, p. 474.

46. *Vital Statistics of New York City and Brooklyn*, pp. 234 ff.

47. Claghorn, "Foreign Immigrant in New York City," *Industrial Commission on Immigration*, XV, 476.

48. *Vital Statistics of New York City and Brooklyn*, pp. 234 ff.   49. *Ibid.*

better neighborhoods. An official report of the 1890s noted: "Of those whose mothers were born in the United States ... there are two quite distinct classes, the prosperous and failures. The prosperous are very prosperous; they live in the best part of the city and have very low death rates ... while the failures are apt to be terrible failures, and when found in the tenement house districts, to furnish very heavy death rates."[50]

The principal changes during the last decade of the nineteenth century in the geographic division of New York's ethnic communities were occasioned by the rapid expansion of the Jewish and Italian populations as the European influx mounted. One observer remarked shortly after the turn of the century that the Jews "on the East Side ... have pressed up through the Tenth and Thirteenth Wards and through the Sixteenth and Eleventh, driving the Germans before them, until it may be said that all of the East Side below 14th Street is a Jewish district." The Germans whom they replaced moved farther uptown, especially to the upper East Side, and above all "to Brooklyn and the suburban districts." The Irish, as a result of the pressure of Italian settlement in their former tenement districts in lower Manhattan tended to move up the West Side.[51]

The general preempting of the newer East Side areas by Germans and the West Side by Irish led Jews and Italians who wished to escape from tenements in Lower Manhattan to move several miles to the north, to Harlem. A "Little Italy" centering around 110th Street soon became established, as did a Jewish settlement, mainly between 97th and 102nd Street.[52]

Religious Groups

While the censuses taken in the latter part of the nineteenth century provide much data useful for measuring the growth of New York's ethnic groups, the statistics available for tracing trends in religious affiliation are inadequate. The number of churches and of communicants, the usual type of information gathered, have been demonstrated to be weak indicators of the actual religious distribution of the population.

In the absence of reliable census statistics, counts of marriages and deaths classified by religious denomination can sometimes serve to produce crude estimates of religious affiliation. The 1865 state census asked married couples if their marriage had occurred during the preceding year, and if so, "in what manner solemnized?"[53] While the returns were admittedly well below the expected,[54] it may be that the reported type of

---

50. *Ibid.*, p. 19.

51. Claghorn, "Foreign Immigrant in New York City," *Industrial Commission on Immigration*, XV, 477, 471.   52. *Ibid.*, 474, 477.

53. *Census of the State of New York for 1865*, pp. 224-25.   54. *Ibid.*, p. lciv.

religious ceremony reflected the distribution of the population by denomination. Table 34 shows the returns for New York and Kings Counties. It
will be seen that in New York County Protestant marriages outnumbered
Roman Catholic by 1.2 to 1.0, while in Kings County the ratio was 1.9
to 1.0.

TABLE 34

Marriages Reported for Census Year 1865* by Type of Religious
Ceremony, New York City and Kings County

Type of religious ceremony	New York City	Kings County
Total	1,532	870
Protestant	640	499
Methodist	154	113
Presbyterian	112	61
Episcopal	107	111
Baptist	94	53
Lutheran	68	38
Dutch Reformed	50	64
Congregational	11	28
Unitarian	9	8
Universalist	3	6
Other Protestant	32	17
Roman Catholic	522	258
Jewish	56	1
Religious, type not specified	16	41
Civil	23	4
Unknown (including declaration before witnesses)	275	67

*Year beginning July 1864 and ending June 1865.
Source: New York Secretary of State, Census of the State of New York for 1865
(Albany, 1867).

Mortality statistics also appear to give evidence that the Roman
Catholic population of New York City, while large in number, was not
yet as numerous as the Protestant. In 1869, of 25,167 New York decedents,
9,935 or 39 percent, were buried in Catholic cemeteries, 13,849 in all
other area cemeteries, and 1,383 outside the New York area.[55] For 1879
the comparable figures for the 28,342 decedents were: Roman Catholic,
11,622 (41 percent); other area, 14,760; outside area, 1,956.[56] Undoubtedly, many Catholics were buried in non-denominational cemeteries.
Over one-fifth of the burials in non-Catholic cemeteries took place at
City Cemetery, where many of the pauper interments may have been of
Catholics. A rough estimate that about 40 percent of the residents of New

55. New York City Board of Health, *Annual Report, 1873*, p. 402.
56. New York City Board of Health, *Annual Report, 1879*, pp. 243, 161.

York City were Roman Catholic in this period does not seem unreasonable when it is conjectured that the mortality among the Catholic population, with its large impoverished immigrant contingent, was somewhat higher than the city average.

The Jewish community's share of the city population rose from less than 5 percent in 1860 to more than 10 percent in 1890. Data from the type of marriage ceremony query of 1865, cited above as a crude measure of religious affiliation, indicated 4.6 percent of the couples who specified one of the three major faiths reported a Jewish service (56 of 1,218). The most reliable population estimate for the era prior to the transformation of New York Jewry from a largely German to a predominately East European origin is 60,000—reported for about 1878 by local sources to the Union of American Hebrew Congregations.[57] The wave of immigrants from Tsarist Russia and the Dual Monarchy doubled and trebled the community in the closing decades of the nineteenth century. In 1890 Philip Cowen, special agent for the U.S. Census Office, placed the size of New York's Jewish population at 175,000.[58]

In Brooklyn Catholics and Jews were relatively less well represented than in New York. If one accepts the 1865 census marriage query as a valid tool then it can be concluded that the Protestant population in Kings County was still almost twice the Catholic. The Jewish community developed slowly in Brooklyn, and as late as 1870 a contemporary estimate was "nearly one thousand families."[59] The Union of American Hebrew Congregations figure for 1878 was about 13,000.[60]

Mortality statistics for Brooklyn also are useful in approximating the size of that city's Roman Catholic population. In 1879, of the 11,528 decedents in Brooklyn, 5,062, or 44 percent, were buried in three Catholic cemeteries.[61] Although the percentage actually was higher than that for New York City deaths the same year, the relatively few potter's field burials in Brooklyn (only 3 percent of all non-Catholic burials) needs to be taken into consideration.

At the 1890 federal census, officials queried sources in each diocese, obtaining statistics on the number of baptized members of the Roman Catholic Church. The bureau, however, excluded an estimated number of baptized persons below the age of nine years from its published figures (the number under nine years was calculated as 15 percent of the total

57. Board of Delegates of American Israelites and the Union of American Hebrew Congregations, *Statistics of the Jews in the United States* (Philadelphia: Union of American Hebrew Congregations, 1880), p. 9.

58. Richard Wheatley, "The Jews in New York," *The Century Magazine*, XLIII, 3 (1892), 323.

59. Henry R. Stiles, *History of the City of Brooklyn* (Brooklyn: pub. by subscription, 1870), III, 816.

60. Board of Delegates, *Statistics of the Jews*, p. 9.

61. Brooklyn Department of Health, *Annual Report 1877 and 1878, with Supplementary Tables for 1879, 1880 and 1881*, p. 119.

population) "in order that the statistics of all denominations might be uniform."[62] The bureau reported 386,200 Catholics in New York City and 204,863 in Kings County.[63] When adjustment is made for the deleted children the totals are approximately 454,400 and 241,000 respectively. As this would indicate only about 30 percent of each area's total population to be Catholic, the estimates clearly need upward revision.

CENSUS UNDERENUMERATION

The decennial census taken in 1890 probably understated the population of New York City more than any other federal census. At least three separate benchmarks tend to make this clear, and while each taken individually might not present a sufficient case, the three combined provide weighty evidence.

New York City statisticians, unable to accept the low figure reported by the Census Office at the 1890 enumeration (1,515,301), pointed to the police registration of October 1890, which returned a population of 1,710,715—almost 13 percent more than the federal figures.[64] Two years later, in 1892, the New York State Census showed 1,801,739 persons in New York City.[65] The federal census of 1890 purported to show an increase of 309,000 persons over the preceding count a decade earlier; the state census of 1892, by contrast, indicated an increase of not less than 286,000 in a time period shorter than two years. The state census gave Kings County a population of 995,276,[66] about 157,000 more than the 1890 federal count (838,547) which had represented a gain of 239,000 in the ten-year period 1880-90. Such large increases in less than two years appear highly improbable. The police census taken of New York City in 1895, which tallied 1,851,060 persons,[67] also appears out of line unless the 1890 federal count is recognized as understated. When this mid-decade figure is compared with data from the preceding and succeeding federal censuses, it appears to show that growth between 1890 and 1895 was close to twice that between 1895 and 1900.

The federal census in 1900 indicated that New York City within the boundaries existing in 1890 had 2,025,515 inhabitants, or 510,000 more than were revealed at the preceding decennial count.[68] Thus, reliance on successive federal returns alone show for New York City *exclusive* of

62. U.S. Census Office, *Report on Statistics of Churches in the United States at the Eleventh Census: 1890* (Washington, 1894), p. 233.   63. *Ibid.*, p. 243.
64. *Annual Report of the Board of Health for 1904*, p. 776.
65. New York State Senate, *Exhibits Showing the Enumeration of the State by Counties, Cities, Towns and Election Districts for the Year 1892*, Senate Report No. 60 (Albany, 1892), p. 6.   66. *Ibid.*
67. *Annual Report of the Board of Health for 1904*, p. 776.   68. *Ibid.*

annexations an average annual growth of 31,000 during 1880-90 and of 51,000 in 1890-1900. Since foreign immigration largely determined the pace of New York's growth, if one accepts the 1890 count at face value, it would follow that migration was much more significant in the 1890s than in the 1880s. Available data, however, make it evident that the opposite was the case. On a national level the Office of Immigration's statistics show 5.2 million immigrants arriving during the decade ending June 30, 1890, and only 3.7 million in that closing June 30, 1900.[69] Furthermore, at the 1900 census inquiry was made of the foreign-born population as to the year of immigration to the United States. "The inquiry was designed in part to afford in connection with the statistics of immigration, a means for determining what proportion of the immigrants of each year or period of years had remained in the country and were still living."[70] For the country as a whole 2,363,000 immigrants reported they had settled in the United States during the preceding ten years (1890-1900), and a considerably larger number—3,163,000, between ten and twenty years prior to the census (1880-90). In New York City the returns showed a similar distribution; 416,000 immigrants had arrived within the preceding decade, while some 432,000 had come in the prior period.[71]. The real excess in the size of the group coming in 1880-90 over the more recent group undoubtedly was greater still since death had more time to take its toll among the earlier immigrants.

A population of about 1.7 million in New York City in 1890 rather than the Census Office's 1.515 million also provides a more reasonable death rate. The average rate of 27.2 deaths per 1,000 population for 1889-91 based on the latter population indicates practically no change in the crude death rate since 1879-81, and that New York's crude death rate was near the very highest among American cities. The sharp downward turn of the death rate to the level in 1900 (21.0 per 1,000 within the old city boundaries) then appears overly dramatic.[72]

69. U.S. Bureau of the Census, Historical Statistics, pp. 55-56.

70. U.S. Bureau of the Census, Thirteenth Census of the United States taken in the Year 1910 (Washington, 1913), I, 1017.

71. U.S. Census Office, Twelfth Census, Vol. I, Part 2, p. 959.

72. The Health Department of New York chose to ignore the 1890 census in its computation of population and of death rates. Based on the Department's estimated population in 1890 of 1,612,559, the average death rate for the years 1889-91 was 24.6 per 1,000. Annual Report of the Board of Health for 1906, pp. 781, 1007. See Appendix Table A-2.

5 The City of Five Boroughs

POPULATION GROWTH, 1900-40

Following the creation of the greater city of New York in 1898 all of the elements necessary for population expansion came into place. These included a large land area (three hundred square miles), a massive cheap labor supply which could man new industries and construct new housing, and the rapid-transit facilities to move the labor force from home to place of work and back again, a substantial rate of natural increase, and a seemingly unlimited free flow of immigrants from abroad. The latter was perhaps the critical factor for it was Europe and not America that was the principal supplier of newcomers to the city.

The growth of American cities during the nineteenth century was very largely due to migration from the Old World, and as a general rule, the greater the size of the city the greater the relative contribution of foreign blood. New York was not atypical of other large American cities. In 1900 84 percent of the city's white heads of families were of foreign birth or the children of immigrants; for all American cities of 500,000 or more residents combined the proportion was 78 percent. Table 35 shows the great dichotomy that existed in 1900 between the foreign-stock representation in large cities and in the balance of the nation.

TABLE 35

Parentage of White Heads of Households for the United States
by Size of Place, 1900

Size of place	Total, all heads of families	Native parentage		Foreign parentage	
		Number	Percent of total	Number	Percent of total
United States	14,063,791	8,080,734	57.5	5,983,057	42.5
Cities of 500,000 plus	1,616,235	356,983	22.1	1,259,252	77.9
New York City	707,843	113,565	16.0	594,278	84.0
Balance	908,392	243,418	26.8	664,974	73.1
Cities of 100,000 to 500,000	1,191,351	356,805	29.9	834,546	70.1
Other urban and rural	11,256,205	7,366,946	65.4	3,889,259	34.6

Source: Same as Table 31.

Immigration from abroad during the first three decades of the twentieth century did not follow quite the same pattern of the earlier era. Certain cities, particularly those located in the Northeast or those experiencing a dynamic period of industrial expansion (such as Detroit), irrespective of their size attracted relatively greater numbers of newcomers than did others. New York was one of the major cities that came to absorb a substantially greater proportion of the incoming tide than previously. In 1900, when 57.5 percent of the white families of the nation were headed by native-born Americans of native parentage, among the fifteen largest cities in only two (Baltimore and Philadelphia) did as many as 30 percent of the white family heads fall into this category.[1] In 1930, however, when exactly the same proportion (57.5 percent) of all white family heads were of native stock as in 1900, in no fewer than nine of the fifteen largest cities at least 30 percent of the white family heads were of native origin.[2] Thus the absence of a significant increase in the proportion of New York City households headed by native whites of native parentage between the years 1900 and 1930 contrasts with the experience in most other American cities. In 1900, 16 percent of New York City's white household heads had native-born parents; in 1930, 18 percent. By and large, the cities that failed to experience relatively strong influxes of Italian or Jewish immigrants during this period had relatively large gains in their native-stock population sector. In Milwaukee, for example, where in 1900 only 9 percent of the white family heads—the smallest proportion of any major city—were not of foreign birth or parentage, the proportion had increased to 25 percent by 1930.[3]

IMMIGRATION

It is frequently not realized that despite New York City's more than fortyfold growth during the nineteenth century the *net* contribution to the city from the American hinterland was, on balance, nil. In 1800 the area within what came to be the five boroughs of New York City contained 79,000 persons,[4] or 1.5 percent of the national population. It may be calculated that approximately 1.6 percent of the country's white residents were then in this area.[5] A century later the federal census classified America's heads of families as either of native or of foreign parentage.

1. U.S. Census Office, *Twelfth Census,* Vol. I, Part 2, based on data in Tables 114, 115.
2. U.S. Bureau of the Census, *Fifteenth Census of the United States, 1930, Vol. VI Families* (Washington, 1933), pp. 11, 56. 3. *Ibid.*
4. U.S. Bureau of the Census, *U.S. Census of Population, 1950,* Vol. II, Part 1 (Washington, 1953), p. 46.
5. About 69,000 of 4,306,000. Derived from U.S. Department of State, *Second Census or Enumeration of the Inhabitants of the United States* (Washington, 1801), pp. 2, 27.

The native parentage group consisted largely of descendants of the residents of the United States in 1800 (the early American stock), though it also included a not insubstantial number of grandchildren of immigrants who had arrived during the nineteenth century. In Table 31 it is seen that New York City in 1900 had only 1.4 percent of the white families in the nation headed by persons of native parentage. Thus, New York's relative share of the white early American stock declined between 1800 and 1900; it follows that New York very likely was more a place of emigration of this stock elsewhere than a destination.

New York City's enormous growth in the nineteenth century came about because of its absorption of proportionately large segments of the immigrant streams from Europe. Table 31 shows the percentage of the total number of families in the United States headed by persons of foreign birth or parentage resident in New York City in 1900. It will be seen that the city had attracted about one-tenth of the German stock and about one-eighth of the Irish stock. But by the close of the nineteenth century Germany and Ireland were no longer the principal sources of American immigrants. Their positions had been taken by Russia, Austria-Hungary, and Italy, and, as Table 31 indicates, much larger proportions of the immigrants originating from these countries chose to settle in New York City. Thus in the early twentieth century, when these three countries provided a large majority of the newcomers to America, a substantially greater proportion of the immigrant arrivals remained in New York City than had previously been the case.

Statistics relating to the period of immigration of the foreign-born population permit the study of the relative attraction of New York City. According to the 1910 census only 11.1 percent of the foreign born who had arrived in the United States in 1890 or earlier were living in New York City compared to 17.1 percent of those who arrived between 1891-95, and 21.2 percent of those who came during 1896-1900. The drawing power of New York City apparently diminished somewhat during the first decade of the twentieth century: 18.6 percent of all immigrants of this period were in New York City in 1910. On the basis of the 1920 census it appears that the relatively downward turn continued during the second decade. The 1930 census, however, shows a sharp reversal occurred during the 1920s. By the late 1920s New York City was absorbing almost one out of every four immigrants from abroad (see Table 36).

The only census to cross-classify country of birth with year of immigration was that of 1930. The data indicate that the rise in the concentration of foreign born in New York City during the 1920s was not due to a differential mix in the source of immigrants—a rise in the proportion settling in New York in comparison with earlier periods occurred among the foreign born from each of the major countries of origin. However, it is interesting to note that this increase was much sharper for the "old" countries of origin than for the "new"; the proportion of German-born and

British-born arrivals in America during the late 1920s who settled in New York City was almost double the pre-World War I percentage, and the proportion from Ireland also increased substantially. By the late 1920s over 40 percent of the Irish newcomers and over 30 percent of the German newcomers were being drawn to New York City, in comparison to 28 percent of the Italian, once considered as especially concentrated in the metropolis (see Table 37). The apparent sharply upward trend toward concentration in New York City among natives of Poland in part reflects the relatively greater proportion of Jews in the over-all movement from Poland in comparison with "ethnic Poles" (Catholic Poles) during the 1920s than was the case previous to 1915.

TABLE 36
Foreign-born Population of New York City by Period of Immigration to the United States, Censuses of 1910-30

Year of immigration	Foreign-born population			Percent of U.S. total in New York City		
	1910	1920	1930	1910	1920	1930
Total	1,944,357	2,028,160	2,358,686	14.4	14.6	16.6
Before 1901	1,015,611	726,634	513,903	13.4	12.6	11.6
Before 1891	592,252	—	—	11.1	—	—
1891-95	198,038	—	—	17.1	—	—
1896-1900	225,321	—	—	21.2	—	—
1901-10	855,521*	742,462	673,927	18.6	18.4	17.6
1901-05	411,842	348,602	—	20.2	19.2	—
1906-10	443,679*	393,860	—	17.3	17.7	—
1911-14	—	333,612	304,822	—	16.2	16.8
1915-19	—	115,132	123,603	—	14.5	16.9
1920-24	—	—	390,288	—	—	22.4
1925-30	—	—	260,793†	—	—	24.9
Not stated	73,225	110,320	91,350	5.5	8.7	15.6

*Through April 15, 1910.   †Through April 1, 1930.
Source: Derived from data in U.S. Bureau of the Census, Thirteenth Census of the United States taken in the Year 1910, Vol. I (Washington, 1913); Fourteenth Census of the United States taken in the Year 1920, Vol. II (Washington, 1922); Fifteenth Census of the United States: 1930, Vol. II (Washington, 1933).

The net migration of foreign-born persons into New York City between successive census dates can be estimated by the residual method. Net migration represents the difference in the number of foreign born residents between the censuses after accounting for deaths among the resident foreign born during the time interval. Several types of errors can affect the accuracy of such an estimate, the most critical relating to the relative completeness of the specific censuses and to the proper reporting of nativity and of country of birth. (Following World War I and the resultant numerous changes in boundaries in the countries of Europe, reporting of country of birth frequently suffered from a lack of comparability.)

TABLE 37

Foreign-born White Population by Period of Immigration to the United States, Principal Countries of Birth; United States and New York City, 1930 Census
(in thousands)

Area and period of immigration	Austria	Germany	Great Britain	Ireland*	Italy	Poland	Russia
United States							
Total	370.9	1,608.8	1,223.2	923.6	1,790.4	1,268.6	1,153.6
Before 1901	99.2	938.6	460.1	429.4	319.2	240.6	242.3
1901-10	141.3	188.6	237.7	167.4	651.9	497.3	465.0
1911-14	57.6	71.4	108.8	60.3	307.6	314.1	220.4
1915-19	8.7	12.8	50.6	26.4	110.3	37.2	42.0
1920-24	38.7	129.5	185.0	75.4	265.7	110.6	123.0
1925-30	9.7	203.6	124.8	109.6	82.1	36.8	23.8
Not reported	15.7	64.4	56.3	55.1	53.6	32.0	37.1
New York City							
Total	127.2	237.6	118.4	220.6	440.2	238.3	442.4
Before 1901	34.5	88.2	29.2	72.9	81.8	33.7	85.4
1901-10	46.0	27.2	23.0	40.3	155.9	77.9	181.3
1911-14	18.7	12.0	9.5	15.5	64.2	48.0	76.7
1915-19	3.4	2.8	6.1	7.9	28.1	9.3	17.5
1920-24	16.8	32.3	20.9	24.8	72.4	48.4	58.5
1925-30	3.9	66.2	22.4	47.0	23.3	15.7	11.3
Not reported	3.7	8.8	7.2	12.1	14.6	5.3	11.6
Percent of U.S. total in New York City							
Total	34.3	14.8	9.7	23.9	24.6	18.8	38.4
Before 1901	34.8	9.4	6.3	17.0	25.6	14.0	35.2
1901-10	32.6	14.4	9.7	24.0	23.9	15.7	39.0
1911-14	32.6	16.8	8.8	25.8	20.9	15.3	34.8
1915-19	39.6	22.1	12.0	30.1	25.5	25.0	41.7
1920-24	43.5	25.0	11.3	32.9	27.2	43.8	47.6
1925-30	40.5	32.5	18.0	42.9	28.4	42.8	47.6
Not reported	23.4	13.6	12.8	22.0	27.2	16.5	31.3

*Includes Irish Free State and Northern Ireland.

Source: U.S. Bureau of the Census, Fifteenth Census, 1930; Population, II (Washington, 1933).

The net migration of foreign born to New York City according to the residual method can be estimated at 942,000 between 1900 and 1910, at 386,000 between 1910 and 1920, and at 657,000 between 1920 and 1930 (see Table 38). An alternative estimate of net migration, not quite identical in concept, can be constructed from data available from a single census, in response to the query on date of arrival asked of immigrants. At the April 15, 1910, census, for example, of the 1,871,132 foreign-born persons in New York City who reported the year of their arrival in the United States 855,521 or 45.7 percent indicated they had come in 1901 or later; assuming a proportionate share of the 73,225 immigrants whose year of arrival was not reported entered during this period, the total number becomes about 889,000. To this figure may be added perhaps 30,000 who came between the census taken June 1, 1900, and the close of 1900 to arrive at a total of approximately 919,000 who would be shown by the census as the net excess of arrivals since the date of the previous count over deaths and return emigration of this group.

For the period between the censuses of 1910 and 1920 the estimated net immigration by the year-of-arrival method differs considerably from that of the residual method. The January 1, 1920, census showed

TABLE 38

Estimated Net Migration of the Foreign-born Population of
New York City by Country of Birth, 1900-10 and 1910-20
(in thousands)

untry of birth	June 1, 1900 Census	April 15, 1910 Census	Jan. 1, 1920 Census	Components of change 1900-10		Components of change 1910-20	
				Deaths	Net migration	Deaths	Net migration
al, foreign born	1,270.1	1,944.4	2,028.2	267.5	941.8	302.6*	386.4
Germany	324.2	278.1	201.9	69.4	23.3	62.9	− 13.3
Ireland	275.1	252.7	203.4	89.2	66.8	76.9	27.6
Russia	182.2†	484.2	543.0	22.4‡	324.4	43.8§	102.6
Italy	145.4	340.8	390.8	24.7	220.1	37.6	87.6
Austria-Hungary	122.0	266.9	307.8	16.5	161.4	26.9	67.8
Great Britain	90.4	103.4	94.7	19.8	32.8	19.6	10.9
Scandinavia	45.3	65.2	67.3	8.0	27.9	9.8	11.9
Canada**	21.9	27.2	27.0	4.4	9.7	4.8	4.6
Romania	10.5	33.6	38.1	1.6	24.7	3.0	7.5
Other	53.1	92.3	154.2	11.5	50.7	17.3	79.2

*Deaths of foreign-born persons less an estimated 800 deaths of natives of United States possessions.

†Includes 1,800 who reported birthplace as Poland and did not specify whether from Austria, Russia, or many. Those who did specify are included with these countries.

‡Includes 1,200 deaths in which birthplace was reported as Poland.

§Includes 2,300 deaths in which birthplace was reported as Poland.

**Includes Newfoundland.

Source: Derived from U.S. Bureau of the Census population data and New York City Department of th mortality data. Calculations based on deaths have been adjusted to account for persons of unknown ity and for fractional parts of calendar years.

1,917,840 immigrants residing in New York City who reported year of arrival, of which 448,744 or 23.4 percent gave the years from 1911 through 1919. Assuming a proportionate share of the 110,320 immigrants not reporting year of arrival came in this period brings the total to 471,000. In addition the newcomers since the last census included those who arrived between April 15 and December 31, 1910, a figure which may be conjectured at 40,000 to 50,000. Thus, on the basis of census data, the net migration of foreign-born persons arriving in the United States between April 15, 1910, and the close of 1919 was in the area of 510,000; on the other hand, the residual method shows a net migration of 386,000. Although the two concepts differ somewhat, it is doubtful this can explain the large divergence. It may be that differences in the relative over-all completeness of the two censuses or error in reporting nativity or year of entry at the 1920 tally affected the estimates of migration.

Greater correspondence between the two measures is shown for the 1920-30 period. Approximately 681,000 immigrants were calculated by the year-of-arrival method (making allowance for the year-not-reported group) as against 657,000 by the residual method. Normally it would be expected that the former method would yield a figure exceeding that of the latter. If it could be assumed that the net movement of foreign-born persons between New York City and the balance of the United States was nil, it would then follow that a figure representing net migration of those foreign born who arrived in the United States in the course of the preceding decade would be greater than that representing net migration of all foreign-born persons in consequence of the return migration during the decade of foreign-born persons resident at the preceding census.

During the first two decades of the present century about two-thirds of the newcomers came from Russia, Austria-Hungary, and Italy. Exact comparison of the contribution of the many source countries is hampered by boundary changes and the creation of several new states following World War I. Thus many of the persons who were reported as born in Austria or Russia at the 1920 census were recorded as born in Poland at the 1930 tally. This name change prevents realistic estimates of net migration between 1920 and 1930 for most of Eastern Europe by means of the residual technique, but, fortunately, in 1930 the census cross-classified year of arrival of immigrants by country of birth. This allows a presentation of estimates of net migration from individual countries between 1920 and 1930 by means of two methods (see Table 39). The comparison for most areas gives gratifyingly close data. In the 1920-30 decade, Germany and Ireland returned to the fore as important areas of origin (though they did not dominate). Immigration from southern and eastern Europe was severly held in check by the stringent quota laws designed for this purpose that took effect in 1924.

Since year-of-arrival data on the foreign-born population ceased with the 1930 census, for the period 1930-40 the residual method provides

TABLE 39
Estimated Net Migration of the Foreign-born Population of New York City, 1920-30; Comparison of Vital Statistics Method and Adjusted Census Migrant Method
(in thousands)

Country of birth	Jan. 1, 1920 Census	April 1, 1930 Census	Components of change 1920-30		Adjusted census immigrants 1920-30*
			Deaths	Net migration	
Total, foreign born	2,028.2	2,358.7	326.8†	657.3	680.7
Italy	390.8	440.2	47.5	96.9	98.9
Ireland	203.4	220.6‡	59.0	76.2	76.0
Germany	194.2	237.6	53.5	96.9	102.3
Great Britain	94.7	118.4	18.8	42.5	46.2
Scandinavia	67.3	86.5	11.0	30.2	32.5
Romania	38.1	46.8	4.7	13.4	9.8
Canada §	27.0	45.4	5.3	23.7	22.4
Russia		442.4	57.1		71.7
Poland		238.3	11.2		65.6
Austria		127.2			21.4
Hungary	849.6	59.9	33.1	175.1	14.3
Czechoslovakia		35.3			8.9
Lithuania		15.0	—		1.7
Latvia		5.2	—		1.4
All other	163.1	239.9	25.6	102.4	107.6

*See text for description of method.

†Foreign-born deaths less estimate of 3,000 deaths of natives of U.S. possessions.

‡Includes Irish Free State and Northern Ireland.

§Includes Newfoundland.

Source: Derived from U.S. Bureau of the Census population data and New York City Department of Health mortality data. Calculations based on deaths have been adjusted to account for persons of unknown nativity and for fractional parts of calendar years.

the chief means of estimating net migration of the foreign born. This yields an estimated net inmigration of 137,700. The calculated changes for individual countries are severely distorted by a marked tendency to report birthplace in pre-World War I rather than postwar boundaries following the shattering of these lines by the events of 1938-39. Jaffe has demonstrated that in comparison with the number expected at the 1940 census the number actually enumerated within the United States was over-reported for countries losing territory after World War I (Austria, Hungary, Russia) and underreported for those gaining territory (Poland, Czechoslovakia).[6] This shift in the designation of country of birth among the East European immigrants explains the apparent large inmigration from Russia and outmigration of natives of Poland occurring in New York City between 1930 and 1940 (see Table 40).

6. Jaffe, *Handbook of Statistical Methods*, p. 93.

TABLE 40

Estimated Net Migration of the Foreign-born White Population
of New York City by Country of Birth,
1930-40 and 1940-50
(in thousands)

Country of birth	April 1, 1930 Census	April 1, 1940 Census	April 1, 1950 Census	Components of change 1930-40		Components of change 1940-50	
				Deaths	Net migration	Deaths	Net migration
Total, foreign born	2,295.2	2,080.0	1,784.2	352.9*	137.7	394.1	98.3
Italy	440.2	409.5	344.1	58.1	27.4	70.2	4.8
Russia	442.4	395.7	314.6	72.2	25.5	83.8	2.7
Germany	237.6	224.7	185.5	47.2	34.3 }	76.0	16.0
Austria	127.2	145.1	124.3	27.7	45.6 }		
Poland	238.3	194.2	179.9	21.5	− 22.6	30.2	15.9
Ireland†	220.6	181.8	144.8	50.5	11.7	44.8	7.7
Great Britain	118.4	97.7	80.0	18.0	− 2.7	17.8	0.1
Scandinavia	86.5	68.5	52.7	12.6	− 5.4	13.5	− 2.3
Hungary	59.9	62.6	52.0	9.7	˙ 12.4	12.6	2.0
Other	324.1	300.2	306.3	35.4	11.5	45.3	51.5

*Includes estimated distribution of deaths in 1933-35 (data not available) by application of average figures for 1932 and 1936.

†Includes Irish Free State and Northern Ireland.

Source: Derived from U.S. Bureau of the Census population data and New York City Department of Health mortality data. Calculations based on deaths have been adjusted to account for persons of unknown nativity, for fractional parts of calendar years, and for reporting on basis of place of occurrence rather than residence.

An approximation of the relative attraction New York City held for the sharply truncated inflow of immigrants during the 1930s can be made on the basis of the migration question asked at the 1940 census: "In what place did this person live on April 1, 1935?" Of the 226,911 foreign-born persons enumerated in the United States in 1940 who were reported as living abroad in 1935, 82,918 or 36.5 percent were in New York City.[7]

The net migration of the native-born population in New York City from census to census can also be estimated by the residual method. However, since determination of the number of births is necessary for this calculation, some adjustment is required for the decade 1900-10 when registration of births in New York was incomplete. The application of this proce-

7. U.S. Bureau of the Census, *Sixteenth Census of the United States, 1940. Population, Internal Migration 1935 to 1940. Social Characteristics of Migrants* (Washington, 1946), pp. 6, 219.

dure indicates a net outflow during each census interval among the native population during the first two decades of this century. Between 1920 and 1930 a net inmigration of native-born persons occurred; however, more detailed analysis shows this was entirely due to the large nonwhite inmigration. As previously, more native whites left New York City than entered during this decade.

INTERNAL MIGRATION

Net migration within the United States masks differences between two distinct streams—inmigrants and outmigrants. Inmigrants to New York City have been predominately natives of native parentage (at least third-generation Americans) while outmigrants from the city have been predominately natives of foreign or mixed parentage (second-generation Americans). Whether second-generation Americans have been more inclined to leave New York City than those of the third generation is not readily ascertainable—what is apparent is that second-generation Americans predominated in the resident native population of New York City and in the outward movement from the city. Thus, as a result of the cross-currents of migration New York City gained native whites of native parentage while losing native whites of foreign or mixed parentage.

Some idea of the dimensions of the net changes may be secured through the use of the census survival techniques of estimating migration.[8] By this method estimates are prepared of the expected number of persons in a given category (in this case, native whites of foreign or mixed parentage and native whites of native parentage) based on a standard set of survival ratios equivalent to the experience of this population as measured between two censuses. The difference between the expected number and the actual number enumerated is attributed to net in- or outmigration.

In the preparation of the data shown in Table 41 net migration of children born during the decade has not been considered because the possible error in converting birth statistics to census survivors in the years before complete registration was achieved within the United States is so large that estimates of migration may become seriously biased. The migration estimates therefore exclude the population under 10 years of age at the later of two censuses, and thus differ from the more inclusive figures of the residual method. Table 41 shows that in each decade between 1900 and 1930 a net outflow of native whites of foreign or mixed parentage occurred, compensated only in part by a net inflow of native

8. For excellent discussion and usage of this technique see: Everett S. Lee, Ann R. Miller, Carol P. Brainerd, and Richard Easterlin, *Population Redistribution and Economic Growth: United States 1870-1950*, Methodological Considerations and Reference Tables (Philadelphia: American Philosophical Society, 1957), I. Further interpretation and a list of 15 references is given in U.S. Bureau of the Census, "National Census Survival Rates, by Color and Sex, for 1950 to 1960," *Current Population Reports*, Series P-23, No. 15 (July 12, 1963).

whites of native parentage. Like their second-generation counterparts, members of the third generation 25 years of age and over at the beginning of a census period tended to move out of New York City during the decade. The age group experiencing the net influx was largely confined to those 10 to 24 years at the beginning of a census interval (20 to 34 years at its close), and among this group the bulk of the newcomers tended to be natives of native parentage.

TABLE 41

Estimated Net Migration of Native White Population of
New York City by Age and Parentage, Census Intervals 1900-40
(in thousands)

Parentage and age at beginning of period	1900-10	1910-20	1920-30	1930-40*
Total native white				
Total	−64.8	− 85.9	−35.4	34.5
Under 5 years	−28.7	− 36.6	−24.2	− 4.6
5-9 years	− 8.5	− 8.9	4.5	16.6
10-14 years	16.2	17.5	54.1	56.1
15-24 years	16.2	14.0	56.9	54.2
25-44 years	−47.3	− 46.6	−78.5	− 63.0
45 and over	−12.7	− 25.3	−48.2	− 24.8
Native white of native parentage				
Total	18.8	54.1	40.5	294.1
Under 5 years	− 7.0	− 8.5	− 9.5	6.3
5-9 years	2.3	4.0	4.0	16.7
10-14 years	15.9	23.7	36.7	51.8
15-24 years	27.2	40.7	56.3	123.1
25-44 years	−12.0	− 0.4	−27.4	67.1
45 and over	− 7.6	− 5.4	−19.6	29.1
Native white of foreign or mixed parentage				
Total	−83.5	−139.9	−75.9*	−259.7
Under 5 years	−21.7	− 28.1	−14.8	− 11.0
5-9 years	−10.7	− 12.8	0.6	0.0
10-14 years	0.3	− 6.2	17.4	4.2
15-24 years	−11.0	− 26.7	0.6	− 68.9
25-44 years	−35.3	− 46.1	−51.1	−130.1
45 and over	− 5.1	− 20.0	−28.6	− 53.9

*Data for 1940 based on 5 percent sample.
Source: Derived from U.S. Bureau of the Census data, utilizing census survival method.

An interesting effect of the crosscurrents of migration within the United States was the gradual relative increase of the third-generation share of a given birth cohort resident in New York. This may be seen in

Table 42, where the proportion of persons of foreign or mixed parentage among the native white population by five-year age intervals is shown for each census from 1890 to 1950. As an illustration, following the approximate native birth cohort of 1880-85 it is seen that in 1890 68.3 percent of this group (then 5-9 years of age) had a foreign-born parent; in 1900 (when 15-19 years of age) 66.3 percent had a foreign-born parent; in 1910 (when 25-29 years) 59.7 percent; in 1920 (then 35-39 years) 56.5 percent; and in 1930 (aged 45-49 years) 56.2 percent.

TABLE 42
Percent of Native White Population of New York City of Foreign or Mixed Parentage by Age, 1890-1950

Age	1890*	1900	1910	1920	1930	1940†	1950‡
Total	64.5	65.0	66.4	66.4	64.9	56.0	50.0
Under 5 years	68.6	70.2	73.9	71.3	61.0	39.2	19.9
5-9 years	68.3	69.3	71.2	74.6	66.6	50.9	27.5
10-14 years	71.6	66.8	69.7	73.6	71.7	59.4	39.0
15-19 years	74.7	66.3	67.7	69.4	74.0	64.5	49.5
20-24 years	70.9	66.5	62.8	64.4	69.0	65.4	54.3
25-29 years	66.9	66.4	59.7	60.1	62.6	62.6	57.8
30-34 years	63.0	65.6	62.1	56.8	60.7	58.9	63.4
35-39 years	54.9 } 64.1		{ 64.3	56.5	58.7	54.4	65.5
40-44 years	42.2 }		{ 64.9	59.4	56.6	52.1	63.3
45-49 years	35.5 } 50.0		{ 65.0	61.4	56.2	50.0	58.9
50-54 years	28.5 }		{ 62.5	62.1	58.9	47.6	57.6
55-59 years	22.6 } 33.5		{ 55.1	62.2	61.4	45.2	56.4
60-64 years	18.3 }		{ 43.7	59.5	62.2	48.5	53.2
65-69 years	16.2 }		{ 35.9	52.5	62.0	51.2	52.2
70-74 years	13.7 } 20.0		{ 29.7	40.5	59.4	50.8	53.6
75 and over	13.0 }		{ 22.1	29.8	46.6	49.2	54.5
Not reported	19.3	6.0	9.8	22.6	35.2	—	—

*New York City and Brooklyn as then constituted.   †Based on 5 percent sample.
‡Based on 20 percent sample.
Source: Derived from U.S. Bureau of the Census data.

Much more familiar than the fact that more native whites moved out of than into New York City is the knowledge that great numbers of residents were from "out of town." Between 1900 and 1940 the number of white residents of New York City who were born outside New York State almost tripled, climbing from 225,000 to 641,000. (The number originating from places in New York State outside of New York City cannot be determined from census classification.) During this period Pennsylvania replaced New Jersey as the principal state of origin of the migrants, while Massachusetts maintained its hold on third place (see Tables 43 and 44).

TABLE 43

Native Population of New York City by State of Birth,
1900-40

Place of birth	1940	1930	1920	1910	-1900
Total	5,316,338	4,571,760	3,591,888	2,822,526	2,167,122
United States	5,238,090	4,512,812	3,577,362	2,818,276	2,164,395
State reported	5,214,657	4,486,050	3,555,363	2,806,077	2,153,663
New York	4,312,100	3,763,213	3,107,563	2,441,765	1,892,719
Other States	902,557	722,837	447,800	364,312	260,944
Pennsylvania	145,869	103,374	62,863	54,904	36,664
New Jersey	128,954	106,800	79,735	69,898	56,568
Massachusetts	76,399	71,405	40,429	34,977	25,235
Virginia	66,014	56,497	33,261	28,862	22,736
South Carolina	62,836	38,075	14,172	8,229	4,398
North Carolina	51,151	31,871	13,668	10,736	6,520
Connecticut	45,687	42,500	27,762	25,235	20,480
Georgia	37,016	26,893	11,775	6,798	3,949
Ohio	29,030	25,844	20,189	16,549	11,847
Illinois	28,961	24,764	18,223	12,938	8,193
Maryland	20,994	20,451	14,336	12,563	9,351
Florida	20,872	12,895	5,418	2,399	1,422
All other	188,774	161,468	105,969	80,224	53,581
State not reported	23,433	26,762	21,999	12,199	10,732
Outlying areas	71,514	53,127	10,307	612	345
Puerto Rico	61,463	*	7,364	554	300
Philippines	2,763	*	773	21	11
Alaska and Hawaii	758	*	238	37	34
All other	6,530	*	1,932†	—	—
U.S. citizens born abroad or at sea	6,734	5,821	4,219	—	—

*Not published.   †Includes Virgin Islands 1,683, Panama Canal Zone 246, Guam 3.
Source: U.S. Bureau of the Census data.

A particularly interesting factor to consider in connection with the surge in New York City's out-of-state native population is that the relative pull of New York City upon the migrant streams from the principal contributing states did not greatly differ in the pre-World War II decades from that in the latter part of the nineteenth century. Table 45 indicates what the percentage of natives of selected states living in New York City were of all those living outside their state of birth in 1900 (which represents the residual effect of movement during the late nineteenth century) and at successive enumerations to 1940. (Unfortunately, the useful tabulations from which these data have been prepared have not been published at more recent censuses.) In general, in 1940 a somewhat larger proportion of the outmigrants were to be found in New York City than in 1900; between 1920 and 1940 the migrant stream in the direction of New York increased from all of the principal source states.

TABLE 44

White and Nonwhite Native Population of New York City
by State of Birth, 1900 and 1940

Place of birth	White		Nonwhite	
	1940	1900	1940	1900
Total	4,897,481	2,108,980	418,857	58,142
United States	4,835,547	2,106,406	402,543	57,989
State reported	4,813,249	2,095,836	401,408	57,827
New York	4,172,227	1,871,157	139,873	21,562
Other States	641,022	224,679	261,535	36,265
Pennsylvania	136,846	35,527	9,023	1,137
New Jersey	121,196	54,902	7,758	1,666
Massachusetts	73,586	24,851	2,813	384
Virginia	12,304	5,693	53,710	17,043
South Carolina	4,961	2,164	57,875	2,234
North Carolina	7,707	1,523	43,444	4,997
Connecticut	44,040	20,025	1,647	455
Georgia	8,328	2,456	28,688	1,493
Ohio	26,695	11,577	2,335	270
Illinois	27,533	8,090	1,428	103
Maryland	13,271	7,231	7,723	2,120
Florida	8,164	900	12,708	522
All other	156,391	49,740	32,383	3,841
State not reported	22,298	10,570	1,135	162
Outlying areas	55,602	308	15,912	37
Puerto Rico	53,323	265	8,140	35
Philippines	885	10	1,878	1
Alaska and Hawaii	551	33	207	1
All other	843	—	5,687	—
U.S. citizens born abroad or at sea	6,332	2,266	402	116

Source: U.S. Census Office, Twelfth Census of the United States Taken in the Year
1900; Population, Vol. I, Part 1 (Washington, 1902); U.S. Bureau of the Census, Sixteenth
Census of the United States; 1940 Population; State of Birth of the Native Population
(Washington, 1944).

NATURAL INCREASE

Both the crude birth rate and the crude death rate tended to decline
in the United States during the first three decades of the twentieth century
(typical of what has been termed "the demographic transition") and the
pattern in New York City did not differ markedly from the national trend
during this period. In the 1930s the city's birth rate was only about half
that at the turn of the century, as was the death rate. In consequence, the
rate of natural increase fell to a very reduced level.

During the first decade of the present century birth registration was
deficient; in 1905, when 85,002 births were registered in New York, the
Health Department conjectured "the true rate in the entire city approxi-

TABLE 45

Percent of Total and of Nonwhite Outmigrants (Persons Born in the State and Living in Other States) from Selected States Living in New York City, 1900-40

State	1940	1930	1920	1910	1900
Total outmigrants					
New Jersey	26.8	25.7	24.0	25.8	24.2
Connecticut	18.2	17.8	14.9	15.1	14.4
Massachusetts	12.4	12.4	9.4	9.8	8.4
Rhode Island	10.2	10.3	7.6	7.7	6.6
Pennsylvania	8.1	6.0	4.7	4.9	3.9
Maine	4.8	4.7	3.4	3.1	2.6
Ohio	2.6	2.2	1.8	1.4	1.1
Illinois	1.7	1.5	1.2	1.0	0.8
Nonwhite outmigrants*					
Maryland	11.4	9.0	—	—	3.7
District of Columbia	17.3	17.2	—	—	14.5
Virginia	17.1	13.4	—	—	6.8
North Carolina	17.4	11.9	—	—	3.7
South Carolina	16.9	10.6	—	—	2.0
Georgia	6.8	4.8	—	—	1.1
Florida	21.9	15.0	—	—	4.5

*Negro only in 1930. Data not available for 1910 and 1920.
Source: Derived from U.S. Bureau of the Census data.

mates 30 per 1,000; in other words over 16,000 births escape registration."[9] However, looking backward, the estimated crude birth rate of 30 per 1,000 may have been slightly too high for this period. Coale and Zelnik, for example, have estimated the crude birth rate of the white population of the United States fell from 28.5 to 27.3 per 1,000 between 1900 and 1910.[10] At the latter date the birth rate for New York City—based on registered births and the midyear population—was 27.0 per 1,000 (see Appendix Table A-3).

An estimate of the New York City birth rate in the year preceding the census of 1900 calculated from the census enumeration of children under one year of age and infant deaths yields a figure of 29.2 per 1,000. For the year ending with the census of 1910 the comparable procedure gives a rate of 26.1 births per 1,000 population. This, it may be noted, differs by only 2 percent from the birth rate for this year calculated from statistics of registered births.[11] The close agreement may be taken as

9. *Annual Report of the Board of Health for 1905*, II, 689.
10. Coale and Zelnik, *New Estimates*, p. 21.
11. Births registered during the period from April 1909 through March 1910 numbered 125,398; based on an estimated mid-period population of 4,700,000 this yields a birth rate of 26.7 per 1,000.

indicative that birth registration was relatively complete by this date (i.e., approximately no more understated than census understatement). It would seem, then, that New York's crude birth rate fell from slightly above the United States level for the white population in 1900 to slightly below in 1910. Thereafter, the rate for New York City declined more sharply than did the general United States birth rate. The crude rate in New York was 17.5 in 1930 and only 14.0 in 1940, while that for the United States in these years was 18.9 and 17.9 per 1,000.[12]

While in some years the crude birth rate for New York City may have been higher than that of the nation, Table 18 indicates that the level of fertility in the metropolis invariably was lower as measured by the fertility ratio (number of children under five years of age per 1,000 women 20-44 years of age) at each census. The explanation for an above-average crude birth rate despite lower fertility is that women 20-44 years of age constituted a substantially larger proportion of the city's population (as a result of the current of immigration) than of the national total.

The age distribution of the component population groups provides part of the explanation for the marked variation in the crude birth rates for the city's ethnic groups early in the century. In 1910, about the earliest year for which birth statistics may be considered realistic, the crude rate of 52.6 births per 1,000 population in the Italian community of New York compared with a rate of 23.8 among the balance of the city's population. The former group's birth rate had fallen sharply by 1920, although at 32.2 per 1,000 population it still held a sizable margin over the 22.3 of the non-Italian population.[13]

The differential fertility of the native and foreign-born women can best be illustrated by data from the 1920 census when special tabulations were prepared showing the age of the population by country of birth of mother for selected countries. Foreign-born white females 20-44 years of age had almost twice the number of children under five years of age (605 per 1,000) as native-born white women (321 per 1,000). Part of this difference could be attributed to a much higher tendency among foreign-born women to be married. Table 46 indicates that 75 percent of all foreign-born women in this category were classified as married against fewer than 60 percent of the native women. Considering only married women aged 20-44 years, the difference in the ratio of children under five years between the two nativity groups diminishes substantially, becoming 808 per 1,000 for foreign-born women and 579 per 1,000 for native-born women.

---

12. Appendix Table A-3; U.S. Department of Health, Education, and Welfare, *Vital Statistics of the United States 1967, Vol. 1 Natality*, p. 3.

13. Rates are based on 28,660 births to Italian-born women in 1910 and 24,895 in 1920 (see Appendix Table A-7); 544,449 persons are classified as of Italian foreign stock in the 1910 census and 772,808 as having Italian mothers in the 1920 census.

TABLE 46
Number of Children Under 5 per 1,000 Women 20-44 Years of Age by Selected Characteristics, New York City, 1920

Race, nativity, and parentage	Women aged 20-44 years			Children under 5 years of age		
					Per 1,000	
	All women	Married women	Percent married	Number	Women	Married women
Total	1,252,208	810,319	64.7	560,869	448	692
White	1,202,830	779,291	64.8	549,402	457	705
Native:						
Native parentage	246,495	139,745	56.7 }	201,158*	321	579
Foreign or mixed parentage	380,886	207,646	54.5 }			
Foreign, Total	575,449	431,900	75.0	348,244†	605	808
Born in Italy	111,678‡	—	—	108,552	972	—
All other	463,771‡	—	—	239,692	517	—
Negro	48,845	30,625	62.7	11,147	228	364
Other races	533	403	75.6	320	600	794

*Children of native white mothers.   †Children of foreign-born white mothers.
‡Estimated; see text.
Source: Derived from data in U.S. Bureau of the Census, Fourteenth Census of the United States Taken the Year 1920, Vol. II (Washington, 1922); Mortality Rates 1910-1920 (Washington, 1923).

The major part of the fertility differential between the two nativity groups resulted from the high fertility pattern of the Italian-born foreign women. An approximation of the age distribution of Italian women in New York City can be developed by assuming a similar distribution to that published for the combined total in a selected group of urban areas.[14] The estimated number of children under five years of age per 1,000 females 20-44 years of age born in Italy so calculated is 972 (see Table 46). This compares with an estimated ratio of 517 per 1,000 among non-Italian foreign-born white women and of 404 among all non-Italian white women (native and foreign).

Unlike the registration of births in New York City, that of deaths is believed to have been adequate well before the dawn of the twentieth century. Differential mortality among the major ethnic groups was a field of interest attracting the attention of eminent statisticians, including those of the Census Office in 1880 and 1890, and the subject continued to be studied in the new century. Following the census of 1910, Dublin compared

14. Of 238,044 women born in Italy enumerated in 1920 in the selected urban areas—New York City, Chicago, Detroit, Milwaukee, Boston, and the state of Rhode Island—150,412, or about 63.2 percent, were 20-44 years of age, according to Niles Carpenter, *Immigrants and their Children*, Census Monograph VII (Washington, D.C.: U.S. Government Printing Office, 1927), p. 17. This percentage when applied to New York City's 176,978 Italian-born women yields 111,678 in the age group.

crude death rates of race stocks in New York State with standardized rates he had developed based on the numbers of deaths in age-nativity groups reported by New York State, and on special tabulations cross-classifying age and birthplace obtained from the U.S. Bureau of the Census.[15]

The crude death rates in New York State for 1910 were highest among Irish-born males and females, next highest for natives of Germany and Great Britain, and lowest among natives of Russia, Austria-Hungary, and Italy. This is not illogical since immigrants from the "new" countries of immigration presumably were younger than those from the "old" countries, who by and large had arrived before the turn of the century. The standardized rates, however, show that after adjusting for the affect of age distribution, mortality among the Irish remained substantially higher than that for any other group; mortality among the German and British stood intermediate, and that among the "newer" immigrant groups was still lowest (see Table 47).

TABLE 47
Crude and Age-adjusted Death Rates* of the Foreign-born Population 10 Years of Age and Over by Country of Birth and Sex, New York State, 1910

Country of birth	Crude death rate		Age-adjusted death rate	
	Male	Female	Male	Female
Foreign born: all	17.5	16.6	17.1	16.2
Austria-Hungary	9.4	7.3	14.3	12.4
Germany	27.7	22.8	17.9	14.4
Great Britain	22.6	16.6	20.8	15.8
Ireland	40.3	34.9	25.9	23.5
Italy	9.0	9.5	12.9	13.7
Russia	7.7	6.8	13.1	12.3

*Per 1,000 population.
Source: Louis I. Dublin: "Factors in American Mortality. A Study of Death Rates in the Race Stocks of New York State, 1910," American Economic Review, VI, 3 (1916).

Another major study made of differential mortality among ethnic groups, and in some ways the most extensive, was that following the census of 1920. This study chose to divide the population groups according to country of birth of mother.[16] Because of assumed discrepancy in reporting

15. Louis I. Dublin, "Factors in American Mortality, A Study of Death Rates in the Race Stocks of New York State, 1910," American Economic Review, VI, 3 (September 1916).
16. U.S. Bureau of the Census, Mortality Rates 1910-1920 (Washington, 1923).

country of birth of mother between the census and the death-record tabula-tion, the national-origin material prepared excluded the East European countries that had experienced extensive boundary revisions in conse-quence of the First World War. Adjusted rates (based on the standard million population of England and Wales in 1901) were computed for the national-origin groups. For only 1.4 percent of deaths in New York City in 1920 was country of birth of mother unknown, and these deaths were distributed proportionate to the known.[17] The derived age-adjusted rates were found to be quite similar among persons of American, British, German, and Italian maternal descent; the Irish, however, experienced a mortality level over 25 percent in excess of that for any of these groups (see Table 48). Both the age-adjusted and the crude death rates of the Jewish population undoubtedly were relatively low. Among the nearly two million persons in New York City in 1920 who had mothers born abroad, in countries other than those distinguished by the Census Bureau for the special mortality analysis tabulations, were included the Jewish masses from Eastern Europe. The low crude death rate of 9.95 per 1,000 for this residual population must have been in large part shaped by the low rate of its Jewish majority. The high crude death rate for the nonwhite popula-tion, like that for the Irish, was due to factors other than age composition; after adjustment for age the gap between the white and nonwhite rates widened rather than decreased (see Table 48).

TABLE 48
Crude and Age-adjusted Death Rates* by Race and by Selected Origins for the White Population, New York City, 1920

Race and country of origin	Crude death rate	Age-adjusted death rate
Total	13.1	14.5
White	12.9	14.2
Country of birth of mother		
United States	12.0	13.7
Germany	17.4	13.0
Great Britain	15.8	13.4
Ireland	20.2	18.1
Italy	12.6	14.0
Nonwhite	19.8	25.5

*Per 1,000 population.
Source: U.S. Bureau of the Census, Mortality Rates 1910-1920 (Washington, 1923).

17. *Ibid.*, p. 13.

Ethnic Groups

The principal statistical frame for the study of changes in the ethnic communities derives from the census classification of the "foreign white stock population," a term the Census Bureau adopted to indicate the total number of foreign-born whites, native whites of foreign parentage (those having both parents born abroad), and native whites of mixed parentage (those having one native-born parent and the other foreign born). Fluctuations of the foreign white stock from census to census indicate growth or decline in the number of immigrants and the children of immigrants. The grandchildren of immigrants have always been included among the "native stock population" where they are indistinguishable from even eighth-generation Americans.

In classifying the country of origin of the foreign stock population, nineteenth-century census statisticians grouped all persons having parents born abroad according to the parents' country of birth; since the turn of the century only the native born have been categorized by parents' birthplace, the foreign born being assigned their own country of birth. This shift in definition produced little difference in the statistics for most countries of origin. However, for a few countries, such as Canada, whose natives include many having parents born elsewhere, the change in concept had a significant effect. The census of 1900 was tabulated by both concepts of parentage classification so that data could be comparable with later as well as earlier enumerations. In Table 49 the distribution of the population of New York City by parentage is shown under the earlier concept for the year 1900 with comparable available figures for the combined total for New York City and Brooklyn for the year 1890. The country of origin of the white population of foreign or mixed parentage is given in Appendix Table C-1. It is to be noted that in 1900, 279 persons classified as whites of native parentage were actually of foreign birth, and these are included in the foreign-stock classification shown in Table 49, which presents the 1900 data under the newer concept.

A new "country of origin" classification—of "mixed foreign parentage" —was introduced in 1900 for persons having foreign-born parents born in different countries, and this was maintained in the 1910 and 1920 enumerations (see Appendix Table C-2). Beginning with the 1930 census this population was classified according to the country of birth of the father and merged with statistics of persons having both parents born in the particular foreign country. The native white population of mixed parentage was classified according to the country of birth of the foreign-born parent at each census.

New York in 1900 was a city in which household heads of Irish or German parentage predominated (see Table 31). The Irish population was not so numerous proportionately as in Boston or Providence and the German population did not approach the preponderant element it did in

TABLE 49

White and Nonwhite Population by Nativity and Parentage, New York City, 1900 and New York City and Brooklyn Combined, 1890

Parentage	White			Nonwhite		
	Total	Native	Foreign	Total	Native	Foreign
Total, 1900	3,369,898	2,108,980	1,260,918	67,304	58,142	9,162
Native parentage	737,756	737,477	279	55,489	55,489	0
Foreign or mixed parents	2,632,142	1,371,503	1,260,639	11,815	2,653	9,162
Foreign parents	2,329,907	1,072,062	1,257,845	9,998	N.A.	N.A.
Mixed parents	302,235	299,441	2,794	1,827	N.A.	N.A.
Father foreign born	198,822	196,706	2,116	1,122	N.A.	N.A.
Mother foreign born	103,413	102,735	678	705	N.A.	N.A.
Total, 1890*	2,285,024	1,387,313	897,711	36,620	32,688	3,932
Native parentage	498.099	493,060	5,039	31,500	N.A.	N.A.
Foreign or mixed parents	1,786,925	894,253	892,672	5,120	N.A.	N.A.
Foreign parents	1,601,082	711,847	889,235	N.A.	N.A.	N.A.
Mixed parents	185,843	182,406	3,437	N.A.	N.A.	N.A.
Father foreign born	127,442	125,450	1,992	N.A.	N.A.	N.A.
Mother foreign born	58,401	56,956	1,445	N.A.	N.A.	N.A.

*New York City and Brooklyn as then constituted.   N.A. = Not available.

Source: U.S. Census Office, Population of the United States at the Eleventh Census, Part 1 (Washington 1895), and Twelfth Census of the United States, taken in the Year 1900. Population Vol. I, Part 1 (Washington 1902).

Cincinnati or Milwaukee. But New York had the rare distinction of being one of very few cities where household heads both of Irish and of German stock outnumbered those of third-generation or later American stock.

Within the brief span of less than a generation the ethnic composition of the metropolis altered radically. Before the second quarter of the twentieth century had begun, persons of Jewish and Italian background had become numerically superior to those of Irish and German descent. Estimates of the growth of the Jewish population have shown considerable variation; unlike other ethnic groups whose numbers—at least in the first and second generation—could be fairly well ascertained from the census classification of the foreign stock by country of origin, the Jews emigrated from several countries. Prior to the 1910 census there was interest in classifying the foreign-stock population by ethnic origin as well as national origin so that the dimensions of groups such as the Jews, the Slovaks, or the Lithuanians, who did not come from their own nation-state, could be measured. This was not achieved, but as a result of this need the classification of the foreign-stock population according to mother tongue spoken (prior to immigration) was instituted. However, such an approach was far from completely satisfactory in delineating ethnic origin; although the "Yiddish mother tongue" classification, for example, included the bulk of the Jewish population of foreign stock, it failed to account for consider-able numbers of Jews of German, French, or other non-Yiddish background.

Two estimates of the Jewish population in New York City developed by more than guesswork deserve attention; significantly, both relied heavily upon data relating to Jewish deaths in their methodology. Henry Chalmers, assuming that Jewish mortality dipped from 15.8 deaths per 1,000 persons in 1901 to 10.5 in 1910, calculated a Jewish population of "at least 510,000" in 1901 and of "close to 1,050,000" in 1910.[18] Compu-tations made by the Jewish Communal Survey of Greater New York indicated a Jewish crude death rate of 7.9 per 1,000 in 1925 and a popula-tion of 1,713,000.[19] The Jewish population thus appears to have more than tripled in size in a very brief period, and much of the growth must be attributed to an outpouring from Russia and to a lesser extent from Austria-Hungary and Romania.

The Italian community during the first decades of the century corre-sponded closely to the census foreign-stock tabulations for a single country and can therefore be measured more accurately than the Jewish popula-tion. The census classification of persons of Italian birth or parentage soared from 218,000 in 1900 to 544,000 in 1910 and 803,000 in 1920. Of this growth about 308,000 can be assigned to the inflow from Italy (see Table 38), and the balance, nearly as large a figure, apparently resulted from natural increase.

There can be little doubt that during the first quarter of the current century the Italian community in New York had by far the highest rate of natural increase of the city's principal ethnic groups. Based on the January 1, 1920, census population the city's crude birth rate in 1920 was 23.6 per 1,000, the death rate 13.0, and the rate of natural increase 10.6 per 1,000. The crude birth rate among the Italian stock was at least 32 (see preceding section), the death rate 12.6; the natural increase, therefore, was in excess of 19 per 1,000.

The Jewish community, for which statistical data are far less defini-tive, probably had the next highest rate of natural growth at this time. It is likely, both in consequence of age structure and because of the high proportion of foreign born in this group, that the crude birth rate was somewhat above the average level of the non-Italian population (22.3 per 1,000), perhaps 25 per 1,000. The crude death rate of the Jewish population, as has been discussed, was remarkably low. Carefully esti-mated at 7.9 per 1,000 in 1925, it probably was in the vicinity of 9-10 in

18. Henry Chalmers, "The Number of Jews in New York City," *Publications of the American Statistical Association*, XIV, 1914-15 (1916), 74.
19. Bureau of Jewish Social Research, *Jewish Communal Survey of Greater New York* (New York: Bureau of Jewish Social Research, 1928), p. 17.

1920. A very rough calculation, then, of the Jewish rate of natural increase in New York City in 1920 is about 15 per 1,000.

The Irish at this period would seem to have experienced an unusually low rate of natural increase, if any at all. The crude birth rate for this community, which unlike the Italian and Jewish components of the population, included many third-generation Americans, quite likely was somewhat below the 22.3 per 1,000 of the non-Italian population of New York in 1920, if only because of its age distribution. On the other hand, its crude death rate probably was not very much less than the 20.2 per 1,000 for the census Irish classification.

The 1930 census was the first after that taken in 1900 to classify heads of families according to nativity and parentage. In addition, this census provided the one occasion when the category "number of children under ten years old" was tabulated not only by nativity and parentage but by specific country of birth of family heads. Calculations based on these tabulations can indicate the minimum number of children under ten for different subcategories of families. The actual number per family cannot be computed, however, since an open-end classification, "six or more children" was used. (The aggregate minimum number of children in all families—1,091,019—was only 2.0 percent less than the total population under the age of ten.) Such statistics provide a crude measure of the differential fertility among New York's ethnic groups. Serious comparison, however, is rendered uneven by the fact that the average age varied considerably among the family heads of different backgrounds. It seems likely, nonetheless, because of the extremely wide range, that although a set of figures standardized for age would alter the child-family ratios of Table 50, the number of children per family for Italian-born heads would still be greatest and those for German-born heads least.

Assuming the parental origin of all white children under ten years of age living in New York in 1930 (1,060,398) approximates that of the 1,043,968 shown in Table 50, then 60.6 percent came from families headed by an immigrant, 24.2 percent from families headed by a native American having at least one foreign-born parent, and 15.2 percent from a family headed by a third-or-later-generation American.[20]

The specific countries of origin of the family heads of the more than 630,000 white children living in immigrant households are shown in Table 50. Among these children were undoubtedly very nearly all of the approximately 27,000 foreign-born persons under the age of ten living in New York City. But the overwhelming bulk were second-generation Americans with two foreign-born parents. The more than 400,000 children in families headed by native whites were largely native whites of native parentage. However, a small group who were second generation,

20. The latter category, it should be noted, also included the Puerto Rican born.

presumably the children of one foreign and one native parent, may be calculated at roughly 45,000. (This represents the difference between the combined number of foreign-born and native of foreign or mixed parentage children and the number of children estimated to be in households having a foreign-born head plus an adjustment for children not living in households.) Hence, although the more than 250,000 children living in families headed by native whites of foreign or mixed parentage were representatives of a chiefly third-generation-American group, a substantial minority presumably were in part second-generation (having one foreign-born parent). Equally complex is the generational status of the approximately 160,000 children in families having heads who were native whites of native parentage. While assuredly fourth- or later-generation Americans predominated in this group, minorities comprised of part third-generation and part second-generation Americans must have been considerable.

TABLE 50

Number of Children Under 10 Years Old in Families by Race, Nativity, and Parentage of Heads and by Country of Birth for Foreign-born White Heads, New York City, 1930

Characteristics of head	Families	Number of children under 10 years old*	Mean number of children per family
Total	1,579,946	1,091,019	0.69
White†	1,513,522	1,043,968	0.69
Native-native parents	254,760	158,369	0.62
Native-foreign or mixed parents	385,574	252,951	0.66
Foreign born	872,756	632,296	0.72
Negro	64,731	45,794	0.71
Other races	1,693	1,257	0.74
Country of birth of foreign-born white			
Austria	53,688	34,515	0.64
Germany	82,448	26,395	0.32
Great Britain	36,418	18,026	0.49
Hungary	22,518	11,266	0.50
Ireland‡	67,784	43,595	0.64
Italy	191,076	216,404	1.13
Poland	94,355	68,828	0.73
Russia	189,917	126,727	0.67
Scandinavia	28,533	13,667	0.48
All other	106,019	72,873	0.69

*See text for derivation.
†Includes 432 "Mexican" family heads with 352 children under 10 years of age, not otherwise classified by nativity and parentage.
‡Includes Irish Free State and Northern Ireland.
Source: Computed from data in U.S. Bureau of the Census, Fifteenth Census of the United States 1930: Population, VI (Washington, 1933); and Special Report on Foreign-born White Families by Country of Birth of Head (Washington, 1933).

To summarize, since heads of families are not uniformly married to spouses of the same generational origin, tabulations of children identified by parentage of family head do not yield exact categories of background. Thus, in the absence of a census query on birthplace of grandparents, the category "native of native parentage" cannot be split so as to obtain a meaningful number of third-generation or of fourth- and later-generation Americans. For rough delineation, however, it may be assumed that a number equivalent to the share of the population representing fourth- and later-generation Americans approximates those in the category, children of family heads of native parentage.

The equivalent concept is important; it recognizes that persons who fit a single category are probably more the exception than the rule. Thus an individual whose background as measured by maternal descent is third-generation American and as measured by paternal descent is fifth-generation American can be considered equivalent to fourth-generation American. Accepting this premise, then the number of children under ten years of age who represent the third-generation American equivalent can be calculated as a residual after excluding children of native white of native-parentage family heads (representing the fourth- and later-generation American equivalent) from the total child population and then deducting the census figure for the foreign stock (foreign born or native born of foreign or mixed parentage) under the age of ten (687,000) from the balance (899,000). The estimate of 212,000 derived in this manner is shown in Table 51.

TABLE 51
Estimate of White Population Under 10 Years Old by Generation Status, New York City, 1930
(in thousands)

Nativity and parentage characteristic	Estimated number of children under 10 by nativity and parentage of parent*	Number of children under 10 by own nativity and parentage†	Estimated "native stock" children under 10 by generation equivalent‡
Total	1,060.1	1,060.1	373.0 Total
Native-native parents	160.9	373.0	160.9 Fourth generation
Foreign stock	899.2	687.2	212.0 Third generation
Native-foreign or mixed parents	256.9	659.8	—
Foreign born	642.3	27.4	—

*Derived by applying factor of 1.0158 to data on number of children in Table 50. Children in "Mexican" families are excluded.

†From U.S. Bureau of the Census, Fifteenth Census of the United States: 1930, Vol. II (Washington, 1933).

‡Method of computation discussed in text.

This table, which shows the third-generational equivalent in the population under ten years of age in 1930, was designed so as to ignore the mixed background of much of the actual portrait by generation and by country of origin. The decennial censuses taken between 1900 and 1940 showed between 12.7 and 16.6 percent of the native-born white persons in New York City who had foreign-born fathers had native-born mothers. Only for the 1930 and 1940 enumerations, however, were classifications prepared which permit the viewing of the mixing or assimilation differential according to the specific country of birth of father. Table 52 shows the wide range among individual countries. It is probably not surprising to find that persons having fathers born in two English-speaking countries— Canada and Great Britain—were most likely to have mothers born in the United States. Despite their language affinity, however, the Irish immigrant males seem to have been less likely to marry American-born women than did German or French males.

TABLE 52

Native White Population with Father Foreign by Country of Birth of Father and Number with Mother Native Born, New York City, 1930 and 1940

Country of birth of father	1930			1940*		
		With native mother			With native mother	
	Total	Number	Percent	Total	Number	Percent
Total, foreign father	2,586,037	374,063	14.5	2,536,960	421,640	16.6
Italy	616,069	79,010	12.8	661,520	110,200	16.7
Russia	484,021	44,875	9.3	503,700	59,740	11.8
Ireland†	333,036	52,820	15.9	287,920	46,140	16.0
Germany	330,719	72,954	22.1	248,900	54,180	21.8
Poland	213,475	14,206	6.7	206,900	21,040	10.2
Austria	154,034	16,229	10.5	167,600	23,200	13.8
Great Britain	107,785	38,088	35.3	92,760	33,420	36.0
Scandinavia	58,380	8,327	14.3	52,640	9,100	17.3
Hungary	51,992	5,153	9.9	56,580	7,460	13.2
Rumania	44,751	4,335	9.7	41,140	5,820	14.1
Czechoslovakia	34,009	3,076	9.0	27,820	3,660	13.2
Canada‡	29,274	12,186	45.0	28,080	11,600	41.3
France	20,958	5,694	27.2	15,960	4,540	28.4
Greece	16,561	1,525	9.2	24,340	3,220	13.2
Lithuania	15,857	1,127·	7.1	17,240	2,100	12.2
All other§	75,116	14,458	19.2	103,860	26,220	25.2

*Based on 5 percent sample.   †Including Irish Free State and Northern Ireland.
‡Including Newfoundland.   §Including not stated.
Source: Derived from data in U.S. Bureau of the Census, Sixteenth Census of the United States: 1940; Population; Nativity and Parentage of the White Population; Country of Origin of the Foreign Stock (Washington, 1943).

Although tabulations were prepared on a national level at the censuses of 1900 through 1930 showing specific country of birth of father for the native-white population cross-classified by country of birth of mother, none were made for individual American cities. It is possible, however, to utilize 1900 census data to estimate for New York City the extent to which native whites having fathers who were born in a given foreign country had mothers who were born in the same foreign country, in another foreign country, or in the United States. This census was the only one to classify the population of mixed foreign parentage in New York City by parental country of origin. These statistics, however, as well as those for the population of mixed parentage (one foreign-born and one native-born parent), were available only for the total white population rather than the native white population. In estimating the parental background of the native white population of mixed nationality it was assumed in Table 53 that the native-born white group had the same proportionate distribution as the total group. This involved minimal chance of error in the case of the population having foreign-born fathers and United States-born mothers, since 98.4 percent (196,706 of 199,044) were native born, but may be off somewhat for the population having fathers and mothers born in different foreign countries where 83.5 percent (106,786 of 127,837) of the total were native.

Table 53, which shows the assimilative picture as of 1900 according to an estimate derived from the census, indicates the wide range in the degree of intermarriage among fathers from different areas. Some 73 percent of the native-born whites who had fathers born in Canada had mothers born elsewhere, but less than 7 percent among persons who had Italian-born fathers had mothers born outside of Italy.

The 1900 census indicated that of 1,268,768 native white persons in New York City who had a foreign-born father, 8.4 percent had a foreign-born mother from a different country. This compared with 15.5 percent who had a native-born mother. At the 1920 census, the only other enumeration where published tabulations yielded such information, almost an identical proportion (8.5 percent) consisted of persons whose mothers originated from a different foreign nation than their fathers (see Table 54).

It is of especial interest to ascertain an age distribution of the native population of mixed foreign parentage since the cohort approach can offer a means of tracing the relative course of assimilation over time. Only the 1920 census provided data from which a close estimate by age can be constructed. Table 55 shows the derivation of this estimate. It will be seen that the cohorts born in the years 1905-14 and 1850-64, periods of heavy immigration or immediately following, show the smallest mixed proportion, while the greatest relative appearance of native mothers occurs among the 1880-89 cohort.

New York City's Negro population experienced phenomenal growth during the early part of the present century, more than doubling between 1900 and 1920 (from 60,666 to 152,467), and then redoubling in the single decade of the 1920s (see Table 69). By 1940 the 458,444 Negroes in the city represented 6.0 percent of the total population, compared with 1.8 percent in 1900. The bulk of this growth was due to migration streams originating in the southern states and in the West Indies. Table 44 shows that the nonwhite native population (always more than 97 percent Negro) throughout the period from 1900 to 1940 generally included two persons born outside of the state for every one native New Yorker.

The data for 1900 indicate that nearly one-half of the native American Negro population born outside of New York State were natives of Virginia. Although Virginia's Negro population continued to move north to New York City, and the community of 17,000 in 1900 rose to 54,000 in 1940, proportionately the state's contribution diminished. The strongest current came from farther south—in the two Carolinas—whose 101,000 nonwhite natives in New York City in 1940 compared with 7,000 in 1900. The pattern of accelerated migration continued down the Atlantic Coast: Georgia and Florida combined were the home states of only 2,000 of New York City's Negro population in 1900, but of 41,000 in 1940.

During the early twentieth century New York City became the goal of an ever-increasing proportion of the Negro population living south of the Mason-Dixon Line. Table 45 indicates that whereas in 1900 only the District of Columbia had sent more than 10 percent of its nonwhite out-migrants to the metropolis, by 1940 at least as significant proportions of the Negro migrants who had left the states of Virginia, North Carolina, South Carolina, and Florida were living in the city.

The number of Negroes in New York City classed among the foreign born increased from 11,757 in 1910 to 30,436 in 1930; and 54,754 in 1920 (see Table 69). In the same period the proportion of the nation's immigrant Negro population living in New York City climbed from 29 percent to almost 56 percent. Table 56 shows the period of immigration to the United States of all foreign-born Negroes living in the United States, as well as the community residing in New York City, at the censuses of 1920 and 1930. It may be concluded that while less than 20 percent of the Negro immigrants who arrived before the turn of the century chose to settle in New York City, close to 70 percent of those who entered in the 1920s established themselves in the nation's largest city.

The absolute decline that took place between 1930 and 1940 in the number of foreign-born Negroes resident in New York City apparently came about as the result of dwindling outmigration from the West Indies during the Depression years. Although data are not available for New York City showing the distribution of the foreign-born Negro population by country of birth, it is evident from the national tallies that the bulk of the immigrants came from the West Indies. Assuming all of the nonwhite natives of the West Indies living in New York City—10,425 in 1910 and

48,263 in 1930—were Negro, then at both censuses over 85 percent of the foreign-born Negro population originated from the Caribbean.

TABLE 53

Native White Population with Father Foreign by Country of Birth of Father and Nativity of Mother (Partly Estimated), New York City, 1900

| Country of origin | Total* | Native† | Foreign born | | |
			Total	Same country as father	Different country ‡
Total, foreign father	1,268,768	196,706	1,072,062	965,276	106,786
Austria	54,527	3,091	51,436	44,644	6,792
Canada	15,289	7,300	7,989	4,192	3,797
France	14,321	3,570	10,751	5,986	4,765
Germany	433,352	76,270	357,082	337,712	19,370
Great Britain	108,080	34,904	73,176	46,424	26,752
Hungary	22,037	1,762	20,275	15,687	4,588
Ireland	380,639	53,493	327,146	312,372	14,774
Italy	73,400	3,085	70,315	68,659	1,656
Poland §	22,135	840	21,295	18,166	3,129
Russia	92,052	2,902	89,150	81,001	8,149
Scandinavia	27,455	3,032	24,423	18,733	5,690
Switzerland	6,706	1,527	5,179	2,680	2,499
All other	18,775	4,930	13,845	9,020	4,825
Percent distribution					
Total, foreign father	100.0	15.5	84.5	76.1	8.4
Austria	100.0	5.7	94.3	81.9	12.5
Canada	100.0	47.7	51.3	27.4	24.8
France	100.0	24.9	75.1	41.8	33.3
Germany	100.0	17.6	82.4	77.9	4.5
Great Britain	100.0	32.3	67.7	43.0	24.8
Hungary	100.0	8.0	92.0	71.2	20.8
Ireland	100.0	14.1	85.9	82.1	3.9
Italy	100.0	4.2	95.8	93.5	2.3
Poland §	100.0	3.8	96.2	82.1	14.1
Russia	100.0	3.2	96.8	88.0	8.9
Scandinavia	100.0	11.0	89.0	68.3	20.7
Switzerland	100.0	22.8	77.2	40.0	37.3
All other	100.0	26.3	73.7	48.0	25.7

*Computed by assuming distribution by country of mother's origin of 102,735 native white persons having mothers born abroad and native fathers similar to that of 103,413 white persons having mothers born abroad and native fathers and subtracting this group from the native white of foreign- or mixed-parentage population (1,371,503).

†Computed by assuming distribution by country of father's origin similar to that of 198,822 white persons having fathers born abroad and native mothers.

‡Computed by assuming distribution by country of father's origin similar to that of 127,837 persons whose parents were born in different foreign countries.

§Poland not specified as Austria, Russia, or Germany.

Source: Derived from U.S. Census Office, Twelfth Census of the United States Taken in the Year 1900; Population, Vol. I Part 1 (Washington, 1902); Thirteenth Census of the United States Taken in the Year 1910 Vol. I (Washington, 1913).

TABLE 54
Native White Population with Foreign Father by Nativity of Mother, New York City, 1900-40*

Nativity of mother	1900	1920	1930	1940†
Total, foreign father	1,268,768	2,146,364	2,586,037	2,536,960
Mother native born	196,706	273,351	374,063	421,640
Mother foreign born	1,072,062	1,873,013	2,211,974	2,115,320
Same country as father	965,276	1,690,131	N.A.	N.A.
Different country	106,786	182,882	N.A.	N.A.
Percent distribution				
Total, foreign father	100.0	100.0	100.0	100.0
Mother native born	15.5	12.7	14.5	16.6
Mother foreign born	84.5	87.3	85.5	83.4
Same country as father	76.1	78.7	N.A.	N.A.
Different country	8.4	8.5	N.A.	N.A.

*Not available for 1910.   †5 percent sample.   N.A. = Not available.

Source: U.S. Census Office, Twelfth Census of the United States, Taken in the Year 1900; Population, Vol. I, Part 1 (Washington, 1902); U.S. Bureau of the Census, Fourteenth Census of the United States Taken in the Year 1920. Vol. II (Washington, 1922); Sixteenth Census of the United States: 1940. Population, Nativity and Parentage of the White Population; Country of Origin of the Foreign Stock (Washington, 1943).

Not all of the Negro population from the Caribbean area were classified in the census as foreign born. Persons born on islands under United States sovereignty—Puerto Rico and the Virgin Islands—are included in the native population of the United States. The census category "Negro," however, when applied to natives of Puerto Rico, is generally regarded as having minimal ethnic significance, and "Negro" Puerto Ricans are usually considered, because of their common cultural background, with other Puerto Ricans. Unfortunately, it has become increasingly difficult to secure data on the natives of the Virgin Islands, the great bulk of whom are Negroes, in successive decennial censuses. At the 1920 census there were 1,997 natives of the Virgin Islands resident in the United States, of whom 1,603 were Negro. In that year 84.3 percent (1,683) were residents of New York City, and 85.6 percent of New York State.[21] Persons of Virgin Islands birth numbered 6,045 in 1930, of whom 5,148 or 85.2 percent were living in New York State.[22] A 1930 figure for New York City was not available. In 1940 no figure was provided for New York State.

21. U.S. Bureau of the Census, Fourteenth Census of the United States, 1920, Vol. II Population (Washington, 1922), pp. 630, 640, 679.

22. U.S. Bureau of the Census, Fifteenth Census of the United States, 1930, Vol. II Population (Washington, 1933), p. 157.

Of all immigrant groups, none (with the possible exception of Virgin Islanders) has so concentrated in New York City as have persons of Puerto Rican origin. Puerto Rico was ceded to the United States by Spain following the Spanish-American War and within a few decades a strong migrant stream from the tropical island in the Caribbean toward the American mainland developed. When legislation was enacted in the 1920s truncating immigration from Europe, this stream grew wider, for any shortage of unskilled cheap labor in American cities meant enhanced opportunities for the Puerto Ricans who, as citizens of an area under United States sovereignty, could freely come and go.

TABLE 55

Native White Population with Father Foreign by Age and Year of Birth Cohort and Number with Mother Native Born (Partly Estimated), New York City, 1920

Age (in 1920)	Birth Cohort	Total, foreign father*	Foreign father and native mother†	
			Number	Percent
Total	—	2,146,364	273,351	12.7
Under 5 years	1915-19	365,537	43,773	12.0
5-9 years	1910-14	358,565	35,638	9.9
10-14 years	1905-09	303,108	30,281	10.0
15-19 years	1900-04	223,158	26,529	11.9
20-24 years	1895-99	203,696	27,180	13.3
25-29 years	1890-94	164,654	26,032	15.8
30-34 years	1885-89	116,903	21,793	18.6
35-39 years	1880-84	97,300	19,271	19.8
40-44 years	1875-79	83,980	14,997	17.9
45-49 years	1870-74	73,525	10,737	14.6
50-54 years	1865-69	60,457	7,224	11.9
55-59 years	1860-64	40,415	4,060	10.0
60-64 years	1855-59	29,724	2,618	8.8
65-69 years	1850-54	14,240	1,411	9.9
70-74 years	1845-49	6,123	894	14.6
75 and over	Before 1845	4,023	779	19.4
Not reported	—	956	134	14.0

*Age computed by adding published distribution of native whites of foreign parentage to calculated distribution of native whites with father foreign and mother native.

†Age distribution calculated as follows: Subtraction from 1,441,860 whites with mother native (published age groups) of 1,164,834 native whites of native parentage (also published) yielded age distribution of 277,026 persons. The age distribution of the 273,351 native whites with foreign father and native mother was then calculated proportionate to that of the 277,026.

Source: Derived from data in U.S. Bureau of the Census, Fourteenth Census of the United States, Vol. II Population 1920 (Washington, 1922); and Mortality Rates 1910-1920 (Washington, 1923).

TABLE 56
Foreign-born Negro Population of the United States and New York City by Period of Immigration, Censuses of 1920 and 1930

Year of immigration	United States 1920	United States 1930	New York City 1920	New York City 1930	Percent of U.S. total in New York City 1920	Percent of U.S. total in New York City 1930
Total	73,803	98,620	30,436	54,754	41.2	55.5
Before 1901	10,105	7,601	1,960	1,374	19.4	18.1
1901-10	16,973	15,356	7,404	6,993	43.6	45.5
1911-19	33,492	29,132	16,691	17,119	49.8	58.8
1920-30*	—	34,954	—	24,291	—	69.5
Not stated	13,233	11,577	4,381	4,977	33.1	43.0

*Through April 1, 1930
Source: Derived from data in U.S. Bureau of the Census, Fourteenth Census of the United States taken in the year 1920, Vol. II (Washington, 1922); Fifteenth Census of the United States: 1930, Vol. II (Washington, 1933).

Table 57 indicates that the Puerto Rican-born population in New York City increased more than eightfold from about 7,000 to 61,000 between 1920 and 1940, and the city's share of the natives of Puerto Rico living in the United States climbed from about 62 percent to almost 88 percent.[23] In 1940, 86.8 percent of the persons of Puerto Rican birth living in New York City were classified by the census as white and 13.2 percent as non-white. By comparison, in 1930, 22.6 percent of the Puerto Ricans in New York were classified as nonwhite. The 1930 census showed 34,756 as white and 10,152 as nonwhite; the 1940 census: 53,323 white and only 8,140 nonwhite.[24]

TABLE 57
Population of Puerto Rican Birth in the United States and New York City, 1910-40

Census year	United States	New York City	Percent of U.S. total in New York City
1910	1,513	554	36.6
1920	11,811	7,364	62.3
1930	52,774	44,908	85.1
1940	69,967	61,463	87.8

Source: U.S. Bureau of the Census, U.S. Census of Population: 1960, Puerto Ricans in the United States (Washington, 1963); Research Bureau, Welfare and Health Council of New York City, Population of Puerto Rican Birth or Parentage; New York City: 1950 (New York, 1952).

23. U.S. Bureau of the Census, U.S. Census of Population: 1960, Puerto Ricans in the United States (Washington, 1963), p. viii.
24. Research Bureau, Welfare and Health Council of New York City, Population of Puerto Rican Birth or Parentage: New York City: 1950 (New York, 1952), p. 2.

RELIGIOUS GROUPS

Pioneer comprehensive studies providing statistical data on the religious distribution of the population of New York City were undertaken by Dr. Walter Laidlaw, founder of the New York Federation of Churches (now the Protestant Council of New York City) shortly before the turn of the century. Laidlaw conducted several population surveys of neighborhoods in New York which gathered information on ethnic and religious background. In December 1902 his publication *Federation* (issued by the Federation of Churches and Christian Organizations in New York City) gave a detailed estimate of the number of Roman Catholics, Jews, and Protestants in the city in 1900. These were derived using the 1900 census nativity and parentage data and assuming that the religious distribution of each foreign-stock group parallelled that for the foreign-stock groups included in the field surveys.[25] Such a procedure might have yielded a good approximation of the city's over-all religious distribution if the surveys had been designed to enumerate a representative sample of the municipal population, but this was not the case. No areas in Queens and Brooklyn, for example, were surveyed. Thus while Laidlaw has received deserved credit as the fountainhead of many meaningful statistical series and as developer of the system of census tracts, his citywide estimates of religious distribution (for later census years, as well as for 1900) are inaccurate, and it is unfortunate they have been frequently cited.

Yet, if cautioned by the knowledge that Laidlaw's estimates are subject to considerable error (relatively much greater for boroughs or smaller areas than for the city as a whole), an examination of his figures may be of benefit, if for no other reason than that alternative more reliable estimates were never constructed. Despite the fact that qualified observers at all familiar with New York's population composition knew as a matter of course that most Italian and Irish immigrants were Catholic, most Russian and Austrian settlers were Jewish, and most German and English newcomers were Protestant, Laidlaw's data were of interest in providing some quantitative criteria.

Laidlaw's estimates of the percentage distribution by religion of the various nativity groups, prepared as part of his computation of the aggregate population by religion, are given in Table 58. In particular, it seems probable that the estimated representation of Jews among the German group is too high, since the population of German descent in Manhattan (where Laidlaw concentrated his surveys) undoubtedly had a much larger relative number of persons of the Jewish religion than was the case outside this borough.

---

25. Laidlaw prepared two estimates for 1900: one categorizing the population as of foreign birth (by birthplace) or of native birth, the second as of foreign stock (by country of origin) or native stock. Computations from the first procedure gave 1,206,955 Catholics, 496,782 Hebrews, and 1,733,405 Protestants; from the second: 1,210,306 Catholics, 597,674 Hebrews, and 1,629,222 Protestants. *Federation*, II, 3 (December 1902), 92-93.

TABLE 58

Estimated Percent Distribution by Religion of Total Population and
Foreign Stock Population from Selected Countries of Origin,
New York City, 1900

Country of origin	All Religions	Catholic	Jewish	Protestant
Total population*	100	35	17	47
Foreign stock				
Austria	100	25	70	5
Bohemia	100	40	10	50
England	100	15	5	80
France	100	65	5	30
Germany	100	15	20	65
Hungary	100	20	70	10
Ireland	100	91	†	9
Italy	100	96	1	3
Poland	100	15	60	25
Romania	100	—	100	—
Russia	100	2	90	8
Scotland	100	10	5	85
Sweden	100	3	†	97

*Includes estimated distribution for the Negro population as follows: 98 percent
Protestant, 2 percent Catholic.
    † Less than one percent.
    Source: Federation, II, 3 (December 1902).

According to the tabulations prepared by Laidlaw, the Protestants
still constituted the largest religious community in New York in 1900,
but after centuries of dominance, they no longer formed a majority.
Roughly about equal numerically were three groups of Protestants: (1)
persons of "old American stock" (at least third-generation Americans);
(2) persons of German parentage; (3) all other origins.

The Catholic population in New York in 1900 undoubtedly exceeded
one million, and assuming Laidlaw's estimate that about 91 percent of the
persons of Irish parentage were Catholic in religion to be correct, then the
Irish comprised a majority of all adherents. The Italians, the next most
sizable Catholic bloc, were about one-third as numerous as the Irish.

The composition of the city's Jewish population had altered radically
between 1880 and 1900. By the latter date the largest component of the
Jewish population was of Russian background. Previously, persons born
in Germany, or of German parentage, had predominated.

It was not until 1935 that the first citywide sample survey was conducted in which the religious distribution of New York's population was
ascertained. This survey originated as part of a study of the city's youth

made by the Research Bureau of the Welfare Council of New York City with the assistance of state and city work-relief authorities and the Works Progress Administration. While the study suffers from the handicap that it relates only to persons 16 to 24 years of age, it nevertheless must be ana-lyzed in detail, by virtue of the fact that it provided the most valuable data by religion for pre-World War II New York.[26]

The welfare council youth survey's important contribution consisted of estimates, yielded for the first time since Laidlaw's surveys a generation earlier, of the distribution by religious affiliation of the population of the city's several major foreign-stock groups. The parallels and divergences with Laidlaw's data are of interest. Again, at least 90 percent of those of Italian and Irish origin showed up as Catholic, and upwards of 90 percent of the Russian and Romanian groups as Jewish. Some discrepancies, such as considerably higher Catholic and lower Jewish percentages among the population originating in Poland and Hungary, might result from one of several possible explanations: unrepresentativeness of the city as a whole in Laidlaw's data, sampling variation in the welfare council study (a random sample of 1 percent of the youth population), real differences between the group aged 16 to 24 years and the aggregate for all ages in 1935, or changes in religious composition among the group from a particular area resulting from immigration patterns occurring during the first three decades of the twentieth century. Other differences that may be noted include substan-tially larger Catholic and somewhat smaller Protestant percentages of the foreign stock of German and English origin in 1935, and a smaller Jewish proportion among the group of German origin (see Table 59).

An opportunity to compare some of the estimated religious distribu-tions by country of origin with still another valuable source of information—the death certificate—came to the fore when deaths in New York City in 1940 were cross-classified by country of birth and type of cemetery, as well as by age of decedent. Table 60 shows the proportions of all decedents in four age groups who were buried in Catholic, Jewish, and Other ceme-teries. The category Other includes not only Protestant but nonsectarian cemeteries and crematories.

Calculating the religion of decedents based upon denomination of cemetery has some built-in limitations. Most Protestants probably were buried in nonsectarian rather than Protestant cemeteries, but evidently a not inconsiderable number of Catholics, as well as a few Jews, were interred in these cemeteries or cremated. Thus the category Other over-states the Protestant group. Conversely, the numbers representing Catholic burials understate the Catholic contingent. For illustration, it may be seen that fewer than 90 percent of all Italian natives were buried in Catholic

---

26. The full study appears in Nettie P. McGill and Ellen N. Matthews, *The Youth of New York City* (New York: Macmillan, 1940).

cemeteries although both Laidlaw and the welfare council indicate over 95 percent of those of Italian background surveyed were Catholic in religion.[27]

Allowing for the limitations of burial data there appears no serious lack of agreement between the religious data by birthplace of decedent in 1940 and the 1935 youth survey for the population of Irish, Italian, and Russian origin. For other groups various degrees of disparity exist, explainable in part, at least, by age differences in the two populations.

Several possible approaches can be assayed in order to construct an estimate of the religious distribution of New York City's population in 1940 that makes use of the detailed mortality tabulations for that year, the country-of-origin data (by age) in the 1940 census, and the 1935 youth survey. Breakdowns in methodology occur, however, when it is realized that the religious distribution shown by the youth survey has validity for only this one segment of the total population, and that the mortality information also is largely confined to a particular age range.

TABLE 59

Estimated Percent Distribution by Religion of Total Youth Population (16-24 Years of Age) by Race and of Foreign Stock Youth Population from Selected Countries of Origin, New York City, 1935

Race and country of origin	All religions	Catholic	Jewish	Protestant	Other*
Total population	100	49	31	18	2
Race					
White	100	50	33	15	2
Negro	100	13	—	85	2
Country of origin					
Austria	100	17	78	3	2
Czechoslovakia	100	60	11	27	2
England	100	29	13	57	1
Germany	100	32	10	58	†
Hungary	100	41	45	13	1
Ireland	100	92	—	8	†
Italy	100	98	†	1	†
Poland	100	43	53	2	2
Romania	100	—	96	—	4
Russia	100	—	95	†	5
Scandinavia	100	11	2	85	2

*Includes religion not reported.   †Less than one percent.

Source: Derived from data in Nettie P. McGill and Ellen N. Matthews; The Youth of New York City (New York: Macmillan 1940).

27. It is worth noting that at the census of Italy taken in 1931, 99.6 percent of those enumerated were Roman Catholics. "Italy," *Encyclopedia Americana* (1957 ed.), XV, 469.

TABLE 60

Deaths of White New York City Residents Recorded in New York City, Selected Age Groups by Country of Birth and Denomination of Cemetery of Burial, 1940

Age group and denomination	Total all areas	Place of birth										
		United States	Austria	Germany	Great Britain	Hungary	Ireland	Italy	Poland	Russia	Scandinavia	Other Foreign*
1-44 years												
All deaths	9,924	7,303	166	227	130	84	328	449	208	433	119	477
Denominational deaths†	9,102	6,697	160	207	119	80	314	433	199	420	99	374
Percent: Total	100.0	100.0	100.0	100.0	100.0	100.0	100.0	100.0	100.0	100.0	100.0	100.0
Catholic	48.0	51.4	16.3	15.0	26.1	13.7	93.0	88.5	22.1	1.4	3.0	27.8
Jewish	24.0	20.5	65.6	14.5	25.2	58.8	—	—	65.3	92.4	1.0	21.1
Other‡	28.0	28.1	18.1	70.5	48.7	27.5	7.0	11.5	12.6	6.2	96.0	51.1
45-54 years												
All deaths	9,877	4,303	498	326	181	182	493	1,100	530	1,225	146	893
Denominational deaths†	8,974	3,861	481	297	154	176	451	1,061	496	1,190	135	672
Percent: Total	100.0	100.0	100.0	100.0	100.0	100.0	100.0	100.0	100.0	100.0	100.0	100.0
Catholic	40.6	45.9	13.5	12.5	31.8	19.3	87.6	87.8	36.5	1.0	3.0	24.5
Jewish	28.0	11.7	73.8	13.8	13.0	53.4	0.2	0.4	52.6	93.0	2.2	25.9
Other‡	31.4	42.4	12.7	73.7	55.2	27.3	12.2	11.8	10.9	6.0	94.8	49.6
55-64 years												
All deaths	14,823	5,532	874	766	330	327	1,014	1,768	713	2,087	288	1,124
Denominational deaths†	13,552	4,883	852	711	283	309	962	1,715	674	2,040	252	871
Percent: Total	100.0	100.0	100.0	100.0	100.0	100.0	100.0	100.0	100.0	100.0	100.0	100.0
Catholic	39.0	43.9	9.4	15.5	26.5	17.2	89.6	89.8	29.5	0.7	3.6	22.3
Jewish	30.3	8.4	80.4	14.9	8.1	63.4	—	0.2	64.9	95.6	1.6	34.4
Other‡	30.7	47.7	10.2	69.6	65.4	19.4	10.4	10.0	5.6	3.7	94.8	43.3
65 years and over												
All deaths	29,367	10,790	1,433	3,039	899	544	2,504	2,773	1,020	3,899	634	1,832
Denominational deaths†	26,739	9,176	1,403	2,873	804	516	2,352	2,701	987	3,847	571	1,509
Percent: Total	100.0	100.0	100.0	100.0	100.0	100.0	100.0	100.0	100.0	100.0	100.0	100.0
Catholic	34.1	36.2	7.1	15.8	25.4	9.5	87.7	89.9	17.6	0.2	3.5	19.9
Jewish	28.8	6.6	84.0	12.9	7.0	73.6	—	0.1	78.8	98.3	0.5	35.2
Other‡	37.1	57.2	8.9	71.3	67.6	16.9	12.3	10.0	3.6	1.5	96.0	44.9

*Including unknown. †Denominational total excludes City Cemetery and out-of-town cemeteries. ‡Other includes Protestant, nonsectarian, and cremation.

Despite these problems, as well as difficulties associated with the incomplete roster of Catholic decedents furnished by the religious auspices of cemetery guidelines, a working estimate of the Catholic population or of the Protestant population could be attempted if one condition existed: consistency in ethnic background independent of age. For example, if at any given age x percent of the Catholic population could be estimated as of Italian origin, then with the aid of the census distribution by age of the Italian foreign-stock population the total Catholic group could be derived. But ethnic distribution diverges markedly along the age scale, both as a result of the different time periods which marked the height of the influx of Irish, Italian, Polish, German, and other streams, and as a consequence of differential fertility. Among the 16-to-24 year-olds surveyed in New York in 1935 (the survivors would be aged 21 to 29 years in 1940), 44.5 percent of those stating they were Catholic were of Italian birth or parentage.[28] On the other hand, of all white decedents aged 65 years or over in 1940 identified as Roman Catholic, only 26.7 percent were of Italian background. This included 26.6 percent born in Italy and 0.1 percent who were born in the United States and had an Italian-born mother.[29]

The Jewish community, unlike the other major religious groups, in 1940 came close to meeting the requisite condition of relative consistency in origin throughout the age structure, and therefore a working estimate can be ventured. The youth survey of 1935 indicated 81.7 percent of the 16-24-year-old Jewish respondents had one or both parents born in Russia, Poland, or Austria.[30] Similarly, according to the death records for New York for 1940, 75.8 percent of the known Jewish decedents aged 65 or over were of this East European background, including 74.6 percent who were foreign born and 1.2 percent who were U.S. born, with mothers born in Russia, Poland, or Austria.[31] Estimates utilized in combining census returns for the population of foreign origin and proportions based on the religious distribution of decedents have been developed stage by stage in Tables 61 through 63.

In Table 61 the method of calculation of the age distribution of the foreign-born Jewish population is demonstrated. Following a slight technical adjustment to make the sample totals agree with the full census count, it is assumed that the Jewish percentage of specific age groups among the aggregate population born in Russia, Poland, and Austria matches their proportion of the decedents in the comparable age group. Then it is assumed the total foreign-born Jewish population at each age

28. McGill, *Youth of New York City*, p. 12.

29. Derived from unpublished data prepared from the records of the New York City Health Department by Herbert Seidman, American Cancer Society, which have been kindly furnished to the writer.

30. Distributed as follows: Russia, 55.4 percent; Poland, 11.0 percent; Austria, 15.3 percent. McGill, *Youth of New York City*, p. 12.

31. See note 29.

interval exhibits the same relationship to the Jewish population born in Russia, Poland, and Austria as the corresponding proportions among decedents interred in Jewish cemeteries. A test of the reasonableness of the derived age structure is presented in Table 62. The estimated distribution is compared with that of the foreign-born population in New York City of Yiddish mother tongue. The fit with this independent measure appears to be close.

TABLE 61
Estimate of Foreign-born Jewish Population of New York City, 1940

Age (years)	Foreign-born white population born in Russia, Poland, and Austria		Estimated Jewish population in 3 areas		Estimated percent of all foreign-born Jews: 3 areas of origin‡	Estimated number of foreign-born Jews
	Sample count	Adjusted*	Percent†	Number		
Under 25	24,300	24,325		19,460		25,310
25-34	87,240	87,325	80.0	69,860	76.9	90,840
35-44	183,800	183,980		147,180		191,390
45-54	219,540	219,755	79.5	174,710	83.6	208,980
55-64	139,960	140,100	86.2	120,770	82.9	145,680
65 and over	79,400	79,480	92.0	73,120	81.0	90,270
Total	734,240	734,965		605,100		752,470

*Sample (5 percent) adjusted to agree to total for full count.
†Based on percent of all deaths in denomination cemeteries.
‡Based on percent of deaths of natives of these countries.
Source: Derived from data in 1940 Census (U.S. Bureau of the Census) and mortality statistics (see Table 60).

TABLE 62
Comparison of Percent Distribution by Age of Estimated Foreign-born Jewish Population and of Census Foreign-born Population Reporting Yiddish Mother Tongue, New York City, 1940

Age (years)	Foreign-born Jewish population*	Foreign-born population with Yiddish mother tongue†
Total, all ages		
Number	752,470	495,420
Percent	100.0	100.0
Under 25	3.4	3.0
25-34	12.1	12.1
35-44	25.4	25.5
45-54	27.8	28.2
55-64	19.4	19.5
65 and over	12.0	11.7

*Figure computed in Table 61.   †Sample of 5 percent.
Source: Derived from unpublished data prepared by U.S. Bureau of the Census of 1940 Census and data in Table 61.

TABLE 63

Derivation of Estimate of Native-born and of Total Jewish Population
25 Years of Age and Over, New York City, 1940

Age (years)	Total native white	Estimate of Jews in native white pop.*		Native white pop. aged 25-54 years: Yiddish mother tongue†		Estimate of native white Jewish pop.‡	Total white	Estimated § total Jews	
		Percent	Number	Number	Percent			Number	Percent
Total	—	—	—	214,860	100.0	—	4,434,762	1,242,080	28.0
25-34	—	—	—	129,120	60.1	292,540	1,282,277	383,380	29.9
35-44	—	—	—	64,620	30.1	146,520	1,198,337	337,910	28.2
45-54	407,571	11.7	47,680	21,120	9.8	47,680	962,597	256,660	26.7
55-64	216,340	8.4	18,180	—	—	—	590,026	163,860	27.8
65 and over	151,533	6.6	10,000	—	—	—	401,525	100,270	25.0

*Based on percent of Jewish among all denominational deaths in age group (see Table 60).

†From unpublished data from 1940 Census (U.S. Bureau of the Census).

‡Computed by assuming 45-54 year-olds as estimated in third column, and applying appropriate percent distributions by age for the native population 25-54 years of Yiddish mother tongue.

§Derived by combining number of foreign-born Jews estimated in Table 61 with number of native-born estimated in preceding columns. Assuming the estimate of 28.0 percent was applicable to the population under 5 as well, then the estimated number of Jews in the total white population (6,977,501) would be 1,954,050.

In estimating the magnitude of the native-born Jewish population, mortality statistics—because of the relatively small number of deaths under 45 years of age—are of limited use, and an additional method must be employed. In Table 63 the estimated number of native-born Jews 45 years of age and over based on mortality data is shown. It is assumed the Jewish proportions among all decedents born in the United States reflects the Jewish percentage of the native population for the given age group. A much greater problem involves the preparation of an estimate of the Jewish population at younger ages.

At the 1940 census a 5 percent sample of all persons—native as well as foreign—were instructed to indicate their mother tongue. The census data on the population whose mother tongue was given as Yiddish generally have been discarded in the measurement studies of the Jewish community because very large numbers reported English or other mother tongues. However, it may well be that while the Yiddish mother tongue group of native birth represented only a fraction of the actual Jewish population, it constituted a fairly representative sample in terms of age, at least among most *adult* ages. For the under 25 years-of-age sector of the Jewish population it can probably be assumed that the not inconsiderable contingent of third-generation Americans made the appearance of a Yiddish-speaking background less common. Also, among the native-born Jewish population at ages 55 years and over (persons born prior to 1885) it may be supposed that Yiddish was not as well represented proportionally as at younger adult ages because a somewhat larger share of this American-born group were the children of German rather than East European parents. Accordingly, in Table 63 only the Jewish native-born population at ages 25 through 54 years are assumed to be distributed similarly to the native-born population at these ages reporting a Yiddish mother tongue in 1940. Since the table already contains an estimate of the native-born group at ages 45-54 years, a little equation-solving easily yields estimates of the 25-34 and 35-44 year-olds.

In Table 63 it will be seen that the computed estimate for the Jewish population 25-34 years of age represents 29.9 percent of the total white population in New York in the specified age group. This is not greatly different from the 1935 youth survey which indicated 32.7 percent of the white total was Jewish.[32] To estimate the total Jewish population in 1940 an arbitrary assumption has been made: it is assumed the same percentage of the city's white population under 25 years of age was of Jewish origin as was estimated for the white population 25 years of age and over (28.0 percent).

A rough estimate of the proportion of the white population of New York City of Roman Catholic background in 1940 would be a figure in the vicinity of the 50 percent indicated by the earlier youth survey. The Protestant proportion undoubtedly was a few percentage points above the 15 percent reported in the same survey.[33] The Negro population remained, as in the past, preponderantly Protestant. Laidlaw had assumed the distribution for 1900 as 98 percent Protestant and 2 percent Catholic.[34] About 86 percent of the Negro youths surveyed in 1935 were Protestant, 12 percent Catholic, and 2 percent of other or not stated religion.[35]

32. McGill, *Youth of New York City*, p. 376.   33. *Ibid*.
34. *Federation*, II, 3 (December 1902), p. 93.
35. Derived from McGill, *Youth of New York City*, pp. 12,376.

6 The Metropolitan Giant

POPULATION GROWTH, 1940-70

By mid-century New York's population growth appeared to have levelled off. The city's 1970 total of 7,895,000 residents was only 5.9 percent more than the figure thirty years earlier, in 1940. With the flow to the suburbs continuing, it is now questionable whether the population in the strict city limits can, in absolute numbers, more than hold its own in the future.

In the 1940s, for the first time in modern New York's history, net migration was negative for the decade. More persons moved from New York than came into the city. Nevertheless, a substantial natural increase (excess of births over deaths) enabled a population gain of 451,000—to 7,892,000 in 1950—the smallest increase in any decade following consolidation. By the 1950s, however, the tide of movement from the city became a flood, exceeding the natural gain and resulting in an absolute loss in population of 110,000. During the 1960s the extensive wave of migration to suburbia continued, but a sizable influx of nonwhites into New York enabled the total population of the city to register a modest increase (113,000).

While the population within the city limits of New York was relatively static after 1950, that in the metropolitan area—however defined—rose uninterruptedly. What was happening in the New York area was not different in principle, only in degree, from what was occurring in most of the nation's major population centers: a mass migration from the center city to the surrounding suburban ring. In New York the movement from the inner core had been part of a continuing process, noted by social scientists for decades. Manhattan, the most densely settled borough, the "Old New York," attained its maximum population in 1910, and by 1930 had lost almost half a million inhabitants (see Table 64). Residents fled the congested areas of the Lower East Side and the Lower West Side for new apartments or houses in the Bronx, Brooklyn, and Queens. Brooklyn and Queens (which quadrupled in population) each gained over one million residents between 1910 and 1940, and the Bronx, which tripled in size during this period, gained more than 950,000 persons. Richmond, with much more modest numbers, doubled in size between 1910 and 1940.

Analysis has demonstrated that within the city limits ever-increasing numbers moved from the inner areas to the outlying zones. Between 1905 and 1925 the proportion of city residents living within four miles of City Hall tumbled from more than one half (54 percent) to less than one-third (29 percent).[1] A contemporary observer noted that "not only has the multiplication of rapid transit routes serving the inner zone facilitated the dispersal of the residential population to outer sections, but it has also aided the trend toward concentration of business uses, which have virtually driven out residences over large areas."[2] By the 1920s improved highways and the growing popularity of the automobile had encouraged an exodus to the outer limits of the city and to suburban communities. The most rapidly growing suburban county—Nassau—adjacent to Queens, more than doubled in population between 1920 and 1930.

The Great Depression retarded the movement to the suburbs in the 1930s, and World War II brought about a further halt in new housing construction in the early 1940s. The post-World War II building boom was spurred by the shortage of housing, rising incomes, the mobility offered by the automobile, and government mortgage policies favoring single-family homes.[3] The first target was vacant land close to the center city. Only Queens and Richmond within the city limits possessed wide areas available for development. In consequence these two boroughs continued to add to their population in the 1950s and 1960s while Manhattan and Brooklyn experienced absolute losses and the population of the Bronx scarcely changed. This has been attributed to a "tendency for population to decline in areas that become fully developed whatever the density that prevailed when they were developed."[4] Growth in the suburbs of New York was phenomenal, with the two Long Island counties alone (Nassau and Suffolk) gaining more than one million residents between 1950 and 1960 (see Table 65).

CHANGES IN POPULATION COMPOSITION

A change in population composition was accelerated by the movement to the suburbs, which largely involved middle-income whites. At the same time two distinct groups of newcomers much lower on the economic scale— Negroes and Puerto Ricans—arrived in New York in growing numbers in search of new opportunity.[5] European immigration, which had once shaped

1. Regional Plan of New York and its Environs, *Regional Survey of New York and its Environs, Vol. II, Population, Land Values and Government* (New York: Committee on Regional Plan of New York and Its Environs, 1929), 99.   2. *Ibid.*, p. 100.

3. William B. Shore, ed., *A Report on the Second Regional Plan* (New York: Regional Plan Association, 1967), p. 66.   4. *Ibid.*, p. 118. For an excellent general account of population trends within the metropolitan area see Edgar M. Hoover and Raymond Vernon, *Anatomy of a Metropolis* (Cambridge, Mass.: Harvard University Press, 1959), Chaps. 1 and 8.

5. For background discussion of these groups see Handlin, *The Newcomers*.

TABLE 64
Population of the Boroughs of New York City
by Race and Nativity, 1900-70

Borough and year	Total	White	Total	Negro	Other	Native	Foreign
			Race			Nativity of white	
			Nonwhite				
Bronx							
1970	1,471,701	1,080,859	390,842	357,681	33,161	N.A.	N.A.
1960	1,424,815	1,256,284	168,531	163,896	4,635	962,967	293,270
1950	1,451,277	1,351,662	99,615	97,752	1,863	977,768	373,894
1940	1,394,711	1,370,319	24,392	23,529	863	909,843	460,476
1930	1,265,258	1,251,823	13,435	12,930	505	774,417	477,406
1920	732,016	726,990	5,026	4,803	223	460,019	266,971
1910	430,980	426,650	4,330	4,117	213	277,715	148,935
1900	200,507	197,923	2,584	2,370	214	136,665	61,258
Brooklyn							
1970	2,602,012	1,905,788	696,224	656,194	40,030	N.A.	N.A.
1960	2,627,319	2,245,859	381,460	371,405	10,055	1,761,548	486,231
1950	2,738,175	2,525,118	213,057	208,478	4,579	1,894,592	630,526
1940	2,698,285	2,587,951	110,334	107,263	3,071	1,820,313	767,638
1930	2,560,401	2,488,815	71,586	68,921	2,665	1,619,741	869,074
1920	2,018,356	1,984,953	33,403	31,912	1,491	1,325,666	659,287
1910	1,634,351	1,610,487	23,864	22,708	1,156	1,039,131	571,356
1900	1,166,582	1,146,909	19,673	18,367	1,306	793,159	353,750
Manhattan							
1970	1,539,233	1,089,302	449,931	380,442	69,489	N.A.	N.A.
1960	1,698,281	1,271,822	426,459	397,101	29,358	936,309	335,601
1950	1,960,101	1,556,599	403,502	384,482	19,020	1,095,497	461,102
1940	1,889,924	1,577,625	312,299	298,365	13,934	1,037,428	540,197
1930	1,867,312	1,633,329	233,983	224,670	9,313	990,417	642,912
1920	2,284,103	2,168,906	115,197	109,133	6,064	1,246,826	922,080
1910	2,331,542	2,266,578	64,964	60,534	4,430	1,162,559	1,104,019
1900	1,850,093	1,808,968	41,125	36,246	4,879	1,026,254	782,714
Queens							
1970	1,986,473	1,695,288	291,185	258,006	33,179	N.A.	N.A.
1960	1,809,578	1,654,959	154,619	145,855	8,764	1,330,414	323,773
1950	1,550,849	1,497,126	53,723	51,524	2,199	1,208,929	288,197
1940	1,297,634	1,270,731	26,903	25,890	1,013	994,143	276,588
1930	1,079,129	1,059,804	19,325	18,609	716	793,547	266,257
1920	469,042	463,661	5,381	5,120	261	351,985	111,676
1910	284,041	280,691	3,350	3,198	152	201,576	79,115
1900	152,999	150,235	2,764	2,611	153	105,620	44,615
Richmond							
1970	295,443	277,604	17,839	15,792	2,047	N.A.	N.A.
1960	221,991	211,738	10,253	9,674	579	186,760	24,946
1950	191,555	185,936	5,619	5,372	247	155,449	30,487
1940	174,441	170,875	3,566	3,397	169	135,754	35,121
1930	158,346	155,606	2,740	2,576	164	116,074	39,532
1920	116,531	114,953	1,578	1,499	79	83,420	31,533
1910	85,969	84,756	1,213	1,152	61	60,478	24,278
1900	67,021	65,863	1,158	1,072	86	47,282	18,581

N.A. = Not available.   Source: U.S. Bureau of the Census data.

TABLE 65
Population of Selected Counties in Metropolitan New York by Race and Nativity, 1900-70

	Race					Nativity of whit	
			Nonwhite				
County and year	Total	White	Total	Negro	Other	Native	Foreig
Nassau (N.Y.)							
1970	1,428,080	1,355,754	72,326	65,679	6,647	N.A.	N.A.
1960	1,300,171	1,258,039	42,132	39,350	2,782	1,138,754	119,2
1950	672,765	655,008	17,757	16,955	802	573,331	81,6
1940	406,748	393,213	13,535	13,226	309	328,966	64,2
1930	303,053	294,769	8,284	7,960	324	231,315	63,4
1920	126,120	122,934	3,186	3,036	150	96,936	25,9
1910	83,930	81,541	2,389	2,317	72	62,217	19,3
1900	55,448	53,093	2,355	2,310	45	42,089	11,0
Rockland (N.Y.)							
1970	229,903	215,625	14,278	13,128	1,150	N.A.	N.A
1960	136,803	129,651	7,152	6,854	298	116,228	13,4
1950	89,276	84,668	4,608	4,483	125	73,227	11,4
1940	74,261	71,038	3,223	3,190	33	59,509	11,5
1930	59,599	57,270	2,329	2,291	38	48,138	9,1
1920	45,548	44,057	1,491	1,471	20	37,096	6,9
1910	46,873	45,317	1,556	1,534	22	35,613	9,7
1900	38,298	36,238	2,060	2,041	19	29,022	7,2
Suffolk (N.Y.)							
1970	1,124,950	1,066,429	58,521	53,340	5,181	N.A.	N.A
1960	666,784	631,997	34,787	33,035	1,752	572,181	59,
1950	276,129	262,537	13,592	13,120	472	218,265	44,2
1940	197,355	188,186	9,169	8,701	468	149,871	38,
1930	161,055	155,243	5,812	5,502	310	120,590	34,
1920	110,246	107,232	3,014	2,814	200	83,344	23,
1910	96,138	93,073	3,065	2,771	294	71,078	21,
1900	77,582	74,298	3,284	3,035	249	59,648	14,
Westchester (N.Y.)							
1970	894,104	802,722	91,382	85,041	6,341	N.A.	N.A
1960	808,891	746,406	62,485	60,455	2,030	645,022	101,
1950	625,816	587,100	38,716	38,061	655	491,031	96,
1940	573,558	541,680	31,878	31,346	532	437,244	104,
1930	520,947	497,312	23,635	23,044	591	376,549	120,
1920	344,436	333,110	11,326	11,066	260	253,105	80,
1910	283,055	273,827	9,228	8,986	242	192,784	81,
1900	184,257	178,742	5,515	5,318	197	132,304	46,
Bergen (N. J.)							
1970	898,012	868,477	29,535	24,915	4,620	N.A.	N.A
1960	780,255	762,790	17,465	16,269	1,196	675,056	87,
1950	539,139	527,938	11,201	10,899	302	451,543	76,
1940	409,646	399,675	9,971	9,733	238	326,630	73,
1930	364,977	355,901	9,076	8,872	204	272,022	83,
1920	210,703	206,443	4,260	4,136	124	152,259	54,
1910	138,002	134,622	3,380	3,295	85	95,239	39,
1900	78,441	75,784	2,657	2,600	57	55,610	20,
Hudson (N.J.)							
1970	609,266	541,778	67,488	61,095	6,393	N.A.	N.A
1960	610,734	568,313	42,421	41,327	1,094	480,381	87,
1950	647,437	623,179	24,258	23,780	478	515,142	108,
1940	652,040	635,583	16,457	16,147	310	497,740	137,
1930	690,730	674,331	16,399	15,970	429	490,172	184,
1920	629,154	619,543	9,611	9,351	260	437,426	182,
1910	537,231	529,747	7,484	7,173	311	354,837	174,
1900	386,048	381,231	4,817	4,439	378	259,964	121,

N.A. = Not available. Source: U.S. Bureau of Census data.

New York's growth, had greatly receded as a result of restrictive legislation. In the decades following 1940 each of the two major internal streams— Negroes from America's southern states and Puerto Ricans from the nation's Caribbean possession—has been more significant to population change in New York than the reduced flow coming from foreign countries.

The net outmigration (excess of persons moving out over those moving in) from New York City of 111,000 between 1940 and 1950 actually masked a net influx of 229,000 nonwhites and of 124,000 Puerto Ricans. (To avoid some slight overlap the latter figure includes only Puerto Ricans reported as white in census counts. U.S. Bureau of the Census procedure classifies Puerto Ricans as both white *and* nonwhite. At the 1940 count 13 percent of all persons born in Puerto Rico were reported as nonwhite; at the 1950 census the proportion was 8 percent; see Table 66.)

The net outflow from New York City of whites, exclusive of Puerto Rican natives, amounted to 464,000 during the 1940s. In computing Puerto Rican immigration, 124,000 is drawn from the white column and 7,000 from the nonwhite, for an aggregate of 131,000 (see Table 66). Between 1950 and 1960 the net loss attributable to outmigration soared to more than 800,000.[6] In this period, however, the Puerto Rican (white) net influx reached 252,000, while the net inward movement of nonwhites fell somewhat, to 174,000. (The nonwhite net migration again includes a small number of Puerto Ricans.) Among the non-Puerto Rican white population of New York City, a massive outmigration of 1,241,000 persons occurred during the 1950s. More than 900,000 of this exodus was absorbed by suburban counties in New York and New Jersey (see Table 67), but several hundred thousand evidently moved to other parts of the country.

A similar situation prevailed in the 1960-70 decade. Although the net outmigration from the central city was not quite so massive, the loss amounted to about a half million persons. Once again this represented the net effect of two divergent currents. The nonwhite population experienced more than double the inmigration of the previous decade, some 436,000 (see Table 67). The white population again was diminished by a net movement beyond the city's boundaries of approximately one million. The suburban counties gained about 400,000 white migrants, a major contribution to their population growth. This suggests, however, that more than half of the net outmigration of whites from New York was directed to other sections of the country (including suburbs or exurbs in Connecticut and in such New Jersey counties as Morris and Middlesex).

6. Statistics representing net outmigration differ slightly in different sources. State and city sources use 816,000 (see Table 66 and New York State Department of Health, *Basic Vital Statistics, New York State 1900-1967*, p. 1) which represents the residual change after accounting for natural increase based on locally prepared vital statistics. Federal sources (see Table 67) use 828,000, which is based on vital statistics from the National Center for Health Statistics with an adjustment for births estimated as unregistered.

TABLE 66
Net Migration of the White Population by Nativity and the Nonwhite Population of New York City, 1940-50 and 1950-60

Population group	April 1 1940 Census	April 1 1950 Census	April 1 1960 Census*	Components of change 1940-50		Components of change 1950-60	
				Natural increase	Net migration	Natural increase	Net migration
Total	7,454,995	7,891,957	7,781,984	548,000	-111,000	707,000	- 816,000
White	6,977,501	7,116,441	6,640,662	479,000	-340,000	515,000	- 990,000
Native born†	4,844,158	5,159,120	4,764,353	878,000	-562,000	922,000	-1,317,000
Puerto Rican born	53,323	173,115	413,649	- 5,000	124,000	- 11,000	252,000
Foreign born	2,080,020	1,784,206	1,463,817	-394,000	98,000	-396,000	76,000
Nonwhite	477,494	775,516	1,141,322	69,000	229,000	192,000	174,000
Puerto Rican born	8,140	14,471	16,061	- 1,000	7,000	- 1,000	2,000

*Figures by nativity based on 25 percent sample, combined figures differ slightly from total.

†Excluding Puerto Rican born (defined as "native" by the Census Bureau).

Source: Derived from U.S. Bureau of the Census population data and vital statistics from the Department of Health of New York City and New York State.

TABLE 67
Net Migration, 1950-60 and 1960-70, by Color: Selected Counties in Metropolitan New York

ea	1950-60			1960-70*		
	Total	White	Nonwhite	Total	White	Nonwhite
w York City	−828,293	−997,657	+169,364	−519,338	−955,013	+435,675
Bronx	−156,163	−194,588	+ 38,425	− 88,308	−255,668	+167,360
Kings	−383,003	−476,094	+ 93,091	−279,994	−469,392	+189,398
New York	−364,401	−324,689	− 39,712	−218,566	−197,457	− 21,109
Queens	+ 67,879	− 6,729	+ 74,608	+ 19,151	− 75,809	+ 94,960
Richmond	+ 7,395	+ 4,443	+ 2,952	+ 48,379	+ 43,313	+ 5,066
burbs: New York State	+927,539	+874,984	+ 52,555	+432,007	+379,810	+ 52,197
Nassau	+462,895	+444,349	+ 18,546	+ 14,390	− 1,941	+ 16,331
Rockland	+ 34,452	+ 32,783	+ 1,669	+ 71,700	+ 66,550	+ 5,150†
Suffolk	+321,953	+304,804	+ 17,149	+328,453	+313,995	+ 14,458
Westchester	+108,239	+ 93,048	+ 15,191	+ 17,464	+ 1,206	+ 16,258
burbs: New Jersey	+ 54,606	+ 41,237	+ 13,369	+ 5,189	− 13,967	+ 19,156
Bergen	+152,847	+148,713	+ 4,134	+ 50,701	+ 41,909	+ 8,792
Hudson	− 98,241	−107,476	+ 9,235	− 45,512	− 55,876	+ 10,364

*Preliminary estimates.

†Estimated by the author. Details by race not shown by the Bureau of the Census.

Source: Gladys K. Bowles and James D. Tarver, Net Migration of the Population, 1950-60, by Age, Sex, d Color. Vol. I, Part 1 (Economic Research Service, U.S. Department of Agriculture, Washington, 1965); and S. Bureau of the Census, "Components of Population Change by County: 1960-1970," Current Population ports, Series P-25, No. 461 (June 28, 1971).

The net migration of the foreign-born white population between 1940 and 1950, as estimated by the residual method, is given in Table 40 as 98,000, or somewhat less than the figure for the previous decade. Actually this method gives results that require some interpretation.

It is probable that more immigrants settled in New York in the forties than in the thirties. But tens of thousands of foreign-born whites, persons who reached New York in an earlier era, undoubtedly accompanied the 562,000 native white net outmigrants principally bound for the suburbs in this period. Thus the 98,000 figure in effect is the remainder when the foreign-born whites who moved from New York are subtracted from the 1940-50 immigrant flow from abroad. A negative net migration (shown for natives of Scandinavia) can result for individual countries of origin if more natives of the foreign country moved out of New York than arrived from overseas. The strength of the movement of some of the foreign born to the suburbs is indicated by the combined increase of 23,387 shown by Nassau and Suffolk counties between 1940 and 1950 in their foreign-born white residents (see Table 65).

In 1940 there were 61,463 persons of Puerto Rican birth in New York City; by 1960 the number had reached 429,710.[7] As citizens of the United States, residents of Puerto Rico were unaffected by the quota restrictions of the 1920s. The movement from Puerto Rico to the mainland, however, did not attain mass proportions until the 1940s. Puerto Rico's simple agricultural economy was unable to absorb a population increase of two percent per year, and the search for employment of the surplus laborers led away from the island. New York, as the terminus of the shipping lines, attracted the bulk of those who emigrated. After World War II the establishment of regular air service between San Juan and New York accelerated the flow.[8] Gradually, however, the percentage of the new arrivals remaining in New York began to diminish. In 1950 about 83 percent of the natives of Puerto Rico living in the United States resided in the metropolis. By 1960, the percentage had declined to just under 70 percent, indicating a diffusion of settlement.[9] By 1970 it was down to about 60 percent.

The burgeoning Puerto Rican migration in the 1940s occurred at a time when the expansion of housing had fallen below the growth of population. The newcomers had to crowd into available space. Puerto Rican geographic distribution followed a pattern analogous to that of other earlier immigrant groups (for example, Germans, Italians, and Jews) in first concentrating in Manhattan and then dispersing to new clusters in the Bronx and Brooklyn. In 1950, 58 percent of the Puerto Rican-born lived in Manhattan, by 1960 the figure was down to 38 percent (see Table 68).

With their mainland-born children the Puerto Rican population in New York City numbered 246,306 in 1950 (3.1 percent of the city's population) and 612,574 in 1960 (7.9 percent). At the latter date in Manhattan and the Bronx about 13 percent of the total population was of Puerto Rican origin. The Puerto Rican population in New York was reported to have climbed to 811,843 by 1970, constituting 10.2 percent of the city's residents. The share of the population that was Puerto Rican reached 21 percent in the Bronx, but in Manhattan, in consequence of a substantial absolute loss, the proportion dropped to 12 percent.[10]

The nonwhite population is comprised of the Negro and of other races, among whom the Chinese predominate. The nonwhite population is often considered as synonymous with the Negro population, but this may be attributed largely to the fact that detailed census statistics have frequently not been available for the Negro group, only for the nonwhite classification. At the 1960 census 95.3 percent of the nonwhite in New York was Negro, 2.9 percent Chinese, 0.5 percent Japanese, and 1.3

7. U.S. Bureau of the Census, *Puerto Ricans*, p. viii.
8. Handlin, *The Newcomers*, pp. 50-56.
9. U.S. Bureau of the Census, *Puerto Ricans*, p. viii.
10. U.S. Bureau of the Census, *Census of Population: 1970*. Final Report PC (1)-C34 (Washington, D.C., 1972), pp. 339, 607, 609.

percent "all other," including Filipinos and American Indians (see Table 69). At the 1970 census the percentage of the nonwhite population in New York that was Negro was down to 90.4, but at least part of the reduction seems to have resulted from faulty census procedures leading to classification of far too many persons in the "all other" race group.[11]

TABLE 68
Persons of Puerto Rican Birth or Parentage by Borough of Residence, New York City, 1930, 1950-70

Borough	1930 Census Puerto Rican birth	1950 Census			1960 Census[†]			1970 Census[‡] Puerto Rican total
		Total	Puerto Rican birth	Puerto Rican parentage*	Total	Puerto Rican birth	Puerto Rican parentage	
New York City	44,908	246,306	187,586	58,720	612,574	429,710	182,864	811,843
Bronx	1,273	61,924	45,599	16,325	186,885	130,184	56,701	316,772
Brooklyn	7,985	40,299	29,949	10,350	180,114	126,223	53,891	271,769
Manhattan	34,715	138,507	108,447	30,060	225,639	161,371	64,268	185,323
Queens	745	4,836	3,056	1,780	17,432	10,508	6,924	33,141
Richmond	190	740	535	205	2,504	1,424	1,080	4,838

*Based on 20 percent sample.   †Based on 25 percent sample.   ‡Based on 15 percent sample.

Source: New York City Department of Health, Weekly Bulletin, XXI, 40 (Oct. 8, 1932); Research Bureau, Welfare and Health Council of New York City, Population of Puerto Rican Birth or Parentage, New York City: 1950 (New York, 1952); U.S. Bureau of the Census, U.S. Census of Population: 1960, Puerto Ricans in The United States PC (2)-1D (Washington, 1963). Census of Population: 1970, Final Report PC (1)-C34 (Washington, 1972).

The study of the Negro population is still further confounded by the inclusion of some Puerto Ricans, since the Census Bureau classifies persons of Puerto Rican origin as both white and nonwhite. Acknowledging that "the commonly held conceptions of race among Puerto Ricans in Puerto Rico, among Puerto Ricans in the United States, and among other persons in the United States are somewhat different," the Census Bureau noted that "differences between successive censuses in the proportion of nonwhite persons among Puerto Ricans may reflect changes in attitudes about racial classification as well as selective migration and differential fertility."[12] Evidently the student of population trends among the American Negro does not have an easy task.

11. The population classified in New York as "all other races" (excluding Negroes, Chinese, Japanese, American Indians, and Filipinos) rose from 7,026 in 1960 to 73,477 in 1970, an increase too large to be credible. Similar changes occurred nationally. The Census Bureau acknowledged there were "many write-in" race categories which were included in Negro and other races and admitted this overstatement resulted from "an undetermined number of persons listing their race as Puerto Rican or Mexican, for example." U.S. Bureau of the Census, "Components of Population Change by County: 1960 to 1970," Current Population Reports, Series P-25, No. 461 (June 28, 1971).

12. U.S. Bureau of the Census, Puerto Ricans, p. ix.

It might be appropriate at this point to note that the New York City Health Department and other city agencies, in order to avoid such statistical overlap and discrepancy, use a three-way mutually exclusive ethnic classification—white, nonwhite, and Puerto Rican.[13]

The Negro population within New York City more than doubled between 1940 and 1960, rising from 458,000 to 1,088,000 (see Table 69). At the latter date Negroes constituted 12.6 percent of the aggregate population. Net migration accounted for the bulk of the gain registered between 1940 and 1950—221,000 out of 289,000. In the succeeding decade, 1950 to 1960, inmigration decreased while the rate of natural increase rose substantially, so that of the increase in the Negro population of 340,000, less than half—about 154,000—resulted from net migration. Unlike the situation prior to 1930, relatively few of the newcomers were from the West Indies. The majority originated from the southern coastal states stretching from Virginia to Florida.

Over the decade ending in 1970 the Negro population of New York City grew by 53 percent, climbing to 1,668,000. Net migration (about 324,000) was more than double that in the 1950-60 decade and accounted for more than half of the substantial increase. Negroes constituted 21.1 percent of the population of New York City in 1970 and 5.9 percent of the total for the four suburban counties in New York State (Nassau, Suffolk, Westchester, and Rockland).

In the late 1960s the West Indies once again became an important source of Negro growth in New York. National statistics indicate the number of immigrants from the Caribbean soared after 1965, and a substantial share of the islanders are reported to have settled in New York. The total number of natives of Jamaica, Trinidad and Tobago, and Barbados who migrated to the United States leaped from 12,477 in the five years ending with fiscal year 1965 to 92,355 in the half decade ending with fiscal year 1970; those from Haiti rose from 9,889 in 1961-65 to 27,648 in 1966-70.[14]

The historic pattern of Negro settlement in New York—in substantial but highly scattered clusters—changed in the second decade of the present century when the rapid expansion of the community strained available housing.[15] A densely settled community developed in Harlem, which by 1930 held 72 percent of Manhattan's and 50 percent of the whole city's Negro population.[16] Between 1940 and 1960 the proportion of New York's

13. See, for example, New York City Department of Health, *Summary of Vital Statistics 1965*, Table 6.
14. U.S. Department of Justice, *Annual Report of the Immigration and Naturalization Service 1970*, p. 64.
15. Handlin, *The Newcomers*, p. 81.
16. Ford, *Slums and Housing*, p. 314. For a highly informative account of the Harlem community see Gilbert Osofsky, *Harlem: The Making of a Ghetto* (New York: Harper and Row, 1963).

black population living in Manhattan declined from 65 to 37 percent. Mass migration was under way to Brooklyn, which increased its Negro population from 107,000 to 371,000 between 1940 and 1960, the newcomers concentrating in the Bedford-Stuyvesant area. This district had contained the largest Negro community in the borough as early as 1920.[17]

TABLE 69

Race of the Population by Nativity, New York City, 1900-70

Nativity and year	All classes	White	Nonwhite					
			Total	Negro	Other races			
					Total	Chinese	Japanese	All other
Total								
70	7,894,862 §	6,048,841	1,846,021	1,668,115**	177,906	69,324	13,968	94,614
60	7,781,984	6,640,662	1,141,322	1,087,931	53,391	32,831	5,991	14,569
50	7,891,957	7,116,441	775,516	747,608	27,908	18,327	3,114	6,467
40	7,454,995	6,977,501	477,494	458,444	19,050	12,753	2,087	4,210
30	6,930,446	6,589,377	341,069	327,706	13,363	8,414	2,356	2,593
20	5,620,048	5,459,463	160,585	152,467	8,118	5,042	2,312	764
10	4,766,883	4,669,162	97,721	91,709	6,012	4,614	1,037	361
00	3,437,202	3,369,898	67,304	60,666	6,638	6,321	286	31
Native*								
60†	6,224,628	5,178,002	1,046,626	N.A.	N.A.	N.A.	N.A.	N.A.
50‡	6,026,450	5,321,650	704,800	N.A.	N.A.	N.A.	N.A.	N.A.
40	5,316,338	4,897,481	418,857	410,026	8,831	4,745	631	3,455
30	4,571,760	4,294,196	277,564	272,952	4,612	1,926	536	2,150
20	3,591,888	3,467,916	123,972	122,031	1,941	1,084	251	606
10	2,822,526	2,741,459	81,067	79,952	1,115	710	92	313
00	2,167,122	2,108,980	58,142	N.A.	N.A.	N.A.	N.A.	N.A.
Foreign born								
60†	1,558,686	1,463,817	94,869	N.A.	N.A.	N.A.	N.A.	N.A.
50‡	1,860,930	1,788,625	72,305	N.A.	N.A.	N.A.	N.A.	N.A.
40	2,138,657	2,080,020	58,637	48,418	10,219	8,008	1,456	755
30	2,358,686	2,295,181	63,505	54,754	8,751	6,488	1,820	443
20	2,028,160	1,991,547	36,613	30,436	6,177	3,958	2,061	158
10	1,944,357	1,927,703	16,654	11,757	4,897	3,904	945	48
00	1,270,080	1,260,918	9,162	N.A.	N.A.	N.A.	N.A.	N.A.

*Includes persons born in U.S. possessions and persons born abroad of American parents.
†Based on 25 percent sample. Combined figures for native and foreign differ slightly from "Total."
‡Based on 20 percent sample. Combined figures for native and foreign born differ slightly from "Total."
§Native and foreign-born populations (per sample) were 6,457,740 and 1,437,058 respectively.
**Native and foreign-born populations (per sample) were 1,506,404 and 159,066 respectively.
N.A. = Not available.
Source: U.S. Bureau of the Census data.

17. Seth M. Scheiner, *Negro Mecca: A History of the Negro in New York City, 1865-1920* (New York: New York University Press, 1965), p. 24.

In the Bronx the Negro population climbed from 24,000 to 164,000 in this period, and in Queens, from 26,000 to 146,000 (see Table 64). Significantly, the geographic trend among the Negro population was following that observed among the white population several decades earlier. And just as Manhattan was the first borough to experience white outmigration (as early as the 1910-20 decade), it is to be noted that the 1950-60 decade witnessed a net outmigration from Manhattan among the nonwhite population of almost 40,000 (see Table 67). Natural increase was barely substantial to permit an overall increase among the Negro community in Manhattan.

Between 1960 and 1970 the movement from Manhattan was so extensive that the number of Negroes residing in this borough actually declined, falling by 17,000 to 380,000. Brooklyn contained by far the largest concentration of the city's Negroes in 1970—some 656,000. The Bronx, with 358,000, more than double its black population ten years earlier, had almost as large a figure as Manhattan.

The Chinese population of New York City, which more than doubled between 1920 and 1940, redoubled between 1940 and 1960, largely as a result of immigration from abroad. In 1940, 8,008 of the 12,753 Chinese—63 percent—were foreign born (see Table 69). Subsequent censuses did not provide breakdowns of the city's Chinese by nativity. However, the 1960 census did report that 18,764 foreign-born nonwhites—12,782 males and 5,982 females—gave their mother tongue as Chinese.[18] It seems probable then that approximately 19,000 of the 32,831 Chinese in New York City in 1960 were foreign born.

The Immigration Act of 1965, which abolished the national-origin quota system, had a profound effect on Chinese immigration to America.[19] In the five-year period subsequent to the new legislation, fiscal years 1966-70, the number of arrivals who were natives of China or Hong Kong quadrupled to 97,987 from the level of 24,294 in the preceding half decade (1961-65).[20] An increasing share of these newcomers to the United States have come to New York City. In 1970, for the first time in American history, New York replaced San Francisco as the home of the largest Chinese community. While the Chinese population in San Francisco rose from 36,445 to 58,696 between 1960 and 1970, that in New York City climbed from 32,831 to 69,324.[21]

The New York Chinese community, like other immigrant groups, has

18. U.S. Bureau of the Census, unpublished tabulations, 1960 census.

19. See Charles B. Keely, "Effects of the Immigration Act of 1965 on Selected Population Characteristics of Immigrants to the United States," *Demography*, VIII, 2 (May 1971), 157-69.

20. *Annual Report of the Immigration and Naturalization Service 1970*, p. 64.

21. U.S. Bureau of the Census, *U.S. Census of Population: 1960, Vol. I, Part 6* (Washington, 1963), p. 141; Vol. I, Part 34 (Washington, 1963), p. 107. U.S. Bureau of the Census, *U.S. Census of Population: 1970*, Final Report PC (1)-B6 (Washington, 1971), p. 102; Final Report PC (1)-B34 (Washington, 1971), p. 87.

dispersed from its concentration in the area of its major early settlement. Chinatown proper, plus the surrounding census tracts (a total of six tracts) had 10,604 Chinese in 1960, not quite one-third of the New York Chinese.[22]

INTERNAL MIGRATION

Census classifications of persons by state of birth and state of residence have been frequently used to estimate intercensal migration streams. However, in addition to the usual problems associated with these statistics (period migration must be deduced from lifetime migration), new difficulties beset those who would make use of such data for examining migration into American cities after 1940. Insurmountable is the absence of state-of-birth tabulations at the 1950 census for individual cities.[23] At the 1960 census some statistics were again provided for state of birth, or rather region of birth, for urban places. But attempts at describing interstate migration streams—at least among the white population—are much confounded by the impact of the post-World War II dispersion of city residents to suburbia.

Table 70 indicates that the number of United States-born whites resident in New York City who were not natives of the Empire State diminished from 641,000 in 1940 to 492,000 in 1960. Declines occurred among whites born in each region of the nation except the West. It would be false, however, to conclude that internal migration directed toward the nation's largest city had ceased; a more logical explanation takes account of the mass exodus from the city proper to the suburban counties. Table 71 shows that the area defined as the New York Standard Metropolitan Statistical Area (New York City and four suburban counties in New York State) in 1960 held 837,630 persons who reported they were natives of one of the 49 states outside New York, and that 41.3 percent of these resided in the suburban counties. It is of interest to note that while 10.9 percent of all native white residents of New York City who reported their state of birth in 1960 were not New Yorkers, the corresponding percentage for residents of the suburban counties was 14.5. Apparently, persons who were interstate migrants (at any prior time period) were proportionately overrepresented in the white movement from city to suburb. Table 71 indicates that this was true for migrants from each of the nation's major regions. A parallel situation—though in much lesser degree—existed among the nonwhite population.

In lieu of state-of-birth statistics, a more appropriate means of studying recent migration streams affecting small areas is provided by the

22. D. Y. Yuan, "Chinatown and Beyond: The Chinese Population in Metropolitan New York," *Phylon*, XXVII, 4 (Winter 1966), 322.

23. The Bureau of the Census classified state of birth only by state of residence in 1950, breaking a series for major cities that stretched all the way back to 1850.

TABLE 70
Native Population by Area of Birth and Color, New York City, 1940 and 1960

Area of birth	1960 Census			1940 Census		
	Total	White	Nonwhite	Total	White	Nonwhi
Total	6,224,628	5,178,002	1,046,626	5,316,338	4,897,481	418,85
United States	5,767,059	4,748,569	1,018,490	5,238,090	4,835,547	402,54
State reported	5,446,628	4,506,357	940,271	5,214,657	4,813,249	401,40
New York	4,498,247	4,014,406	483,841	4,312,100	4,172,227	139,87
Other States	948,381	491,951	456,430	902,557	641,022	261,53
Other Northeast	320,366	291,096	29,270	430,293	408,158	22,13
North Central	99,928	87,837	12,091	117,930	111,221	6,70
South	500,561	89,977	410,584	330,151	100,687	229,46
West	27,526	23,041	4,485	24,183	20,956	3,22
State not reported	320,431	242,212	78,219	23,433	22,298	1,13
Outlying areas	442,170	416,576	25,594	71,514	55,602	15,91
U.S. citizens born abroad or at sea	15,399	12,857	2,542	6,734	6,332	40

Source: U.S. Bureau of the Census, Sixteenth Census of The United States: 1940 Population, State of Birth of The Native Population (Washington, 1944); U.S. Census of Population: 1960 Detailed Characteristics; New York, PC (1)-34D (Washington, 1962).

TABLE 71
White and Nonwhite Native Population by Area of Birth, New York Standard Metropolitan Statistical Area, 1960

Area of birth	White			Nonwhite		
	Total SMSA	In four suburban counties*		Total SMSA	In four suburba counties*	
		Number	Percent		Number	Perce
Total	7,650,187	2,472,185	32.3	1,186,878	140,252	11.8
United States	7,204,085	2,455,516	34.1	1,157,606	139,116	12.0
State reported	6,873,109	2,366,752	34.4	1,060,242	119,971	11.3
New York	6,035,479	2,021,073	33.5	537,980	54,139	10.1
Other States	837,630	345,679	41.3	522,262	65,832	12.6
Other Northeast	487,291	196,195	40.3	33,229	3,959	11.9
North Central	155,997	68,160	43.7	13,814	1,723	12.5
South	153,292	63,315	41.3	470,087	59,503	12.7
West	41,050	18,009	43.9	5,132	647	12.6
State not reported	330,976	88,764	26.8	97,364	19,145	19.7
Outlying areas	426,572	9,996	2.3	26,374	780	3.0
U.S. citizens born abroad or at sea	19,530	6,673	34.2	2,898	356	12.3

*Counties are Nassau, Rockland, Suffolk, and Westchester.
Source: U.S. Bureau of the Census, U.S. Census of Population: 1960; Detailed Characteristics; New Y PC (1)-34D (Washington, 1962); U.S. Census of Population: 1960, State of Birth, PC (2)-2A (Washington, 1!

published data based on the query on place of residence five years prior to the census date, asked at the 1940 and 1960 censuses. The data have various limitations, however, among them a deficiency in the count of migrants, particularly for Negroes, being outstanding. Also, these migrant statistics exclude children under five years of age and (like tabulations based on state-of-birth information) those persons who moved during the period under study but died before the census, as well as those who moved out of the country.[24]

Table 72 shows that about 163,000 whites and 29,000 nonwhites living in New York City in 1940 reportedly had been residents of states other than New York in 1935. At the 1960 census the corresponding figures—relating to residence in 1955—were 148,000 and 58,000 respectively (see Table 73). Furthermore, at the latter date approximately 106,000 whites and 17,000 nonwhites who reported an out-of-state origin were living in four suburban counties, indicating that many who moved to metropolitan New York probably settled directly in the ring, bypassing the central city. In addition the suburban counties showed, as expected, an enormous influx of 424,000 persons who had been resident in New York City five years earlier, while only 59,000 1955 residents of the ring were living in the city in 1960.

In comparing the statistics for 1935-40 with those for 1955-60 it must be realized that the detailed data on immigrants to New York are limited to New York City proper at the former period and to the aggregate of New York City and four suburban counties (the New York Standard Metropolitan Statistical Area) in the latter. The ideal comparison would be of inmigrants to the whole metropolitan area at both dates, but unfortunately the earlier census did not provide county data. Nevertheless, the 1960 SMSA statistics permit more meaningful comparison than would a similar tabulation for the city alone, since a very large share of the more recent migrants settled in the suburban ring.

Since the white migrant stream and the nonwhite migrant stream have been quite dissimiliar in origin, it is more meaningful to study each separately. Table 74 shows the ten states sending the largest number of white immigrants to the New York area in 1955-60. An important finding demonstrated here is that the percentage of all persons moving from each of these states who chose to settle in New York was smaller in 1955-60 (despite an expanded definition of New York) than it had been in 1935-40. Thus New York did not have the same drawing power in the 1950s, relative to other areas, that it possessed during the Depression years.

24. For a discussion of some of the serious inadequacies of these data see Karl E. Taueber and Alma F. Taueber, "The Changing Character of Negro Migration," *American Journal of Sociology,* LXX (January 1965), 429-41.

TABLE 72

Migration Status, 1935-40, of the 1940 Population of
New York City, 5 Years of Age and Older by Color and Nativity

Migration status	Total	Color		Nativity*	
		White	Nonwhite	Native	Foreign
Total: 1940 Census	7,021,101	6,574,262	446,839	5,316,338	2,138,657
Nonmigrants	6,645,985	6,236,752	409,233	5,070,096	2,009,783
Inmigrants from					
Balance of N.Y. State	40,248	39,252	996	33,101	7,147
Other U.S.	192,751	163,298	29,453	165,492	27,259
Abroad	101,971	98,845	3,126	19,053	82,918
Not reported	40,146	36,115	4,031	28,596	11,550

*Includes children under five years of age (all nonmigrants).
Source: U.S. Bureau of the Census, Sixteenth Census of The U.S.: 1940 Population;
Internal Migration 1935 to 1940; Age of Migrants (Washington, 1946); and Social
Characteristics of Migrants (Washington, 1946).

Although the number of outmigrants from New Jersey and Pennsylvania—traditionally the two leading states of origin of New York newcomers—during 1955-60 was more than double the 1935-40 level, about the same number of migrants from these states settled in New York in each period.

The nonwhite movement into New York City largely originated from the southern Atlantic coast states. Table 75 indicates that the two Carolinas, Virginia, and Georgia were the principal places of origin of nonwhite immigrants in the 1930s and the 1950s. With the exception of Virginia, the percentage of these states' nonwhite outmigrants who headed for New York was higher during 1955-60 than the relative level two decades earlier. Thus, the relative loss of attraction New York possessed for white migrants did not apply among nonwhites.

There can be little doubt that the outmigration from New York was considerably larger during the period 1955-60 than in 1935-40, although even approximate measurement is handicapped by the difference in the geographic units for which data were published at the 1940 and 1960 censuses, as well as the quality of the data. Following the 1940 enumeration the Census Bureau pointed out that the number of outmigrants from large cities "is undoubtedly overstated.... This overstatement results from a tendency of migrants from the suburbs of an urban place ... to give the urban place as their former residence. This is particularly true of migrants who had moved long distances.... A similar bias does not occur in the classification of inmigrants by 1940 place of residence since the 1940 place of residence is based on the classification of the place at which the person was enumerated."[25]

25. U.S. Bureau of the Census, *Sixteenth Census of the United States 1940, Internal Migration, 1935 to 1940: Age of Migrants* (Washington, 1946), p. 3.

TABLE 73
Migration Status, 1955-60, of the 1960 Population of Metropolitan New York 5 Years of Age and Older by Color

Migration status	New York SMSA			New York City			Outside New York City		
	Total	White	Nonwhite	Total	White	Nonwhite	Total	White	Nonwhite
Total: 1960 Census	9,682,272	8,552,568	1,129,704	7,096,339	6,096,074	1,000,265	2,585,933	2,456,494	129,439
Nonmigrants	8,346,764	7,385,805	960,959	6,423,452	5,548,283	875,169	1,923,312	1,837,522	85,790
Inmigrants from									
Balance of SMSA*	483,983	465,559	18,424	59,491	54,635	4,856	424,492	410,924	13,568
N.Y. State Outside SMSA	38,250	36,307	1,943	18,346	16,877	1,469	19,904	19,430	474
Other U.S.	328,767	253,827	74,940	205,920	148,168	57,752	122,847	105,659	17,188
North and West (excl. N.Y. State)	204,307	188,267	16,040	122,794	109,712	13,082	81,513	78,555	2,958
South	124,460	65,560	58,900	83,126	38,456	44,670	41,334	27,104	14,230
Abroad	271,363†	246,530	24,833	234,787	211,819	22,968	36,576	34,711	1,865
Not Reported	213,145	164,540	48,605	154,343	116,292	38,051	58,802	48,248	10,554

*Balance inside or outside city.   †Includes 70,579 persons of Puerto Rican birth.

Source: U.S. Bureau of the Census, U.S. Census of Population: 1960; General Social and Economic Characteristics, New York PC (1)-34c (Washington, 1962); U.S. Census of Population and Housing: 1960; Census Tracts, PHC (1)-104, Part 2 (Washington, 1962).

TABLE 74
Number of White Outmigrants 5 Years Old and Over, Principal States of Origin of White Inmigrants to New York Area, 1940 and 1960

State of residence in 1935 or 1955	1940 Census			1960 Census		
	Total outmigrants 1935-40	Inmigrants to New York*	Percent of total	Total outmigrants 1955-60	Inmigrants to New York†	Perce of tota
New Jersey	155,688	40,525	26.0	367,505	46,723	12.
Pennsylvania	298,750	28,339	9.5	647,322	24,635	3.
California	206,831	7,707	3.7	780,459	18,640	2.
Massachusetts	140,305	13,715	9.8	332,535	17,172	5.
Connecticut	61,703	10,157	16.5	164,894	16,820	10.
Florida	87,672	4,569	5.2	348,854	14,283	4.
Illinois	339,436	9,295	2.7	696,712	12,579	1.
Ohio	242,412	6,502	2.7	604,964	10,853	1.
Maryland	67,848	2,926	4.3	239,802	8,156	3.
Virginia	102,668	2,393	2.3	364,883	7,762	2.

*New York City.　　†New York SMSA.

Source: U.S. Bureau of the Census, Sixteenth Census of The U.S.: 1940 Population. Internal Migration 1935 to 1940 Color and Sex of Migrants (Washington, 1943); U.S. Census of Population: 1960. Mobility for States and State Economic Areas, PC (2)-2B (Washington, 1963).

TABLE 75
Number of Nonwhite Outmigrants 5 Years Old and Over, Principal States of Origin of Nonwhite Inmigrants to New York Area, 1940 and 1960

State of residence in 1935 or 1955	1940 Census			1960 Census		
	Total outmigrants 1935-40	Inmigrants to New York*	Percent of total	Total outmigrants 1955-60	Inmigrants to New York†	Perc of tota
North Carolina	29,744	4,225	14.2	73,613	15,959	21.
South Carolina	33,619	5,421	16.1	62,355	14,711	23.
Virginia	24,780	3,735	15.1	48,221	7,268	15.
Georgia	48,391	2,529	5.2	65,304	5,005	7.
Alabama	36,522	858	2.4	58,080	3,463	6.
New Jersey	8,039	2,339	29.1	21,014	3,401	16.
Florida	13,740	1,632	11.9	32,287	3,314	10
Pennsylvania	12,075	1,781	14.7	31,273	3,186	10
Maryland	7,816	861	11.0	19,852	1,939	9
District of Columbia	9,217	817	8.9	23,418	1,776	7

*New York City.　　†New York SMSA.　　Source: Same as Table 74.

As similar inaccuracy was deduced for the 1960 count, the Census Bureau chose not to tabulate much data on outmigrants for central cities but rather for metropolitan areas as a unit. Table 76 therefore compares a probably somewhat exaggerated number of outmigrants from New York City in the five years preceding the 1940 census with outmigrants from an aggregate area embracing New York and four suburban counties in the five years prior to the 1960 census. The intra-New York State migrant figures are not at all comparable since at the earlier census those who moved from the city to the four suburban counties (perhaps the bulk of the outmigrants within New York State) are included.

The somewhat larger territory composing the New York area in 1960, however, does not begin to account for the much greater magnitude of the movement to the balance of the United States shown at the later census. The number of outmigrants who went to Florida more than quadrupled, while the volume of the flow to several other states, most notably California, more than doubled. Migration to New Jersey deserves special consideration, inasmuch as a major share is represented by the suburban or exurban exodus. In reality, a.substantial number of the outmigrants to New Jersey remained within what may be considered the New York metropolitan ring. Some of these movers may merely have exchanged one suburban home (in say, Westchester County) for another (in Bergen County, for example).

TABLE 76
Place of Destination of Outmigrants 5 Years Old and Over from New York Area, 1940 and 1960

State	1940 Census Total* outmigrants 1935-40	White	Nonwhite	1960 Census Totalt outmigrants 1955-60	White	Nonwhite
Areas	423,872	404,062	19,810	721,184	671,227	49,957
New York State (balance)	166,719	158,510	8,209	86,706	80,088	6,618
Other United States	257,153	245,552	11,601	634,478	591,139	43,339
New Jersey	64,933	63,231	1,702	159,536	151,461	8,075
Florida	19,903	19,223	680	96,741	94,229	2,512
California	32,559	31,808	751	81,012	76,454	4,558
Connecticut	20,132	19,530	602	40,471	38,992	1,479
Pennsylvania	19,828	18,809	1,019	34,718	31,707	3,011
Massachusetts	13,939	13,552	387	28,295	26,885	1,410
Virginia	6,706	5,383	1,323	18,117	15,554	2,563
Illinois	8,879	8,625	254	15,832	14,936	896
Maryland	6,438	5,992	446	15,175	13,883	1,292
Ohio	7,243	6,906	337	14,270	13,182	1,088
Texas	3,772	3,644	128	12,174	10,989	1,185
North Carolina	3,242	2,406	836	10,258	7,062	3,196
Other states	43,625	40,846	2,779	107,879	95,805	12,074

*From New York City.   tFrom New York SMSA.   Source: Same as Table 74.

NATURAL INCREASE

The natural increase component of New York City's population movement for the decade 1940-50 (547,709) was approximately double the figure for the preceding decade (266,038).[26] This could be principally attributed to the substantial rise of the birth rate during and immediately following World War II from the very low level of the Depression years. The city's birth rate, which had fallen without interruption from 23.1 per 1,000 in 1921 to a nadir of 13.4 per 1,000 in 1936, began to revive in the early 1940s. After reaching a postwar high of 21.6 per 1,000 in 1947, the rate leveled off to between 19.0 and 20.5 per 1,000 during the years 1948-65. It dipped below 18 per 1,000 after 1966 (see Appendix Table A-3).

The crude death rate, on the other hand, showed comparatively little change during this period. A rate close to 11 per 1,000 occurred in 1921, as well as in 1930. From 1932 through 1956 the rate remained slightly below 11 (the record low was 10.3) except during the years in which major influenza epidemics were present. Since 1957 the rate has annually exceeded 11 per 1,000.

While age-specific death rates for New York City show substantial reductions in mortality over the decades,[27] the gradual aging of the population has meant that increasingly larger proportions have become subject to the higher mortality of the elderly. The age composition of the population has steadily shifted: in 1930, 3.8 percent of the population was 65 years of age or older; in 1950, 7.7 percent; in 1970, 12.0 percent (see Appendix Table B-1).

Differential fertility in New York City has been a recurrent phenomenon. Typically newcomers from rural environments have tended to maintain fertility rates in excess of the host ethnic categories. In the early 1900s New York's Italian population was characterized by birth rates well above those of the balance of the community. In the post-World War II period, Negroes and Puerto Ricans have exhibited birth-rate levels markedly higher than those of the non-Puerto Rican white population.

Table 77 shows both crude birth rates and fertility rates (births per 1,000 women aged 15 to 44 years) for color and ethnic groups in New York City in 1950 and 1960. At each date the birth rate of Puerto Rican New Yorkers was over twice that among the white population exclusive of the Puerto Rican segment. The birth rates shown for the nonwhite population were considerably above those for whites, but not so high as among Puerto Ricans. The detailed breakdown reveals that the apparent slight increase in the white birth rate between 1950 and 1960 (from 18.0 to 18.4 per 1,000) was entirely due to change in the Puerto Rican component of this

26. New York State Department of Health, *Annual Report 1950*, II xi.
27. See New York City Department of Health, *Summary of Vital Statistics 1965*, Table 15, for age-specific death rates for each census period from 1900 through 1960.

population. The birth rate of the non-Puerto Rican white population actually declined during this period.

Comparison may be made not only among the ethnic communities comprising New York City's population but also with each group's counterpart outside the city. As indicated by data in Table 78, Puerto Ricans living in New York City in 1960 had a slightly higher fertility rate than Puerto Ricans in their home island, while both whites and nonwhites living in New York had lower rates at every age than was true in the United States as a whole.[28] A partial explanation for the very low level of the white birth rates in New York City is the heavy percentage of Jewish women included in the population. Recent studies have shown that Jewish fertility is the lowest among the major religious groups in the United States.[29]

Puerto Rican women living in New York had higher birth rates at young ages (under 25 years) and lower birth rates at older ages than did residents of Puerto Rico. Among nonwhites, with each advance in age women in New York showed an increase in their percentage difference below the national age-specific rate. Among the white (non-Puerto Rican) population of New York almost the opposite situation could be described; birth rates for women approached the higher level of the national age-specific rate with each successive age group up through 30-34 years, but the relationship did not hold for women at older ages.

RELIGIOUS GROUPS

The most reliable data yet produced about the religious composition of New York City's population are based on a household survey conducted in the first half of 1952 by the Health Insurance Plan (HIP) of Greater New York. A total of about 4,200 households were chosen for interview on the

28. As 11 percent of New York's white female population at ages 15 to 44 years was of Puerto Rican birth, the non-Puerto Rican white population was thought to be more comparable to the white category as used in U.S. statistics. Nationally, only 0.6 percent of all white females in the fertile age groups were natives of Puerto Rico (from data in U.S. Bureau of Census, *Puerto Ricans*). No statistics are available at the national level concerning the fertility rate of all Puerto Ricans in the United States.

29. The national Current Population Survey taken in 1957 indicated 1,749 children ever born per 1,000 ever-married Jewish women 15 to 44 years of age and 2,218 children ever born per 1,000 ever-married Jewish women 45 years old and over. Comparable figures for all American ever-married white women were 2,164 and 2,759 respectively. U.S. Bureau of the Census, *Statistical Abstract of the United States 1958*, p. 41. Reasons for low Jewish fertility, including late marriage, as well as "atomization, disillusionment, and secularization," are discussed by Nathan Goldberg, "The Jewish Population in America, 1917-1947: Population Growth and Birth Rate," *The Jewish Review*, V (January-December 1948), 30-55. Another study found that Protestant-Jewish differences in fertility were virtually eliminated when socio-economic characteristics were controlled by matching. Ronald Freedman, Pascal K. Whelpton, and John W. Smit, "Socio-Economic Factors in Religious Differences in Fertility," *American Sociological Review*, XXVI (August 1961), 608-14.

basis of area probability sampling. The results subsequently received wide study.[30] The 1952 survey revealed the approximate religious distribution of the city's total population to be: Catholic, 47.6 percent; Jewish, 26.4 percent; Protestant, 22.8 percent; other and not reported, 3.2 percent. Over 51 percent of the white population was reported in households headed by a person of Catholic background, close to 30 percent Jewish, and 16 percent Protestant. Among the nonwhite population, over 80 percent were in families headed by a person of Protestant background (see Table 79).

The age composition of each of the religious elements in New York's white population was associated both with the relative historical arrival point and the recent fertility of the group. The Catholic community, with the highest birth rate, was relatively overrepresented at the younger ages.

TABLE 77
Birth Rates and Fertility Rates by Color and Ethnic Group, New York City, 1950 and 1960

Color and ethnic group	Birth rate (per 1,000 population)		Fertility rate (per 1,000 women aged 15-44 years)	
	1950	1960	1950	1960
Total: New York City	19.0	20.3	77.3	96.8
Color				
White	18.0	18.4	74.9	91.4
Nonwhite	29.0	30.9	94.3	121.2
Ethnic group				
Puerto Rican	37.4	39.2	135.6	165.8
White excluding Puerto Rican	17.3	16.4	72.5	82.9

Source: Derived from U.S. Bureau of the Census population data and births in New York State Department of Health, Annual Report, 1950, 1960. Births of Puerto Rican natives which are given by place of occurrence in vital statistics of the Department of Health, New York City, are assumed to be approximately identical with births by place of residence.

30. A detailed summary of the study is given in *Health and Medical Care in New York City*, prepared by the Committee for the Special Research Project in the Health Insurance Plan of Greater New York (Cambridge, Mass.: Harvard University Press, 1957). Statistics for religious groups are highlighted in Neva R. Deardorff, "The Religio-Cultural Background of New York City's Population," *Milbank Memorial Fund Quarterly*, XXXIII, 2 (April 1955), 152-60. Additional details relating to the Jewish population are given in Ben B. Seligman, "The Jewish Population of New York City: 1952," in Marshall Sklare, ed., *The Jews. Social Patterns of an American Group* (Glencoe, Ill.: The Free Press, 1958), pp. 94-106.

TABLE 78
Birth Rates by Age of Mother for Color and Ethnic Groups in New York City and for Similar Groups Outside the City, 1960
(births per 1,000 women)

Color/ethnic group by place	All women aged 15-44 years	15-19 years	20-24 years	25-29 years	30-34 years	35-39 years	40-44 years
White							
New York City*	82.9	29.7	167.9	169.2	98.2	44.2	9.7
United States	113.2	79.4	252.8	194.9	109.6	54.0	14.7
Percent difference N.Y.C. from U.S.	− 26.8	− 62.6	− 33.6	− 13.2	− 10.4	− 18.1	−34.0
Nonwhite							
New York City	121.2	154.3	258.2	167.0	97.2	50.4	12.6
United States	153.6	158.2	294.2	214.6	135.6	74.2	22.0
Percent difference N.Y.C. from U.S.	− 21.1	− 2.5	− 12.2	− 22.2	− 28.3	− 32.1	−42.7
Puerto Rican							
New York City†	165.8	161.1	323.2	200.4	119.0	68.2	21.5
Puerto Rico (all residents)	158.4	95.8	279.8	235.0	155.0	107.5	50.2
Percent difference N.Y.C. from P.R.	+ 4.7	+ 68.2	+ 15.5	− 14.7	− 23.2	− 36.6	−57.2

*Exclusive of persons born in Puerto Rico.   †Persons born in Puerto Rico.
Source: Derived from U.S. Bureau of the Census population data and births in New York State Department of Health, Annual Report, 1960. Births of Puerto Rican natives which are given by place of occurrence in New York City Department of Health, Vital Statistics 1956 to 1963 (New York, 1964), are assumed to be approximately identical with births by place of residence.

TABLE 79
Percent Distribution by Religion, Population of New York City by Color, 1952
(per HIP survey)

Religion	Total	White	Nonwhite
All groups	100.0	100.0	100.0
Catholic	47.6	51.5	13.8
Jewish	26.4	29.7	—
Protestant	22.8	16.0	80.7
Other	1.6 }	2.8	5.5
Not reported	1.6 }		

Source: HIP survey percentages found in Neva R. Deardorff, "The Religio-Cultural Background of New York City's Population," The Milbank Memorial Fund Quarterly, XXXIII, 2 (April, 1955), 160.

The Protestants, the majority group in an earlier day, had a relatively large share of the aged. The Jewish community's low fertility was evinced by its lower-than-average share of the population under 15 years of age, while survivors of the heavy immigration of the first quarter of the current century were responsible for the disproportionate concentration at ages 45 to 64 years.

Applying to the 1950 census populations at each of four broad age groups, the percentage distribution by religion obtained in the HIP survey yields an estimate of the actual number of white residents by religion and age. The totals for each religious group, when converted to percentages, agree very closely with the overall HIP proportions for each identical category (see Table 80).

Studies of mortality differentials in New York City by religion seem to have come into their own in the 1950s. The most comprehensive was that by Seidman, Garfinkel, and Craig, covering almost all deaths in the city of white residents in 1949-51; others were prepared by McMahon and Keller and by Liberson.[31]

Some well-known differences in religious background by country of origin for the immigrant population are clearly shown in Table 81, which is based on deaths in the years 1949-51. Most decedents from Ireland and Italy were buried in Catholic cemeteries; most decedents from Scandinavia in Protestant or nonsectarian cemeteries; and most from Austria, Hungary, Poland, and Russia in Jewish cemeteries.

Among the native-born white population the differentials by denomination of cemetery are closely associated with age. As Table 82 indicates, among native whites the percentage buried under Protestant or nonsecretarian as well as other (including cremation) auspices in 1949-51 tended to rise for each successively older age class, while the percentage of Catholic and particularly of Jewish burials tended to diminish. This of course corresponded to the fact that older Catholics and Jews were predominantly of foreign rather than of native birth, while this was not true among Protestants.

Seidman and co-workers ultimately classified deaths as Jewish or non-Jewish. Although the largest number of interments included in their three-year (1949-51) census study period took place in Catholic cemeteries, and practically all of these undoubtedly were of Catholics, a substantial number of Catholics were believed to have been buried in

31. Herbert Seidman, Lawrence Garfinkel, and Leonard Craig, "Death Rates in New York City by socio-Economic Class and Religious Group and by Country of Birth, 1949-1951," *Jewish Journal of Sociology*, IV, 2 (December 1962); Brian MacMahon and Ernest K. Koller, "Ethnic Differences in the Incidence of Leukemia," *Blood*, XII, 1 (January 1957); Vaun A. Newill, "Distribution of Cancer Mortality Among Ethnic Subgroups of the White Population of New York City, 1953-58," *Journal of the National Cancer Institute*, XXVI (1961), 405-17; David M. Liberson, "Causes of Death among Jews in New York City in 1953," *Jewish Social Studies*, XVIII, 2 (April 1956).

nonsectarian cemeteries, some of which set aside hallowed grounds for this purpose. Because these burials could not be easily distinguished from those of the many Protestants interred in nonsectarian cemeteries it was not feasible to classify Catholics and Protestants separately.[32] Thus, analysis on the basis of mortality statistics must largely be confined to the Jewish population.

TABLE 80
Estimated Distribution of White Population of New York City by Age Group (1950 Census) and Religion

Age	Total	Percent distribution by religion per HIP survey			
		Catholic	Jewish	Protestant	Other and not reported
All ages*	100.0	51.5	29.7	16.0	2.8
Under 15 years	100.0	56.5	27.2	14.2	2.1
15-44 years	100.0	55.1	28.3	13.9	2.7
45-64 years	100.0	44.5	32.7	19.8	3.0
65 years and over	100.0	43.6	32.2	21.3	2.9
	Estimated age distribution (1950 census)† (in thousands)				
All ages‡	7,116.6	3,682.1	2,100.6	1,143.8	189.9
Under 15 years	1,462.9	826.5	397.9	207.7	30.7
15-44 years	3,253.7	1,792.8	920.8	452.3	87.8
45-64 years	1,822.9	811.2	596.1	360.9	54.7
65 years and over	577.1	251.6	185.8	122.9	16.7

*Including age not stated.

†Calculated by applying percent distributions above to number of persons in each age group.

‡Sum of individual age groups. The following aggregate percent distributions by religion are derived: Catholic, 51.7; Jewish, 29.5; Protestant, 16.1; all other and not reported, 2.7.

Source: HIP survey percentages found in source for Table 79.

Aside from the primary aim of establishing mortality differentials the data gathered by Seidman are useful in estimating the size of the Jewish community (by other than the survey method), and in the calculation of some detailed birthplace characteristics not otherwise available. An estimate prepared by Seidman, based on skillful use of mortality statistics, arrived at a Jewish population of 2,189,000 in 1950, or 30.8 percent of the white (study) population of New York.[33] This figure is about 89,000 larger than that calculated from the HIP study (see Table 80). Most of the difference results from divergence for the group under 15 years of age, where the small number of deaths involved makes such estimation subject to a particularly wide range of error. Seidman calculated that 31.6 percent

32. Seidman, *et al.*, "Death Rates in New York City," pp. 256-58.   33. *Ibid.*

of the white study population in this broad age group was Jewish, compared to only 27.2 percent given in the HIP survey. Numerically this amounted to an excess of about 64,000.

In utilizing the mortality statistics to derive data on the origin of the Jewish population, it can be assumed that within each age-sex group of the population the distribution by country of birth corresponds to that among decedents. This percentage distribution is presented in Table 83.

TABLE 81

Percent Distribution of Deaths of Foreign-born White New York City
Residents Recorded in New York City by Country of Birth
and Sex According to Denomination of Cemetery
of Burial, 1949-51

Country of birth and sex	Total		Denomination of cemetery			
	Number	Percent	Catholic	Jewish	Protestant and nonsectarian	Other*
Austria, total	8,913	100.0	11.9	74.4	8.0	5.7
Male	4,888	100.0	12.1	73.1	7.9	6.8
Female	4,025	100.0	11.7	76.0	8.1	4.3
Germany, total	11,028	100.0	13.1	18.5	43.6	24.9
Male	6,065	100.0	12.3	18.1	40.3	29.3
Female	4,963	100.0	14.0	19.0	47.5	19.5
Great Britain, total	4,293	100.0	23.4	11.4	44.6	20.6
Male	2,379	100.0	21.6	12.0	43.9	22.5
Female	1,914	100.0	25.6	10.7	45.5	18.2
Hungary, total	3,475	100.0	13.4	59.7	15.8	11.1
Male	1,820	100.0	13.0	57.0	16.1	14.0
Female	1,655	100.0	13.8	62.7	15.6	8.0
Ireland, total	11,352	100.0	86.0	0.2	8.5	5.3
Male	5,231	100.0	82.5	0.2	10.0	7.3
Female	6,121	100.0	89.1	0.2	7.2	3.6
Italy, total	20,029	100.0	88.0	0.2	9.5	2.3
Male	12,017	100.0	86.1	0.2	10.6	3.2
Female	8,012	100.0	90.9	0.1	8.0	1.0
Poland, total	9,725	100.0	20.6	71.2	4.3	3.9
Male	5,413	100.0	21.2	68.4	5.0	5.5
Female	4,312	100.0	19.9	74.7	3.6	1.9
Russia, total	22,634	100.0	0.5	93.1	3.4	3.0
Male	12,672	100.0	0.7	91.1	4.6	3.7
Female	9,962	100.0	0.4	95.7	1.9	2.1
Scandinavia, total	3,412	100.0	2.8	0.5	72.3	24.4
Male	2,034	100.0	3.3	0.6	67.7	28.4
Female	1,378	100.0	2.0	0.4	79.0	18.5
Other foreign, total	13,173	100.0	21.4	27.3	36.7	14.6
Male	7,849	100.0	20.1	24.8	39.5	15.6
Female	5,324	100.0	23.4	31.0	32.5	13.1

*Includes cremation, City Cemetery, or out-of-town burial.

Source: Derived from unpublished data prepared from records of the New York City Health Department by Herbert Seidman, American Cancer Society.

TABLE 82

Percent Distribution of Deaths of White New York City Residents
25 Years of Age and Over, Recorded in New York City
by Nativity, Age, and Sex According to
Denomination of Cemetery of Burial,
1949-51

Nativity, age, and sex	Total		Denomination of cemetery			
	Number	Percent	Catholic	Jewish	Protestant and nonsectarian	Other*
United States						
25-34 years, total	3,073	100.0	46.2	21.5	23.5	8.7
Male	1,499	100.0	43.4	19.7	28.4	8.5
Female	1,574	100.0	49.0	23.2	18.9	8.9
35-44 years, total	7,365	100.0	47.6	21.4	19.9	11.1
Male	4,176	100.0	47.7	20.4	21.3	10.6
Female	3,189	100.0	47.5	22.7	18.0	11.8
45-54 years, total	13,796	100.0	42.9	17.2	27.4	12.5
Male	8,589	100.0	41.6	16.4	29.2	12.8
Female	5,207	100.0	45.0	18.5	24.4	12.2
55-64 years, total	19,062	100.0	39.0	12.8	34.2	14.0
Male	11,862	100.0	36.3	12.9	36.2	14.6
Female	7,200	100.0	43.5	12.7	30.8	13.0
65-74 years, total	18,929	100.0	38.3	8.2	36.2	17.3
Male	10,272	100.0	36.0	8.0	36.8	19.2
Female	8,657	100.0	41.1	8.4	35.5	15.0
75 years and over, total	18,197	100.0	31.2	7.0	42.0	19.7
Male	7,305	100.0	30.3	6.8	42.0	20.9
Female	10,892	100.0	31.9	7.2	42.0	18.9
Foreign born						
25-34 years, total	300	100.0	33.7	26.7	25.7	14.0
Male	140	100.0	32.9	19.3	30.7	17.1
Female	160	100.0	34.4	33.1	21.2	11.2
35-44 years, total	2,191	100.0	36.9	31.9	20.5	10.6
Male	1,236	100.0	36.6	27.5	24.5	11.3
Female	955	100.0	37.3	37.7	15.4	9.6
45-54 years, total	10,791	100.0	35.5	35.4	19.6	9.4
Male	6,746	100.0	34.8	33.2	21.4	10.7
Female	4,045	100.0	36.7	39.2	16.7	7.3
55-64 years, total	26,666	100.0	34.9	39.5	17.2	8.4
Male	16,666	100.0	33.3	37.5	19.3	9.9
Female	10,000	100.0	37.6	42.7	13.8	5.9
65-74 years, total	36,166	100.0	33.5	42.3	15.7	8.5
Male	20,431	100.0	32.1	40.9	16.7	10.4
Female	15,735	100.0	35.3	44.1	14.5	6.1
75 years and over, total	31,772	100.0	32.1	39.2	20.1	8.6
Male	15,064	100.0	30.9	39.8	19.0	10.3
Female	16,708	100.0	33.2	38.6	21.1	7.1
Puerto Rican born						
25 years and over, total	1,839	100.0	21.0	0.1	69.3	9.6
Male	875	100.0	19.9	0.0	69.6	10.5
Female	964	100.0	22.0	0.2	69.0	8.8

*Includes cremation, City Cemetery, or out-of-town burial.   Source: See Table 81.

TABLE 83

Percent Distribution of Deaths of Foreign-born White New York City
Residents Recorded in New York City with Burial in a
Jewish Cemetery by Sex, Age, and Country
of Birth, 1949-51

Sex and country of birth	Total all ages	Age				
		35-44 years	45-54 years	55-64 years	65-74 years	75 years and over
Male						
Number of deaths	23,228*	340	2,238	6,257	8,349	5,997
Percent, total	100.0	100.0	100.0	100.0	100.0	100.0
Russia	49.7	33.3	45.0	50.5	51.4	49.7
Poland	15.9	25.0	20.6	17.4	15.1	13.3
Austria	15.4	13.5	13.4	14.4	15.5	17.1
Germany	4.7	10.3	3.8	3.6	4.5	5.9
Hungary	4.5	4.7	3.6	3.5	4.5	5.8
Great Britain	1.2	3.2	2.9	1.4	0.9	0.7
Other foreign	8.6	10.0	10.7	9.2	8.1	7.5
Female						
Number of deaths	19,668†	360	1,587	4,269	6,937	6,443
Percent, total	100.0	100.0	100.0	100.0	100.0	100.0
Russia	48.5	35.5	45.1	48.6	49.4	49.3
Poland	16.4	25.3	20.7	17.2	16.2	14.3
Austria	15.5	11.4	13.6	15.3	16.5	15.4
Germany	4.8	8.1	3.9	2.9	4.0	6.8
Hungary	5.3	5.0	5.0	4.8	5.3	5.6
Great Britain	1.0	3.3	2.7	1.3	0.8	0.7
Other foreign	8.5	11.4	9.0	9.9	7.8	7.9

*Includes 47 deaths of persons under 35 years of age.
†Includes 72 deaths of persons under 35 years of age.
Source: See Table 81.

The largest proportion among foreign-born persons buried in Jewish cemeteries were natives of Russia (49.7 percent of males, 48.5 percent of females), followed by natives of Poland (15.9 percent of males, 16.4 percent of females), and of Austria (15.4 percent of males, 15.5 percent of females).

An estimate of the total number of foreign-born Jews has been derived by assuming that Jews in each age-sex group bear the same percentage to the total population in that group (given in the 1950 census) as Jewish deaths hold to all deaths. The percentages of Jewish deaths shown in Table 83, however, have been adjusted upward slightly to allow for the deaths of Jews who were not buried in Jewish cemeteries. According to one informed estimate for a date close to this period (1953), in addition to nearly 20,000 burials in Jewish cemeteries "from 200 to 300 Jews were buried in nonsectarian cemeteries, 600 to 800 in crematories, a total of about 1,000 in both."[34] Therefore, an upward adjustment in the percent-

34. Liberson, "Causes of Death," *Jewish Social Studies*, XVIII, 2 (April 1956), 85.

ages of deaths which may be considered as of Jewish persons seems a necessary step in the estimation. An adjustment of 5 percent for males, and of 2.5 percent for females appears reasonable. The resultant totals for age-sex groups have then been distributed by country of birth by applying the percentages given in Table 83. The result (shows in Table 84) yields an estimate of about 680,000 foreign-born Jews resident in New York City in 1950. This is equivalent to 32.5 percent of the estimated Jewish population (2,100,000) based on HIP data.[35]

TABLE 84
Estimated Foreign-born Jewish Population by Age, Sex, and Country of Birth, New York City, 1950

Sex and country of birth	Total all ages	Under 35 years	35-44 years	45-54 years	55-64 years	65-74 years	75 years and over
Total	679,520	55,530	95,635	180,270	188,030	121,450	38,605
Sex							
Male	313,030	20,170	37,780	84,785	93,260	58,790	18,245
Female	366,490	35,360	57,855	95,485	94,770	62,660	20,360
Country of Birth							
Russia	295,160	7,440	33,150	81,175	93,135	61,155	19,105
Poland	132,175	13,995	24,070	37,260	32,495	19,010	5,345
Austria	94,895	5,165	11,690	24,355	27,950	19,470	6,265
Germany	39,020	9,775	8,550	6,950	6,110	5,175	2,460
Hungary	31,815	3,275	4,665	7,865	7,860	5,950	2,200
Great Britain	12,830	945	3,140	4,985	2,480	1,020	260
Other foreign	73,625	14,935	10,370	17,680	18,000	9,670	2,970

Source: Based on data in Tables 82 and 83. See text for explanation of method of estimation.

NATIVITY, PARENTAGE, AND ETHNIC ORIGIN

The foreign stock, as termed by the census, comprises the foreign-born population plus the native population of foreign or mixed parentage (first- and second-generation Americans). Third and subsequent generations are described as "native of native parentage."[36] While some type of

35. It may be of interest to note that a sample survey taken in 1951 in the second-largest Jewish community in the nation, Los Angeles, indicated 32.1 percent of the population was foreign born. Fred Massarik, *A Report on the Jewish Population of Los Angeles 1959* (Research Service Bureau, Jewish Federation Council of Greater Los Angeles, 1959), p. 18.
36. U.S. Bureau of the Census, *U.S. Census of Population: 1960. Nativity and Parentage* (Washington, 1965), p. ix.

tabulation for New York City by nativity and parentage has been available for the white population at every census taken in the present century, the 1960 count was the only enumeration to provide some details for the non-white population.

Table 85 shows the foreign white stock in New York City by nativity and parentage for each census from 1900 to 1960. The number of foreign-born whites reached a peak of 2,295,000 in 1930, and the subsequent decline has resulted from the reduced level of immigration to the United States following the restrictive legislation of the 1920s and the loss through death of the earlier immigrants. The number of white natives of foreign or mixed parentage also is indicated to have reached a high in 1930, when, 2,789,000 strong, they outnumbered the first generation.

Close examination of the statistics for 1940, however, reveals serious understatement for this group relative to other censuses. At this enumeration, for the first time in census history, some questions (including parentage) were asked on a (5 percent) sample basis. Nonresponse was greater for items included in the sample than for those questions asked of all persons. It is logical to assume that there was a tendency among some enumerators to overlook completely questions asked only of one person in twenty. Whenever this happened and parentage was not reported, the assignment made, according to census editing procedures, was to native of native parentage. In addition, there was a tendency in the sample coding to classify persons as native white of native parentage at the expense of other white categories.[37]

Some idea of the magnitude of the group not properly classified in 1940 may be derived from a look at the categorization of cohorts of native whites at the surrounding censuses. For example, in 1940 only 52.1 percent of the native whites in New York City at ages 40-44 years (persons born around 1895-1900) were shown as of foreign stock. But at the 1930 census 60.7 percent of the persons 30-34 years of age (also born around 1895-1900), and at the 1950 census 57.6 percent of the persons 50-54 years old (similarly, born abound 1895-1900) were of foreign stock. Thus the 1940 percentage falls considerably short of the 58-60 percent that would be expected on the basis of the 1930 and 1950 patterns. Similar shortcomings are noted for virtually every adult age in 1940 (see Table 42).

A corrected version of the 1940 count of second-generation Americans in New York City undoubtedly would indicate that the numerical peak was achieved at this date, rather than in 1930. The second-generation population in New York experienced a small decline in the 1940s and a major one in the 1950s, occurring both through death of this gradually aging group, and through large-scale migration to the suburbs and elsewhere.

37. U.S. Bureau of the Census, *Sixteenth Census of the United States 1940, Population. Nativity and Parentage of the White Population. Country of Origin of the Foreign Stock* (Washington, 1943), p. 7.

TABLE 85

Nativity and Parentage of the Foreign White Stock,
New York City, 1900-60

Census year	Total foreign white stock	Foreign born white	Native white of foreign or mixed parentage			
			Total	Both parents foreign	Father foreign	Mother foreign.
1960*	3,622,929	1,463,821	2,159,108	1,537,839	408,086	213,183
1950	4,444,141	1,784,206	2,659,935†	1,972,200	459,890	227,845
1940	4,831,580	2,080,020	2,751,560‡	2,115,320	421,640	214,600
1930	5,084,066	2,295,181	2,788,885	2,211,974	374,063	202,848
1920	4,294,629	1,991,547	2,303,082	1,873,013	273,351	156,718
1910	3,747,844	1,927,703	1,820,141	1,445,465	374,676	
1900	2,632,421	1,260,918	1,371,503	1,072,062	196,706	102,735

*Based on 25 percent sample.
†Figures for native white based on 20 percent sample.
‡Figures for native white based on 5 percent sample.
Source: U.S. Bureau of the Census data.

With the end of mass immigration from abroad (except from Puerto Rico) and the aging of the foreign born, the child-producing population in New York shifted from first- to second-generation American. This is reflected by the data in Table 42, which can be utilized to conclude that the half-decade 1935-40 was the first after the opening half of the nineteenth century in which fewer than 50 percent of the white newborn had at least one foreign-born parent. A decade later, in 1945-50, only about one-fifth of the white births were to immigrant parents. The 1950 census also revealed, in contrast to the experience at every previous census in which such information was reported, that a majority of all white persons under 20 years of age were not of foreign stock.

In recent years analysis of the census category "native white of native parentage" has been confounded by the inclusion of Puerto Ricans within the same rubric. By 1960 more than one of every six New Yorkers in this category was of Puerto Rican origin. Hence in the tracing of cohorts of native-born whites over time the closed population implied by the word *native* becomes fiction. Furthermore, in the study of assimilation, of differential economic status, of fertility patterns, or of other demographic features, the supposed native stock must include a large number of Spanish-speaking immigrants to the mainland and their children. To adjust for this distortion, as well as to improve comparability with prior censuses, it is advisable to separate the Puerto Rican population from the residual native-white-of-native-parentage group whenever possible. This has been accomplished in Table 86, which shows by age group the percentages of the native white population who were the children of immigrants at the 1950 and 1960 censuses. (Corresponding material for earlier censuses was given in Table 42.) It is interesting to note that among the native white population, 35 years of age and over, second-generation Americans were relatively more numerous in 1960 than in 1910.

At the same time, most young (under 35 years of age) New Yorkers were not of foreign stock; a majority in 1960 consisted of third-generation (or even fourth-generation) Americans. Since the country of origin of the grandparents of third-generation Americans is not ascertained by the census, the numbers belonging to each ethnic group who are not among the foreign stock cannot be stated with any precision. Nevertheless, much attention has been focussed on the ethnic group, which some experts have considered not a survival from the age of mass immigration but a new social form.[38] One study made in the early 1960s identified all New Yorkers by ethnic categories because these seemed "to be meaningful for present-day New York City."[39]

The demographic characteristics of New York City's largest ethnic group—the Jewish community—which, as has been seen, originated from several nations, can probably best be studied through sample surveys of the HIP type. But in the study of other of New York's sizable ethnic communities—most prominent, the Italian—review of the decennial census returns for the foreign stock can play a very large part.

TABLE 86

Percent of Non-Puerto Rican Native White Population of New York City
of Foreign or Mixed Parentage by Age, 1950 and 1960

Age	1950*	1960†
Total, all ages	52.2	47.0
Under 5 years	20.9 ⎫	
5-14 years	34.2 ⎭	20.8
15-24 years	55.2	34.9
25-34 years	63.4	54.2
35-44 years	67.1	67.1
45-54 years	60.2	68.9
55-64 years	56.4	60.7
65-74 years	54.1	55.5
75 years and over	55.4	48.1

*Based on 20 percent sample.   †Based on 25 percent sample.
Source: Derived from statistics of the U.S. Bureau of the Census given in Appendix
Tables B-2 and B-6.

38. Nathan Glazer and Daniel P. Moynihan, *Beyond the Melting Pot* (Cambridge, Mass.: MIT Press, 1963), pp. 16-19. In one sense Glazer and Moynihan's whole book deals with ethnicity.

39. Jack Elinson, Paul W. Haberman, and Cyrille Gell, *Ethnic and Educational Data on Adults in New York City 1963-1964* (New York: School of Public Health and Administrative Medicine, Columbia University, 1967), p. i.

The foreign white stock of Italian origin has been first in numerical importance, representing over one-fifth of the total white population of foreign birth or parentage at each census since 1930 (see Appendix Table C-2). Next in importance has been the foreign white stock originating from Russia; at least nine-tenths of this group is of Jewish background. Ireland, Germany, Poland, Austria, Great Britain, and Hungary were each the origin of between 2 and 12 percent of the foreign white stock between 1930 and 1960.

The distribution of the foreign white stock from the principal areas of origin at the censuses of 1930, 1940, and 1960 by age and nativity category is presented in Appendix Table B-3. (Similar data were not available from the 1950 census.) In 1930 a majority of the foreign-born white from virtually every country were under 45 years of age; in 1960 most persons of foreign birth—except for natives of Germany, Czechoslovakia, and Canada—were over 55 years of age. The age composition of the native white of foreign or mixed parentage reflects the location in time of the major peak of immigration of their parents. Thus in 1930, the second generation of Italian, Russian, Polish, Austrian, and Hungarian descent were overwhelmingly under 25 years of age, while large majorities of the second-generation British, Irish, and Germans were above 25 years of age. By 1960, in consequence of reduced migration in the recent period, relatively few of the native whites of foreign or mixed parentage were under 25 years of age. However, the age distribution still reflected the timing of immigration of the first generation. Less than 15 percent of the second generation of Italian origin, for example, were 55 years of age and over, compared with over 30 percent of those of German or Irish origin.

When comparative statistics by country of origin (such as those in Appendix Table C-2) are examined, differences over time in the classification of given countries must be considered. The classic illustration of error occurred at the 1950 census when the statement of instruction to the enumerators that had appeared on the 1930 and 1940 census schedules to distinguish between Ireland and Northern Ireland was deleted. As a result, for the decade 1940 to 1950 the number of persons classified as having been born in Northern Ireland decreased by about 90 percent.[40] To provide comparability between censuses it seems advisable to combine data for Ireland (the Republic of Ireland) and Northern Ireland (part of the United Kingdom) whenever possible.

A review of census figures has indicated "that a completely accurate count of the foreign stock from the countries whose boundaries were changed as the result of World War I has never been achieved."[41] In general, Austria, Hungary, and Russia have been overreported at the expense of Poland, Czechoslovakia, and Yugoslavia. However, the

---

40. U.S. Bureau of the Census, *U.S. Census of Population: 1950, Nativity and Parentage* (Washington, 1954), p. 5.   41. *Ibid.*

patterns of over or underreporting have varied from census to census. What can appear to be an increase due to immigration may actually result from a classification change. A case in point: Yugoslavia. This foreign-stock group increased in number between 1950 and 1960, in contrast to the experience of almost every other European nationality. Census statisticians attributed the "growth" to the revision of procedures for processing entries of "Austria-Hungary," noting that "the apparent understatement in the number of persons of Yugoslavian origin, which was evident in the data for 1950, does not exist in the published 1960 statistics."[42]

Between 1930 and 1960, aside from the explainable increase for Yugoslavia, the foreign white stock population from Greece was the only European contingent to show notable growth (see Appendix Tables C-2 and C-3). The foreign white stock with this national background numbered 43,833 in 1930 and 55,584 in 1960. This growth is closely related to the fact that the Greek influx was the last of the many migration streams from Europe; the peak number of foreign-born natives of Greece was not reached until 1950. Second-generation whites of Greek descent were predominantly young, and therefore not subject to high mortality.

Of the numerous declines registered by the different country-of-origin groups the greatest proportionately has occurred among persons of Swedish origin. The 27,473 counted in 1960 was less than half the 66,978 enumerated in New York City in 1930.

In the 1950s, when the Puerto Rican population in the United States more than doubled, immigrants from other Caribbean islands also made proportionate gains, although on a considerably smaller scale. The number of natives of both Cuba and the Dominican Republic doubled between 1950 and 1960, and much of the inflow was directed toward New York City. New York State (separate figures were not available for New York City) contained 14,531 natives of Cuba in 1950 (white and nonwhite) and 30,632 in 1960, of whom 28,567 were in New York City. The 9,223 immigrants from the Dominican Republic living in New York City in 1960 represented no less than 78 percent of the total within the nation.[43]

Comparison in depth of foreign-stock groups can only be made between the 1930 and 1960 census returns. As noted earlier, the data for 1940 relating to the native population of foreign or mixed parentage have serious understatement, and unfortunately, very few details were published for 1950. Table 87 provides an illustrative comparison of the Italian foreign-stock population in 1930 and in 1960 within comparable age cohorts. It will be seen that persons of first- or second-generation Italian

42. U.S. Census of Population: 1960, Nativity and Parentage, p. x.
43. U.S. Census of Population: 1950, Nativity and Parentage, p. 73; U.S. Bureau of the Census, U.S. Census of Population: 1950, Nonwhite Population by Race (Washington, 1953), p. 82. U.S. Census of Population: 1960, Detailed Characteristics, New York PC (1)-34D, p. 99; Detailed Characteristics, United States Summary, p. 366; unpublished tabulations from the 1960 census made available by Martin Oling, New York City Planning Commission.

stock comprised 16.2 percent of the white population living in New York City in 1930 and 14.2 percent of the non-Puerto Rican whites in 1960. (The attempts to survive the 1930 age cohorts are rendered more difficult in terms of maintaining a closed population if Puerto Ricans—overwhelmingly inmigrants since 1930—are included.) The decline in the percentage of Italian origin reflects the fact that ethnic Italians of the third generation are not included in the census classification. After 1930 an ever-increasing share of the additions to New York's Italian community undoubtedly consisted of third-generation Americans (native whites of native parentage). Table 87 indicates that among white children in New York City 5 to 14 years of age in 1930, 22.7 percent were of Italian foreign stock. These same children were at the 1960 census at ages 35 to 44 years, and approximately the same proportion were again of Italian foreign stock. If one assumes ethnic Italians were proportionately represented at the younger ages, then in 1960 probably at least 22 percent of all white (excluding Puerto Rican) New Yorkers under 25 years of age were of Italian origin. This of course is in contrast to the census percentage—6.7 percent—which was limited in its measurement to the first- and second-generation group.

TABLE 87

Population of Italian Foreign Stock by Age Group Expressed as a Census Survival Cohort, New York City, 1930 and 1960

Age in 1930	Age in 1960	Census population, 1930		Census population, 1960*	
		Number	Percent of all white	Number	Percent of all non-Puerto Rican white
Total, all ages	Total, all ages	1,070,355†	16.2	858,601‡	14.2
—	Under 25 years	—	—	133,400	6.7
Under 5 years	25-34	100,832	19.8	137,898	18.3
5-14	35-44	251,732	22.7	182,243	22.2
15-24	45-54	228,774	18.7	171,020	18.6
25-44	55-74	320,507	13.8	203,225	15.0
45-64	75 and over	140,809	12.2	30,815	14.9
65 and over	—	27,219	10.5	—	—
Not reported	—	482	8.9	—	—

*Based on 25 percent sample.

†Since the foreign-born population under age 10 was not further subdivided by country of origin it was assumed that as in the general white population 79.7 percent were 5 to 9 years and 20.3 percent under 5 years. The Italian-born population under 10 years numbered 5,375.

‡Includes 942 persons classified as nonwhite.

Source: Derived from statistics of the U.S. Bureau of the Census given in Appendix Tables B-1, B-3, and B-6.

Some control for the effects of the migration from abroad of immigrants arriving after 1930 can be introduced by excluding foreign-born whites from consideration, and studying population movement solely among native whites of foreign or mixed parentage. Analysis based on survival of two age cohorts of white second-generation Americans living in New York City can provide clues important to a comparison of persons of Italian origin with persons of other backgrounds. Since outmigration from the city has been the predominant trend among the second-generation population of all origins, the principal measure produced by obtaining a ratio of survivors in 1960 per 100 members of the same population cohort in the 1930 census is of the relative impact of outmigration. Table 88 indicates that Italian-origin whites were least likely among major second-generation groups to have removed from New York City between 1930 and 1960. Persons of East European background (overwhelmingly Jews) occupied an intermediate position, while those of German background were most likely to have departed from the city.

TABLE 88
Cohorts of Native Whites of Foreign or Mixed Parentage, Selected Countries of Origin (of Parents), Aged 5-14 Years and Aged 15-24 Years in 1930, Followed to 1960, New York City
(in thousands)

Cohort and origin	1930 Census	1960 Census*	1960 survivors as percent of 1930 population
Population { 5-14 years in 1930 / 35-44 years in 1960 }			
Total	734.0	456.3	62.2
Italy	241.9	158.5	65.5
Russia, Poland, Austria, Hungary	306.5	188.5	61.5
Ireland, United Kingdom	70.8	38.8	54.8
Germany	25.8	13.1	50.6
All other	88.9	57.4	64.6
Population { 15-24 years in 1930 / 45-54 years in 1960 }			
Total	712.3	449.6	63.1
Italy	193.8	129.3	66.7
Russia, Poland, Austria, Hungary	301.9	190.8	63.2
Ireland, United Kingdom	88.3	52.3	59.3
Germany	47.2	26.2	55.5
All other	81.1	51.0	62.9

*Based on 25 percent sample.
Source: Derived from statistics of the U.S. Bureau of the Census given in Appendix Table B-3.

Many of the outmigrants from New York City moved no farther than the suburban counties. This is demonstrated in Table 89 which shows for the foreign-stock population of Italian origin the number residing in each county of the New York Standard Metropolitan Statistical Area in 1930 and 1960. This information, invaluable for the study of Italian migration streams within the metropolitan area, indicates that the areas of heaviest Italian concentration in 1930—Brooklyn and Manhattan—experienced substantial declines over the following decades. Within the city, only Queens showed a marked increase in its population of Italian origin. The four suburban counties witnessed heavy inmigration and increased their share of the area's Italian stock from 10.3 percent in 1930 to 23.8 percent in 1960.

The nonwhite population of foreign stock was classified by country of origin in 1960, but not by individual race. It may be assumed that among the 40,983 persons born or having parents born in the countries of Asia, race approximates national origin. The nonwhite foreign stock from China, for example, numbering 28,687, was close to the total number of Chinese enumerated in New York City (32,831). Very nearly all of the 121,539 nonwhite foreign stock from continents other than Asia may be assumed to be Negro. The great majority of these were West Indians (see Table 90).

TABLE 89

Population of Italian Foreign Stock in New York
SMSA by County of Residence, 1930 and 1960

Area	Number		Percent distribution	
	1930	1960*	1930	1960
Total, New York SMSA	1,192,746	1,126,843	100.0	100.0
New York City	1,070,355	858,601	89.7	76.2
Bronx	165,004	161,974	13.8	14.4
Kings	487,344	372,518	40.9	33.1
New York	260,702	89,434	21.9	7.9
Queens	127,381	201,698	10.7	17.9
Richmond	29,924	32,977	2.5	2.9
Suburbs	122,391	268,242	10.3	23.8
Nassau	24,652	108,646	2.1	9.6
Rockland	5,384	7,888	0.5	0.7
Suffolk	10,273	53,996	0.9	4.8
Westchester	82,082	97,712	6.9	8.7

*Based on 25 percent sample.

Source: Derived from data in U.S. Bureau of the Census, Fifteenth Census of the United States: 1930, Vol. III, Part 2 (Washington, 1933); U.S. Census of Population: 1960; General Social and Economic Characteristics, New York PC (1)-34C (Washington, 1962).

TABLE 90
Nativity and Parentage of Nonwhite Foreign Stock
by Country of Origin, New York City, 1960

Area	Total	Foreign born	Native born
Total	162,522	94,869	67,653
China	28,687	18,602	10,085
Japan	5,350	3,415	1,935
Philippines	3,844	2,849	995
Other Asia	3,102	2,348	754
Cuba	4,140	2,608	1,532
Dominican Republic	1,614	1,041	573
Haiti	2,584	1,916	668
Other West Indies	85,749	47,313	38,436
Panama	6,078	4,469	1,609
All other	21,374	10,308	11,066

Source: Unpublished statistics, U.S. Bureau of the Census.

As early as 1930 a majority of the foreign-born Negro population in the United States were residents of New York City (see Table 56). The foreign-born Negro population in the nation, unlike whites of foreign birth, had gradually increased in number by 1960. Nevertheless, the geographic detail provided by the Census Bureau for Negroes diminished almost to the vanishing point over the succeeding decades. The 1940 count was the last (prior to 1970) in which statistics were published for New York City.

In 1950, of 113,842 immigrant Negroes in the United States, 59,527 were enumerated in New York State, where it may be assumed all but a small number were residents of New York City.[44] In 1960 the foreign-born Negro population in the United States reached a new high of 125,322.[45] In the absence of even a figure for New York State, an estimate for New York City must be rough. Probably the best approximation of the foreign-born Negro population may be derived by assuming the number close to the total immigrant nonwhite population born in areas outside Asia. The estimate, based on data given in Table 90, is 67,655. The 1970 census showed the total for New York City had more than doubled to 159,066.

THE METROPOLITAN AREA

A review of population trends in New York City cannot be considered complete with an analysis only of what has transpired within the city

44. *U.S. Census of Population: 1950, Nonwhite Population by Race*, p. 84.
45. U.S. Bureau of the Census, *U.S. Census of Population: 1960, Nonwhite Population by Race* (Washington, 1963), p. 89.

limits. Increasingly, metropolitan New York—the city and its surrounding ring of counties—has become a more meaningful focus for study. Even in the first quarter of the present century tens of thousands of suburbanites commuted daily to workplaces in the central city. Since World War II there has been a commuter explosion, reflecting the mass exodus of urban residents to suburban locations. In addition, much industry has relocated beyond the city, producing to some extent reverse commuter streams. The patterns of the outward spread of settlement from New York have been quite complex. Indeed, a new literature has developed dealing with the subject.[46]

While it is not always easy to define a metropolitan area in contemporary America, where the accessibility provided by the automobile has rendered many old political boundaries obsolete, no area is so difficult to categorize as the New York metropolitan area. Just what configuration of territory is most appropriate would seem to depend upon the intent of the user of data. The boundaries defined range from the nine-county New York Standard Metropolitan Statistical Area of the U.S. Census Bureau (the five counties within the city plus Nassau, Rockland, Suffolk, and Westchester in New York State) to the twenty-two-county New York Metropolitan Region, embracing areas in New York, New Jersey, and Connecticut, of the Regional Plan Association. The use of different definitions can, of course, result in the appearance of very different, if not contradictory, data.[47]

Although no one definition can suit all purposes, it nevertheless is of value to see what counties are most appropriately associated with metropolitan New York in terms of the most traditional measure—job location. The county of residence of the approximately one-half million persons living outside New York City who indicated at the 1960 census that their place of employment was within the city is to be seen in Table 91. The percentage of the labor force these workers represented of all employed residents of their respective areas of residence is also given. The three counties sending the largest number of their residents to New York workplaces—Nassau, Westchester, and Bergen—accounted for more than half of the entire commuter inflow. Furthermore, among residents living in each of these three counties, more than 20 percent of all those who were employed worked in New York City. Over 15 percent of the labor force in three other counties—Suffolk, Hudson, and Rockland—also were employed

46. See, for example, the books in the New York Metropolitan Region Study, particularly Hoover and Vernon, *Anatomy of a Metropolis.*

47. This commonsense maxim is not infrequently overlooked. Net total inmigration between 1950 and 1960 to the area defined as the New York SMSA was 99,000; on the other hand, in the areas termed the New York Metropolitan Region the net total inmigration was 704,000. Derived from data in U.S. Bureau of the Census. "Components of Population Change, 1950 to 1960," *Current Population Reports*, Series P-23, No. 7 (November 1962).

in New York City. It would seem that any definition of metropolitan New York should include these six counties.[48]

The population composition of each of these counties by race and nativity at each federal census from 1900 to 1970 is shown in Table 65. Nassau County more than tripled in population between 1940 and 1970, while the number of persons residing in Suffolk County, farther out on Long Island, multiplied more than fivefold. Bergen County more than doubled and Rockland County more than tripled in this period. Westchester County, an older suburban area containing such established cities as Yonkers, Mount Vernon, and New Rochelle, grew more moderately. On the other hand, Hudson County has declined continuously since its peak level was reached in 1930. Hudson County has quite correctly been described as part of the inner core of the region rather than a sector of the suburban ring.[49] Its old congested cities—Jersey City, Bayonne, and Hoboken—have much the same industrial character of parts of Brooklyn, Queens, and Manhattan.

TABLE 91

Labor Force Resident in Selected Counties
Working in New York City, 1960

Area	Number of persons (in thousands)	Percent of labor force residing in county working in New York City
Nassau County, N.Y.	182.6	40.5
Westchester County, N.Y.	84.7	28.0
Bergen County, N.J.	64.9	22.3
Suffolk County, N.Y.	33.6	16.7
Hudson County, N.J.	37.1	15.9
Rockland County, N.Y.	6.9	15.8
Putnam County, N.Y.	1.0	9.8
Union County, N.J.	13.8	7.3
Morris County, N.J.	6.2	6.9
Fairfield County, Conn.	16.4	6.4
Greenwich Town	4.1	19.9
Balance of county	12.3	5.5
Essex County, N.J.	19.2	5.6
Monmouth County, N.J.	5.9	5.3
Middlesex County, N.J.	7.2	4.7
Passaic County, N.J.	6.2	4.1
Somerset County, N.J.	2.0	3.9

Source: Derived from data in U.S. Bureau of the Census, U.S. Census of Population: 1960; Journey to Work, Final Report PC(2)-6B (Washington, 1963).

48. Bergen and Hudson, the two New Jersey counties, are not included by the Census Bureau in the New York SMSA despite their meeting the rule regarding integration which states that "a county is regarded as integrated with the county or counties containing the central cities of the area if . . . 15 percent of the workers living in the county work in the county or counties containing central cities of the area." For discussion on this point, see Ira Rosenwaike, "A Critical Examination of the Designation of Standard Metropolitan Statistical Areas," *Social Forces*, XLVIII, 3 (March 1970), 330-31.

49. Hoover and Vernon, *Anatomy of a Metropolis*, p. 7.

Three New Jersey counties—Essex, Union, and Morris—are classified by the U.S. Census Bureau as comprising the Newark Standard Metropolitan Statistical Area. In each of these counties about 5 to 7 percent of the resident labor force works in New York City. Newark (1950 population—439,000; 1970 population—382,000), like New York City, has lost heavily to suburbs since World War II, although the remainder of Essex County has continued to grow. Some of the suburbs in these three counties, as well as in Monmouth County, are more oriented toward New York than to Newark. The expanding commuter fields (areas sending commuters to a particular workplace) of New York have led to rapid growth in the peripheral counties of New Jersey, especially Bergen, Morris, and Middlesex, which have also attracted former residents of Newark, Jersey City, Elizabeth, and Paterson. These older New Jersey cities have been described as becoming satellites of New York, engulfed or surrounded by the New York metropolitan area.[50]

Suburbia has also extended north of Westchester County into Putnam County, almost 10 percent of whose labor force commutes to New York City. While it is by far the least populous of the counties shown in Table 91, it is currently the fastest growing suburban area in the state. Putnam County increased its population by 79 percent between 1960 and 1970, reaching a total of 56,696 at the latter date.[51]

Of the territory surrounding New York City probably none has so many overlapping commuter fields as Fairfield County, Connecticut. New York's commuting field reaches in and overlaps in complex ways the labor markets of Stamford, Norwalk, Bridgeport, and even Waterbury and New Haven.[52] In consequence, a dual personality has been attributed to Fairfield County.[53] A group of suburbs, extending from the New York State line, led by Greenwich (20 percent of whose resident labor force works in New York City), have Manhattan as their nucleus, but much of the county's economic life focuses on Bridgeport (1970 population 157,000), an old industrial center and the second largest city in Connecticut.

It is essential that New York (and other major cities) be defined in terms of a metropolitan area when studying internal migration streams in the United States after World War II. Limiting analysis to the central city itself, the urban to suburban flow obscures all other movements. During the 1940s and the 1950s, as in every measurable period over the preceding century, the nation's largest metropolitan area functioned more as a point

50. John E. Bebout and Ronald J. Grele, *Where Cities Meet: The Urbanization of New Jersey* (Princeton, N.J.: Van Nostrand, 1964), p. 79.
51. U.S. Bureau of the Census, *U.S. Census of Population: 1970 Final Report PC (1)-B34* (Washington, 1971), p. 72.
52. U.S. Bureau of the Census, *Metropolitan Area Definition: A Re-Evaluation of Concept and Statistical Practice.* Bureau of the Census Working Paper No. 28 (Washington, 1969), p. 27.
53. Hoover and Vernon, *Anatomy of a Metropolis*, p. 4.

of origin of migrants than as a destination among the native-born population within the United States. The growth of the New York City area continually has been dependent upon successive waves arriving from overseas. Equally consistent has been the powerful tide of outmigration of native New Yorkers.

It would be interesting to measure the important contribution of natives of New York City in the more rapidly expanding metropolitan and nonmetropolitan areas of the nation. This cannot be done with any accuracy, however, since federal censuses have not classified birthplace beyond state of birth. Nevertheless, since the 1960 census did provide statistics of migrants between 1955 and 1960 cross-classified by place of origin and destination, the movement of New Yorkers in this half-decade can be traced. It has already been seen (Table 76) that 721,184 persons whose place of residence in 1955 was the New York SMSA were counted as residents of other areas in the nation in 1960. By comparison, only 367,017 persons living in the New York SMSA in 1960 reported they had lived elsewhere in the United States in 1955, resulting in a net loss to the New York SMSA through internal migration of 354,167 persons in the five-year span.

The net outflow in 1955-60 was particularly strong to two widely separated areas: metropolitan Los Angeles (40,930 persons) and Florida (79,144 persons). Of the net movement to Florida, 32,579 was directed toward metropolitan Miami (Dade County) and 46,565 to the balance of the Sunshine State. The New York SMSA also experienced a net loss in its population exchange with most of the major metropolitan areas. The combined net loss resulting from the excess of outmigrants over inmigrants equalled 33,255 for the inter-metropolitan movement between the New York SMSA and the ten metropolitan areas ranking after New York and Los Angeles (Chicago, Philadelphia, Detroit, San Francisco-Oakland, Boston, Pittsburgh, St. Louis, Washington, Cleveland, and Baltimore).[54]

Is the net migration loss figure of 354,167 in the 1955-60 period excessive because outmigration, when measured in terms of the rather restricted boundaries of the SMSA, includes the movement to New Jersey suburbs? This question might be answered by compiling mobility data that would provide a figure of net migration for a metropolitan area embracing the New York SMSA plus Bergen and Hudson counties in New Jersey (the two New Jersey counties most closely linked to New York City, as demonstrated in Table 91). The published census statistics do not enable such a compilation, since detailed mobility data for Bergen and Passaic counties are combined. However, an extended area consisting of

---

54. These migration statistics are derived from U.S. Bureau of the Census, *U.S. Census of Population: 1960. Mobility for Metropolitan Areas* (Washington, 1963), Table 2; also *U.S. Census of Population: 1960. Mobility for States and State Economic Areas* (Washington, 1963), Table 16.

the New York SMSA and the three New Jersey counties, while not the most desirable choice, may give somewhat more meaningful a picture than that presented by New York SMSA statistics alone. Hudson County, according to the 1960 census statistics of population mobility, had a net loss due to internal migration in 1955-60 of 57,343 (38,605 inmigrants versus 95,948 outmigrants). Bergen and Passaic experienced a combined net gain of 20,300 persons (149,727 inmigrants versus 129,427 outmigrants). Of the net loss of 354,167 that has been noted for the New York SMSA about one-seventh—52,753 persons—are accounted for by population transfers with these neighboring counties. When the interchange between the New Jersey areas is considered (a net loss by Hudson to Bergen and Passaic of 24,251 persons), the merged picture is of a net loss through internal migration beyond the boundaries of the combined twelve-county area of 400,896 persons. This consists of a net loss from the New York SMSA amounting to 302,414 persons, of 40,535 persons from Hudson County, and of 58,947 from Bergen and Passaic.[55]

Accordingly, we find that when the mobility statistics for the population of the New Jersey counties most associated with New York City are combined with those for the New York SMSA, the net outmigration from the merged area is greater than the loss from the New York SMSA alone. By whatever definition is used then, the New York metropolitan area is evinced as having a role as a source of internal migrant streams more prominent than its role as a recipient.

At the 1960 census 2,710,697 persons who were born in New York State were enumerated within the United States living outside their state of birth. States containing the largest number of natives of New York were: New Jersey (600,109), California (400,763), and Florida (286,940).[56] Although it is not possible to estimate how many of these migrants were natives of New York City, it seems reasonable to suggest their number runs to more than one half of the total.

Of the 990,488 persons classified as outmigrants from New York State in the 1955-60 period, no fewer than 64 percent lived in the New York SMSA in 1955. Among outmigrants from New York State moving to New Jersey during 1955-60, 88 percent originated from the New York SMSA (159,536 of 181,346). Among outmigrants from the Empire State in this half-decade, 62 percent of those who moved to Florida, and a like percentage of those who moved to California, had been residents of the nine-county New York SMSA in 1955.[57]

55. Derived from U.S. Bureau of the Census, *Mobility for Metropolitan Areas*, Table 2.

56. U.S. Bureau of the Census, *U.S. Census of Population: 1960. State of Birth* (Washington, 1963), pp. 8, 21.

57. U.S. Bureau of the Census, *Mobility for States and State Economic Areas*, Table 16, Table 35.

At the 1960 census 1,359,892 natives of states other than New York were counted living in the New York SMSA.[58] Conversely, it may be very crudely calculated that perhaps 1.7 to 1.8 million natives of the New York SMSA were then living outside of New York State. The dimensions of outmigration from metropolitan New York thus appear very great, and not unworthy of detailed study.

CONCLUSION

In summary, the relatively insignificant growth between 1940 and 1970 in New York's total population—from 7.5 to 7.9 million—masked very dramatic shifts in population composition within the city. The white population (exclusive of Puerto Ricans) experienced unparalleled massive losses through outmigration in this period, falling from approximately seven million to five million. By contrast, the number of Negro residents grew extremely rapidly, from 458,000 to 1,668,000. The Puerto Rican population also increased with startling speed, climbing from an insignificant group of under 100,000 to a major segment approaching one million.

In the same time period (1940 to 1970) the population living in four suburban counties in New York State (Nassau, Suffolk, Westchester, and Rockland) rose from 1.3 million to 3.7 million. The extensive loss in the white population within the central city to a considerable extent could be attributed to movement to these counties. Nevertheless, the whole New York metropolitan area experienced substantial net outmigration of whites to other sections of the nation. Opportunities in Los Angeles, Washington, D.C., and other growth areas attracted the city's youth, while retirement havens in Florida beckoned the aged. New York has long been justly famous as a city attracting vast numbers of immigrants from around the globe; it should also be viewed as a metropolis that has perpetually sent out across the country a large proportion of its native sons.

58. U.S. Bureau of the Census, *State of Birth*, p. 175.

Appendix A

BIRTH AND DEATH STATISTICS
NEW YORK CITY, 1804-1969

Tables A-1 through A-11 have been compiled from data appearing in reports (usually annual) of the Health Departments of the City of New York and of the State of New York. The pre-1900 statistics are from the *Annual Report of the Board of Health for . . . 1906* of the New York City Health Department.

APPENDIX A

TABLE A-1
Recorded Deaths in New York City, 1804-1900, and in Brooklyn, 1866-1900

Year	Deaths	Year	Deaths	Year	Deaths
New York City					
1804	2,084	1837	8,626	1870	27,175
1805	2,297	1838	7,911	1871	26,976
1806	2,174	1839	7,910	1872	32,647
1807	2,236	1840	8,469	1873	29,084
1808	1,950	1841	9,093	1874	28,727
1809	2,038	1842	9,154	1875	30,709
1810	2,073	1843	8,659	1876	29,152
1811	2,431	1844	8,890	1877	26,203
1812	2,503	1845	10,122	1878	27,008
1813	2,335	1846	11,411	1879	28,342
1814	1,844	1847	14,844	1880	31,937
1815	2,511	1848	14,892	1881	38,624
1816	3,000	1849	22,605	1882	37,924
1817	2,409	1850	15,826	1883	34,011
1818	3,106	1851	20,738	1884	35,034
1819	3,178	1852	20,196	1885	35,682
1820	3,522	1853	21,979	1886	37,351
1821	3,422	1854	28,473	1887	38,933
1822	3,212	1855	24,448	1888	40,175
1823	3,551	1856	21,748	1889	39,679
1824	4,224	1857	22,811	1890	40,103
1825	4,920	1858	23,269	1891	43,659
1826	4,961	1859	22,745	1892	44,329
1827	5,139	1860	24,760	1893	44,486
1828	4,843	1861	24,525	1894	41,175
1829	4,734	1862	23,150	1895	43,420
1830	5,522	1863	26,617	1896	41,622
1831	6,347	1864	25,792	1897	38,877
1832	10,257	1865	25,767	1898	40,438*
1833	5,689	1866	26,815	1899	39,911*
1834	8,937	1867	23,159	1900	43,227*
1835	7,096	1868	24,889		
1836	8,068	1869	25,167		
Brooklyn					
1866	8,683	1878	11,075	1890	19,827
1867	8,389	1879	11,569	1891	21,349
1868	8,750	1880	13,222	1892	20,807
1869	8,759	1881	14,533	1893	21,017
1870	9,546	1882	15,014	1894	21,183
1871	10,259	1883	13,758	1895	22,568
1872	10,648	1884	14,116	1896	22,501
1873	10,968	1885	15,369	1897	20,674
1874	11,011	1886	15,790	1898	21,989*
1875	12,470	1887	17,078	1899	21,649*
1876	12,334	1888	16,061	1900	23,507*
1877	11,362	1889	18,480		

*Within boundaries prior to consolidation of 1898.

TABLE A-2
Death Rates in New York City and Brooklyn, 1866-1900
(per 1,000 population)

Year	New York City	Brooklyn	Year	New York City	Brooklyn
1866	34.9	27.5	1883	25.8	22.0
1867	28.6	25.1	1884	25.8	21.9
1868	29.2	24.7	1885	25.6	23.1
1869	28.1	23.3	1886	26.0	22.7
1870	28.8	24.0	1887	26.3	23.3
1871	28.2	24.8	1888	26.4	21.2
1872	33.7	24.8	1889	25.3	23.6
1873	29.6	24.5	1890	24.9	24.5
1874	27.9	23.7	1891	26.3	25.6
1875	29.4	25.8	1892	26.0	24.2
1876	27.1	24.7	1893	25.3	23.7
1877	23.7	22.0	1894	22.8	22.0
1878	23.7	20.8	1895	23.2	22.7
1879	24.1	21.0	1896	24.8	21.8
1880	26.4	23.3	1897	20.0	19.4
1881	31.0	24.8	1898	20.5*	20.0
1882	29.6	24.8	1899	19.8*	19.1
			1900	21.0*	20.1

*Within boundaries prior to consolidation of 1898.

TABLE A-3
Birth and Death Rates in New York City, 1900-69
(per 1,000 population)

Year	Birth Rate	Death Rate	Year	Birth Rate	Death Rate
			Recorded		
1900	N.A.	20.6	1915	27.0	14.6
1901	N.A.	19.7	1916	25.9	14.6
1902	N.A.	18.3	1917	26.2	14.5
1903	N.A.	17.6	1918	25.2	17.9
1904	N.A.	19.6	1919	23.4	13.3
1905	N.A.	17.9	1920	23.4	12.9
1906	N.A.	17.9	1921	23.1	11.1
1907	N.A.	18.0	1922	21.8	11.7
1908	N.A.	16.1	1923	21.3	11.4
1909	N.A.	15.9	1924	21.1	11.5
1910	27.0	16.0	1925	20.4	11.4
1911	27.6	15.5	1926	19.5	11.8
1912	27.3	14.7	1927	19.6	10.7
1913	26.8	14.6	1928	18.8	11.6
1914	27.4	14.6	1929	18.2	11.3
			1930	17.7	10.8
			Resident		
1930	17.5	11.0	1950	19.0	10.4
1931	16.3	11.3	1951	19.7	10.5
1932	15.4	10.8	1952	19.8	10.7
1933	14.4	10.8	1953	19.5	10.9
1934	14.0	10.9	1954	19.7	10.5
1935	13.8	10.7	1955	19.8	10.8
1936	13.4	11.0	1956	19.9	10.8
1937	13.8	10.9	1957	20.2	11.2
1938	13.6	10.3	1958	20.4	11.3
1939	13.6	10.5	1959	20.5	11.4
1940	14.0	10.5	1960	20.3	11.4
1941	14.9	10.3	1961	20.5	11.5
1942	17.0	10.3	1962	20.2	11.6
1943	17.3	11.2	1963	20.6	11.8
1944	15.7	10.6	1964	20.3	11.6
1945	16.4	10.6	1965	19.5	11.6
1946	19.3	10.4	1966	18.8	11.7
1947	21.6	10.7	1967	17.8	11.6
1948	19.7	10.9	1968	17.3	11.8
1949	19.4	10.4	1969	17.8	11.4

N.A. = Birth rates not shown for these years as birth registration was incomplete.

TABLE A-4
Recorded Births and Deaths by Color, New York City, 1910-40

Year	Births			Deaths		
	Total	White	Nonwhite	Total	White	Nonwhite
1910	129,080	127.022	2,058	76,742	74,330	2,412
1911	134,544	132,209	2,335	75,423	72,980	2,443
1912	135,655	133,215	2,440	73,008	70,424	2,584
1913	135,134	132,699	2,435	73,902	71,421	2,481
1914	140,647	138,115	2,532	74,803	72,141	2,662
1915	141,256	138,615	2,641	76,193	73,430	2,763
1916	137,664	135,095	2,569	77,801	75,084	2,717
1917	141,564	138,516	3,048	78,575	75,606	2,969
1918	138,046	134,700	3,346	98,119	94,208	3,911
1919	130,377	126,697	3,680	74,433	71,053	3,380
1920	132,856	128,646	4,210	73,249	69,864	3,385
1921	134,241	129,689	4,552	64,257	61,223	3,034
1922	129,684	124,979	4,705	69,690	66,376	3,314
1923	129,160	123,982	5,178	69,452	65,875	3,577
1924	130,436	124,618	5,818	71,252	67,415	3,837
1925	128,790	122,478	6,312	71,864	67,614	4,250
1926	125,515	119,028	6,487	76,082	71,496	4,586
1927	128,889	121,556	7,333	70,430	65,889	4,541
1928	126,332	119,009	7,323	78,091	72,701	5,390
1929	124,404	116,982	7,422	77,482	72,356	5,126
1930	122,811	115,114	7,697	74,888	69,430	5,458
1931	115,621	108,340	7,281	77,418	71,612	5,806
1932	109,878	102,544	7,334	74,319	68,856	5,463
1933	103,500	96,314	7,186	75,153	69,438	5,715
1934	101,239	94,410	6,829	75,857	70,095	5,762
1935	100,657	93,677	6,980	75,057	69,075	5,982
1936	98,507	91,744	6,763	77,638	71,340	6,298
1937	101,988	94,411	7,577	77,465	71,264	6,201
1938	102,045	94,390	7,655	73,775	68,003	5,772
1939	102,261	94,461	7,800	75,439	69,572	5,867
1940	107,287	99,005	8,282	76,008	70,177	5,831

TABLE A-5

Resident Births by Race and Nativity, New York City,
1940-67

Year	Total all births	White			Nonwhite		
		Total	Native*	Foreign	Total	Negro	Other races
1940	104,646	96,365	76,788	19,577	8,281	8,082	199
1941	111,536	102,795	84,039	18,756	8,741	8,512	229
1942	128,542	119,482	100,199	19,283	9,060	8,877	183
1943	131,228	121,176	102,482	18,694	10,052	9,867	185
1944	119,910	109,067	93,337	15,730	10,843	10,638	205
1945	126,101	114,315	99,206	15,109	11,786	11,576	210
1946	149,334	134,666	119,209	15,457	14,668	14,403	265
1947	167,571	149,251	132,489	16,762	18,320	17,954	366
1948	153,997	133,786	119,227	14,559	20,211	19,443	768
1949	152,196	130,582	116,490	14,092	21,614	21,413	201
1950	150,373	127,874	113,927	13,947	22,499	21,590	909
1951	155,302	131,536	117,561	13,975	23,766	22,904	862
1952	155,955	131,761	117,647	14,114	24,194	23,330	864
1953	153,055	128,182	114,955	13,227	24,873	24,057	816
1954	154,975	128,532	115,166	13,366	26,443	25,620	823
1955	155,438	127,293	113,925	13,368	28,145	27,284	861
1956	156,034	125,948	112,276	13,672	30,086	29,154	932
1957	158,228	126,852	112,789	14,063	31,376	30,448	928
1958	159,286	125,891	111,515	14,376	33,395	32,403	992
1959	159,470	124,704	109,835	14,869	34,766	33,646	1,120
1960	157,711	122,485	107,546	14,939	35,226	34,035	1,191
1961	160,128	122,694	106,720	15,974	37,434	36,251	1,183
1962	157,750	118,981	102,433	16,548	38,769	37,544	1,225
1963	160,779	119,160	101,589	17,571	41,619	40,180	1,439
1964	159,164	116,601	98,413	18,188	42,563	41,114	1,449
1965	153,128	110,960	92,872	18,088	42,168	40,578	1,590
1966	147,415	106,310	88,317	17,993	41,105	39,609	1,496
1967	140,347	100,830	82,542	18,288	39,517	37,844	1,673

*Includes nativity not stated.

TABLE A-6

Resident Deaths by Race and Nativity, New York City,
1940-67

Year	Total all deaths	White				Nonwhite		
		Total	Native	Foreign	Not stated	Total	Negro	Other races
1940	78,404	70,177*	32,867*	36,448*	862*	5,831*	5,616*	215*
1941	77,327	71,063	32,708	37,476	879	6,264	5,974	290
1942	78,016	72,032	33,696	37,478	858	5,984	5,730	254
1943	85,418	78,769	36,471	41,324	974	6,649	6,342	307
1944	80,646	73,941	34,196	38,859	886	6,705	6,427	278
1945	81,618	74,772	34,652	39,159	961	6,846	6,514	332
1946	80,737	73,692	33,891	38,689	1,112	7,045	6,745	300
1947	83,448	76,158	35,117	39,633	1,408	7,290	7,027	263
1948	84,864	76,966	35,172	40,126	1,668	7,898	7,604	294
1949	81,543	74,000	34,244	38,248	1,508	7,543	7,288	255
1950	82,278	74,419	34,481	38,413	1,525	7,859	7,596	263
1951	82,869	74,960	34,493	38,987	1,480	7,909	7,626	283
1952	84,694	76,277	35,355	39,419	1,503	8,417	8,109	308
1953	85,648	77,247	35,623	39,971	1,653	8,401	8,082	319
1954	82,624	74,385	34,638	38,227	1,520	8,239	7,927	312
1955	85,038	76,273	35,673	39,101	1,499	8,765	8,452	313
1956	84,429	75,386	35,601	38,346	1,439	9,043	8,716	327
1957	87,577	77,420	36,552	39,446	1,422	10,157	9,747	410
1958	87,946	77,650	37,710	38,448	1,492	10,296	9,929	367
1959	88,845	77,963	37,604	38,679	1,680	10,882	10,488	394
1960	88,943	77,771	38,111	37,958	1,702	11,172	10,785	387
1961	89,899	78,135	38,386	37,932	1,817	11,764	11,355	409
1962	90,431	78,277	39,002	37,523	1,752	12,154	11,730	424
1963	92,432	79,730	39,802	38,060	1,868	12,702	12,259	443
1964	91,135	78,106	39,619	36,858	1,629	13,029	12,561	468
1965	91,159	77,822	39,803	36,327	1,692	13,337	12,859	478
1966	92,226	78,372	40,466	36,265	1,641	13,854	13,404	450
1967	91,054	76,761	39,966	35,244	1,551	14,293	13,806	487

*By place of occurrence. Aggregate by place of occurrence: 76,008.

TABLE A-7
Recorded Births by Birthplace of Mother, New York City, 1910-32

Year	Total all births	United States*	Foreign† Total	Austria-Hungary	England, Scotland	Germany	Ireland	Italy	Russia, Poland	All other
1910	129,080	40,411	88,669	12,558	1,898	4,732	7,774	28,660	26,714	6,3:
1911	134,544	43,952	90,592	14,521	2,274	5,253	7,669	28,652	25,759	6,4
1912	135,655	43,725	91,930	14,778	2,138	4,160	7,842	30,044	25,714	7,2
1913	135,134	44,345	90,789	14,392	2,085	3,653	7,671	29,976	25,412	7,6
1914	140,647	46,104	94,543	15,244	2,069	3,620	7,293	31,598	26,861	7,8
1915	141,256	48,147	93,109	15,476	2,040	3,267	7,188	30,235	26,741	8,1
1916	137,664	48,853	88,811	14,518	1,856	3,032	6,745	29,541	25,360	7,7
1917	141,564	49,922	91,642	14,933	1,979	2,904	6,963	29,876	26,768	8,2
1918	138,046‡	—	—	—	—	—	—	—	—	—
1919	130,377	52,025	78,352	12,115	1,598	1,938	5,748	24,632	23,089	9,2
1920	132,856	56,929	75,927	10,633	1,672	1,631	5,767	24,895	21,770	9,5
1921	134,241	58,157	76,084	9,787	1,778	1,587	5,641	25,239	21,598	10,4
1922	129,684	57,610	72,074	8,959	1,738	1,377	5,234	24,123	20,127	10,5
1923	129,160	58,475	70,685	8,148	1,882	1,388	5,087	23,106	20,108	10,9
1924	130,436	60,974	69,462	7,726	1,888	1,628	4,916	22,324	18,878	12,1
1925	128,790	61,979	66,811	7,073	2,002	1,851	4,787	20,905	18,199	11,9
1926	125,515	62,430	63,085	6,346	2,033	2,101	4,723	19,158	16,566	12,1
1927	128,889	66,409	62,480	6,027	2,100	2,450	5,098	18,514	15,919	12,3
1928	126,332	67,532	58,800	5,512	2,131	2,673	5,301	16,446	14,899	11,8
1929	124,404	67,887	56,517	4,977	2,135	2,846	5,608	15,048	13,633	12,2
1930	122,811	69,260	53,551	4,435§	2,180	2,978	5,840	13,791	12,420**	11,9
1931	115,621	67,507	48,114	3,592§	2,094	2,750	5,857	11,964	10,705**	11,1
1932	109,878	67,039	42,839	2,981§	1,882	2,645	5,750	10,211	9,330**	10,0

*Includes nativity not reported.　　　†Includes U.S. possessions.　　　‡Nativity not available.

§Beginning 1930 data available separately for Austria and Hungary as follows: Austria, 1930, 3,288; 19 2,656; 1932, 2,149; Hungary, 1930, 1,147; 1931, 936; 1932, 832.

**Beginning 1930 data available separately for Russia and Poland, as follows: Russia, 1930, 8,958; 1931 7,541; 1932, 6,427; Poland, 1930, 3,462; 1931, 3,164; 1932, 2,903.

TABLE A-8

Recorded White Births by Birthplace of Mother,
New York City, 1935-40

Birthplace	1935	1936	1937	1938	1939	1940
Total white births	93,677	91,744	94,411	94,390	94,461	99,005
United States	62,836	63,522	67,622*	70,053	73,967	79,116
Puerto Rico	†	†	1,828	1,709	‡	‡
Foreign countries	30,841	28,215	26,778	22,623	20,488	19,862
Austria	1,483	1,227	1,148	946 ⎱	2,836	2,969
Germany	2,501	2,129	2,204	2,104 ⎰		
Great Britain	1,611	1,521	1,458	1,265	1,247	1,207
Hungary	623	546	533	459	449	467
Ireland	5,137	4,966	4,731	4,257	3,999	3,731
Italy	6,281	5,548	5,078	4,565	3,956	3,692
Poland	2,477	2,331	2,333	2,141	2,064	2,020
Russia	4,303	3,785	3,480	2,956	2,434	2,293
All other	6,425	6,162	3,985	3,930	3,503	3,483
Not stated	—	7	11	5	6	27

*Includes 20 births to mothers born in U.S. possessions other than Puerto Rico.
†Included with foreign-born mothers.
‡Included with mothers born in the United States.

TABLE A-9

Recorded Deaths by Birthplace of Decedent, New York City, 1900-32

Year	Total all deaths	Native	Foreign born Total*	Austria†	Germany	Great Britain‡	Ireland	Italy	Poland	Russia	Scandinavia	All other	Not stated
1900	70,872	45,356	24,873	955	7,257	1,942	9,299	1,620	88	1,241	731	1,740	643
1901	70,720	44,139	25,901	1,005	7,277	2,025	9,664	1,928	67	1,410	740	1,785	680
1902	68,085	43,539	23,929	1,089	6,652	1,816	8,255	2,048	78	1,475	761	1,755	617
1903	67,864	41,829	25,405	1,240	6,845	1,928	8,864	2,220	97	1,745	729	1,737	630
1904	78,060	48,387	28,784	1,411	7,767	2,059	9,743	2,764	119	2,087	842	1,992	889
1905	73,714	46,279	26,992	1,358	7,018	1,926	9,207	2,448	140	2,047	760	2,088	443
1906	76,203	47,552	28,191	1,521	6,946	2,057	9,104	2,850	185	2,516	861	2,151	460
1907	79,205	49,034	29,661	1,732	7,198	2,117	9,497	2,995	163	2,670	890	2,399	510
1908	73,072	45,933	26,721	1,751	6,493	1,878	8,237	2,581	123	2,659	820	2,179	418
1909	74,105	46,363	27,359	1,833	6,645	1,916	8,210	2,824	122	2,776	833	2,200	383
1910	76,742	47,711	28,663	1,877	6,765	1,947	8,594	3,017	160	3,091	899	2,313	368
1911	75,423	45,815	29,125	1,960	6,836	2,024	8,548	3,125	145	3,281	875	2,331	483
1912	73,008	44,205	28,361	2,043	6,479	1,881	7,972	3,177	166	3,323	876	2,444	442
1913	73,902	44,447	29,043	2,130	6,501	1,953	7,938	3,445	174	3,502	933	2,467	412
1914	74,803	43,966	30,490	2,324	6,836	1,839	7,977	3,599	157	4,020	870	2,868	347
1915	76,193	45,254	30,648	2,597	6,549	2,011	7,958	3,593	165	4,173	974	2,628	291
1916	77,801	46,362	31,092	2,603	6,555	1,972	8,080	3,628	189	4,328	998	2,739	347
1917	78,575	45,534	32,665	2,797	6,549	2,063	8,241	3,959	251	4,599	1,052	3,154	376
1918	98,119	57,537	40,218	3,997	6,243	2,143	7,742	6,589	509	6,937	1,423	4,635	364
1919	74,433	43,493	30,588	2,840	5,410	1,875	6,160	4,196	442	5,011	1,109	3,545	352
1920	73,249	43,121	29,778	2,824	5,411	1,687	5,680	4,225	657	4,862	909	3,523	350
1921	64,257	36,856	27,082	2,545	4,772	1,573	5,158	3,836	668	4,511	889	3,130	319
1922	69,690	39,696	29,667	2,670	5,071	1,684	5,698	4,239	842	4,958	941	3,564	327
1923	69,452	37,893	31,102	2,405	5,275	1,754	6,073	4,328	946	5,190	982	4,149	457
1924	71,252	39,443	31,232	2,268	5,290	1,758	5,719	4,332	1,056	5,380	1,039	4,390	577
1925	71,864	38,643	32,632	2,400	5,249	1,864	5,870	4,584	1,155	5,666	1,138	4,706	589
1926	76,082	41,547	33,840	2,492	5,306	2,005	6,048	4,963	1,273	5,920	1,110	4,723	695
1927	70,430	37,937	31,768	2,422	4,968	1,787	5,384	4,558	1,266	5,490	1,118	4,775	725
1928	78,091	42,667	34,591	2,528	5,173	1,897	5,778	5,138	1,410	6,179	1,191	5,297	833
1929	77,482	40,886	35,774	2,753	5,198	1,950	5,691	5,482	1,455	6,607	1,248	5,390	822
1930	74,888	39,247	34,822	2,694	5,032	1,825	5,316	5,213	1,541	6,624	1,285	5,292	819
1931	77,418	40,561	36,025	2,817	4,925	1,861	5,503	5,560	1,827	6,638	1,245	5,649	832
1932	74,319	38,040	35,513	2,755	4,864	1,757	5,159	5,500	1,917	6,851	1,182	5,528	766

TABLE A-10
Recorded Deaths by Birthplace of Foreign-born White Decedents, New York City, 1935-48

Year	Total	Germany, Austria*	Great Britain	Hungary	Ireland†	Italy	Poland	Russia	Scandinavia	All other‡
35	34,617§	—	—	—	—	—	—	—	—	—
36	36,388	7,382	1,807	1,111	5,018	5,912	2,201	7,431	1,310	4,216
37	36,513	7,341	1,837	1,115	4,843	6,184	2,337	7,389	1,237	4,230
38	34,941	6,965	1,669	1,131	4,513	5,884	2,412	7,369	1,209	3,789
39	36,120	7,170	1,758	1,158	4,682	6,039	2,593	7,569	1,265	3,886
40	36,448	7,476	1,624	1,167	4,434	6,194	2,537	7,768	1,258	3,990
41	35,955	7,227	1,636	1,125	4,296	6,436	2,464	7,697	1,184	3,890
42	36,218	7,342	1,662	1,189	4,249	6,370	2,486	7,745	1,247	3,928
43	39,991	7,749	1,838	1,252	4,751	6,997	2,906	8,653	1,383	4,462
44	37,591	7,207	1,678	1,245	4,167	6,772	2,883	8,095	1,317	4,227
45	37,850	7,111	1,698	1,193	4,289	6,649	2,869	8,254	1,368	4,419
46	37,214	7,014	1,664	1,174	4,142	6,709	3,084	7,779	1,292	4,356
47	38,022	7,329	1,672	1,225	4,101	6,770	3,196	8,054	1,263	4,412
48	38,325	7,086	1,725	1,212	4,211	6,943	3,189	7,786	1,271	4,902

*Austria separately available only for 1936 (2,769) and 1937 (2,789).
†Includes Irish Free State and Northern Ireland.
‡Includes Puerto Rico, 1935-37.
§Not available by country.

TABLE A-11
Recorded Births and Deaths of Puerto Ricans by Color, New York City, 1950-69

Year	Births			Deaths		
	Total	White	Nonwhite	Total	White	Nonwhite
1950	9,206	8,672	534	734	682	52
1951	10,479	9,896	583	906	834	72
1952	12,215	11,316	899	1,041	973	68
1953	14,431	13,530	901	1,094	1,044	50
1954	16,891	15,918	973	1,100	1,045	55
1955	18,365	17,289	1,076	1,149	1,105	44
1956	19,545	18,551	994	1,230	1,177	53
1957	20,553	19,593	960	1,422	1,342	80
1958	21,863	21,007	856	1,500	1,411	89
1959	22,894	21,829	1,065	1,600	1,525	75
1960	24,022	23,007	1,015	1,703	1,622	81
1961	24,746	23,738	1,008	1,781	1,682	99
1962	24,975	24,033	942	1,836	1,758	78
1963	25,563	24,549	1,014	1,930	1,845	85
1964	25,081	23,973	1,108	1,937	1,848	89
1965	24,498	23,332	1,166	2,058	1,985	73
1966	23,907	22,772	1,135	2,165	2,072	93
1967	23,578	22,423	1,155	2,379	2,268	111
1968	23,641	22,487	1,154	2,613	2,502	111
1969	24,364	22,949	1,415	2,682	2,630	52

Appendix B

AGE DISTRIBUTION OF POPULATION
BY RACE, SEX, NATIVITY, AND PARENTAGE,
NEW YORK CITY, 1910-70

Tables B-1 through B-6 have been compiled from published and unpublished data prepared by the U.S. Bureau of the Census. The unpublished material includes the age distribution by parentage in 1950 and 1960 (in Table B-2), and the age distribution of the foreign white stock in 1960 (in Table B-3).

TABLE B-1
Age by Race and Sex, New York City, 1910-70

Age, race, sex	1970	1960	1950	1940	1930	1920	191
All Classes							
Total, all ages	7,894,862	7,781,984	7,891,957	7,454,995	6,930,446	5,620,048	4,766,
Under 5 years	615,831	686,717	665,889	433,894	535,600	560,869	507,
5-9 years	631,748	595,847	535,039	470,556	577,284	536,490	438,
10-14 years	624,166	575,321	443,599	561,108	575,300	494,867	422
15-19 years	602,327	486,851	467,065	606,942	599,286	453,758	457,
20-24 years	649,640	482,522	598,718	649,153	687,417	545,660	531,
25-29 years	596,566	513,629	665,245	697,153	695,984	575,915	499,
30-34 years	479,020	542,769	638,249	691,027	649,576	513,204	422
35-39 years	444,931	546,966	668,845	669,421	621,248	474,270	382
40-44 years	470,704	524,381	642,065	628,714	518,588	379,366	309
45-49 years	479,839	550,310	590,622	550,743	422,063	318,933	246
50-54 years	462,177	534,526	556,389	467,020	340,807	266,750	191
55-59 years	463,418	499,493	450,515	346,871	246,277	179,209	122
60-64 years	426,617	428,825	364,482	267,974	190,527	136,721	94
65-69 years	355,284	344,063	274,343	190,439	127,356	80,743	62
70-74 years	270,715	240,101	170,654	120,675	77,327	50,207	39
75 and over	321,879	229,663	160,238	103,305	59,819	45,281	33
Not reported	—	—	—	—	5,987	7,805	6
Male, all ages	3,703,355	3,719,257	3,821,788	3,676,293	3,472,956	2,802,638	2,382
Under 5 years	313,235	347,721	339,620	221,415	272,438	283,873	255
5-9 years	321,899	301,648	272,154	238,798	291,782	269,451	219
10-14 years	316,375	290,330	225,342	283,453	290,263	248,289	210
15-19 years	297,738	234,746	226,849	300,717	293,740	219,332	216
20-24 years	292,295	222,238	278,921	304,862	327,734	249,761	251
25-29 years	282,673	250,455	313,432	322,558	341,448	280,340	253
30-34 years	230,692	262,584	296,280	331,782	327,685	263,065	219
35-39 years	212,063	257,498	309,773	330,950	319,859	247,263	196
40-44 years	219,947	239,550	309,289	317,471	272,868	195,778	161
45-49 years	219,952	252,224	290,311	282,769	219,600	167,078	127
50-54 years	206,750	252,415	275,471	243,321	175,346	135,986	98
55-59 years	207,093	239,484	226,273	178,162	123,128	90,152	61
60-64 years	191,700	202,238	182,687	132,668	92,494	67,768	45
65-69 years	152,179	159,119	129,975	89,275	60,451	38,341	29
70-74 years	111,494	109,623	78,275	54,474	35,866	22,658	17
75 and over	127,270	97,384	67,136	43,618	25,243	18,861	13
Not reported	—	—	—	—	3,011	4,642	
Female, all ages	4,191,507	4,062,727	4,070,169	3,778,702	3,457,490	2,817,410	2,384
Under 5 years	302,596	338,996	326,269	212,479	263,162	276,996	25
5-9 years	309,849	294,199	262,885	231,758	285,502	267,039	219
10-14 years	307,791	284,991	218,257	277,655	285,037	246,578	21
15-19 years	304,589	252,105	240,216	306,225	305,546	234,426	24
20-24 years	357,345	260,284	319,797	344,291	359,683	295,899	28
25-29 years	313,893	263,174	351,813	374,595	354,536	295,575	24
30-34 years	248,328	280,185	341,969	359,245	321,891	250,139	20
35-39 years	232,868	289,468	359,072	338,471	301,389	227,007	18
40-44 years	250,757	284,831	332,776	311,243	245,720	183,588	14
45-49 years	259,887	298,086	300,311	267,974	202,463	151,855	11
50-54 years	255,427	282,111	280,918	223,699	165,461	130,764	9
55-59 years	256,325	260,009	224,242	168,709	123,149	89,057	6
60-64 years	234,917	226,587	181,795	135,306	98,033	68,953	4
65-69 years	203,105	184,944	144,368	101,164	66,905	42,402	3
70-74 years	159,221	130,478	92,379	66,201	41,461	27,549	2
75 and over	194,609	132,279	93,102	59,687	34,576	26,420	1
Not reported	—	—	—	—	2,976	3,163	

Age by Race and Sex, New York City, 1910-70

e, race, sex	1970	1960	1950	1940	1930	1920	1910
White							
tal, all ages	6,048,841	6,640,662	7,116,441	6,977,501	6,589,377	5,459,463	4,669,162
der 5 years	422,343	546,341	587,649	403,239	508,017	549,402	500,248
years	424,062	479,069	480,051	436,484	552,381	527,392	433,026
14 years	431,798	482,318	395,131	524,420	556,345	486,682	417,490
19 years	437,045	417,639	419,714	571,412	577,773	443,874	451,190
24 years	498,830	400,847	528,325	607,184	647,688	525,313	519,033
29 years	443,136	423,310	576,951	644,590	645,175	551,787	483,004
34 years	340,879	443,393	559,352	637,687	606,675	492,773	409,658
39 years	321,779	447,292	591,483	614,219	582,334	454,256	371,130
44 years	355,541	441,286	577,915	584,118	491,452	365,974	302,418
49 years	376,368	478,891	537,558	518,427	402,047	309,299	240,808
54 years	378,743	476,722	515,331	444,170	328,270	260,721	187,668
59 years	396,377	449,792	424,385	331,865	239,582	176,154	120,279
64 years	372,680	394,363	345,577	258,161	186,582	134,629	93,117
69 years	312,979	319,756	260,166	183,669	124,936	79,596	61,620
74 years	243,564	224,486	163,173	117,370	76,058	49,507	38,832
and over	292,717	215,157	153,680	100,486	58,621	44,643	33,139
t reported	—	—	—	—	5,441	7,461	6,502
le, all ages	2,851,687	3,189,229	3,463,354	3,455,003	3,304,524	2,723,217	2,334,844
der 5 years	215,643	277,751	300,273	206,210	258,656	278,238	252,414
years	216,942	243,521	245,018	221,887	279,622	265,031	216,652
14 years	220,021	244,560	201,466	265,679	281,121	244,567	208,305
19 years	217,211	202,816	205,191	284,588	284,300	215,034	213,313
24 years	228,709	187,605	250,448	289,049	310,184	240,623	245,687
29 years	216,387	210,541	274,980	301,328	316,776	268,596	245,945
34 years	169,297	218,857	262,010	308,050	305,416	252,786	213,241
39 years	157,231	212,252	275,347	304,806	299,480	236,810	190,638
44 years	169,154	202,187	278,752	294,594	258,440	188,458	157,148
49 years	173,375	219,735	264,550	266,165	209,088	161,596	124,697
54 years	170,195	225,570	254,833	231,787	168,740	132,741	96,733
59 years	178,335	215,999	213,279	170,782	119,658	88,628	60,102
64 years	168,750	185,715	173,727	127,865	90,618	66,755	44,425
69 years	134,286	147,819	123,694	86,370	59,482	37,847	29,209
74 years	100,047	102,762	75,069	53,153	35,387	22,402	17,611
nd over	116,104	91,539	64,717	42,690	24,830	18,639	13,684
reported	—	—	—	—	2,726	4,466	5,040
ale, all ages	3,197,154	3,451,433	3,653,087	3,522,498	3,284,853	2,736,246	2,334,318
er 5 years	206,700	268,590	287,376	197,029	249,361	271,164	247,834
years	207,120	235,548	235,033	214,597	272,759	262,361	216,374
4 years	211,777	237,758	193,665	258,741	275,224	242,115	209,185
9 years	219,834	214,823	214,523	286,824	293,473	228,840	237,877
4 years	270,121	213,242	277,877	318,135	337,504	284,690	273,346
9 years	226,749	212,769	301,971	343,262	328,399	283,191	237,059
4 years	171,582	224,536	297,342	329,637	301,259	239,987	196,417
9 years	164,548	235,040	316,136	309,413	282,854	217,446	180,492
4 years	186,387	239,099	299,163	289,524	233,012	177,516	145,270
9 years	202,993	259,156	273,008	252,262	192,959	147,703	116,111
4 years	208,548	251,152	260,498	212,383	159,530	127,980	90,935
9 years	218,042	233,793	211,106	161,083	119,924	87,526	60,177
4 years	203,930	208,648	171,850	130,296	95,964	67,874	48,692
9 years	178,693	171,937	136,472	97,299	65,454	41,749	32,411
4 years	143,517	121,724	88,104	64,217	40,671	27,105	21,221
nd over	176,613	123,618	88,963	57,796	33,791	26,004	19,455
reported	—	—	—	—	2,715	2,995	1,462

Age, race, sex	1970	1960	1950	1940	1930	1920	1910
Negro							
Total, all ages	1,668,115	1,084,862*	749,080†	458,444	327,706	152,467	91,70
Under 5 years	175,584	135,513	75,795	29,691	26,920	11,147	6,67
5-9 years	191,721	111,124	55,030	33,134	24,365	8,833	5,11
10-14 years	177,269	89,812	47,530	35,848	18,662	7,961	4,85
15-19 years	150,079	67,000	46,400	34,678	21,120	9,592	6,28
20-24 years	133,815	77,972	68,330	41,099	38,658	19,499	12,36
25-29 years	136,030	84,183	84,790	50,978	48,661	22,870	15,38
30-34 years	121,624	94,231	76,480	51,180	40,533	19,302	11,91
35-39 years	109,730	95,255	74,125	52,186	36,924	18,795	10,16
40-44 years	104,058	78,229	61,265	41,789	25,515	12,447	6,55
45-49 years	94,425	67,277	50,680	30,381	19,057	9,029	4,5
50-54 years	76,241	54,004	38,155	21,468	11,922	5,549	2,96
55-59 years	60,952	46,590	24,405	14,251	6,365	2,828	1,75
60-64 years	48,674	32,255	17,515	9,285	3,767	1,873	1,18
65-69 years	37,990	23,627	13,970	6,521	2,331	1,114	7
70-74 years	24,036	14,326	7,650	3,197	1,236	682	44
75 and over	25,887	13,464	6,960	2,758	1,184	627	44
Not reported	—	—	—	—	486	319	2
Male, all ages	761,933	496,648	336,860	205,727	156,968	72,351	42,14
Under 5 years	88,433	67,690	38,160	14,706	13,431	5,466	3,2
5-9 years	96,750	55,796	27,280	16,442	11,894	4,271	2,4
10-14 years	88,641	44,420	22,930	17,294	8,987	3,602	2,2
15-19 years	72,905	30,347	20,825	15,574	9,169	4,089	2,6
20-24 years	55,953	33,107	27,215	15,251	16,664	8,427	5,1
25-29 years	58,288	37,128	36,070	20,008	22,779	10,615	6,9
30-34 years	52,921	40,521	32,460	21,924	20,121	9,273	5,7
35-39 years	47,924	42,455	31,725	23,418	18,539	9,316	5,0
40-44 years	45,450	34,382	27,770	20,299	12,909	6,437	3,2
45-49 years	41,864	29,593	23,370	14,802	9,607	4,902	2,1
50-54 years	32,819	24,163	18,420	10,251	6,032	2,779	1,3
55-59 years	25,621	21,017	11,665	6,675	3,155	1,307	7
60-64 years	20,021	14,421	7,805	4,311	1,708	800	5
65-69 years	15,311	10,355	5,710	2,676	891	462	3
70-74 years	9,655	6,215	3,160	1,219	448	241	1
75 and over	9,377	5,038	2,295	877	400	212	1
Not reported	—	—	—	—	234	152	1
Female, all ages	906,182	588,214	412,220	252,717	170,738	80,116	49,5
Under 5 years	87,151	67,823	37,635	14,985	13,489	5,681	3,4
5-9 years	94,971	55,328	27,750	16,692	12,471	4,562	2,7
10-14 years	88,628	45,392	24,600	18,554	9,675	4,359	2,6
15-19 years	77,174	36,653	25,575	19,104	11,951	5,503	3,6
20-24 years	77,862	44,865	41,115	25,848	21,994	11,072	7,2
25-29 years	77,742	47,055	48,720	30,970	25,882	12,255	8,4
30-34 years	68,703	53,710	44,020	29,256	20,412	10,029	6,1
35-39 years	61,806	52,800	42,400	28,768	18,385	9,479	5,1
40-44 years	58,608	43,847	33,495	21,490	12,606	6,010	3,2
45-49 years	52,561	37,684	27,310	15,579	9,450	4,127	2,4
50-54 years	43,422	29,841	19,735	11,217	5,890	2,770	1,6
55-59 years	35,331	25,573	12,740	7,576	3,210	1,521	9
60-64 years	28,653	17,834	9,710	4,974	2,059	1,073	6
65-69 years	22,679	13,272	8,260	3,845	1,440	652	4
70-74 years	14,381	8,111	4,490	1,978	788	441	2
75 and over	16,510	8,426	4,665	1,881	784	415	3
Not reported	—	—	—	—	252	167	1

Age by Race and Sex, New York City, 1910-70

Age, race, sex	1970	1960	1950	1940	1930	1920	1910
Other races							
Total, all ages	177,906	56,633*	28,025†	19,050	13,363	8,118	6,012
Under 5 years	17,904	5,717	2,445	964	663	320	156
5-9 years	15,965	4,945	1,045	938	538	265	123
10-14 years	15,099	4,183	1,430	840	293	224	83
15-19 years	15,203	2,057	1,225	852	393	292	146
20-24 years	16,995	3,548	2,280	870	1,071	848	471
25-29 years	17,400	4,747	2,900	1,585	2,148	1,258	762
30-34 years	16,517	5,360	2,435	2,160	2,368	1,129	882
35-39 years	13,422	4,478	2,595	3,016	1,990	1,219	929
40-44 years	11,105	3,598	2,495	2,807	1,621	945	918
45-49 years	9,046	3,410	2,705	1,935	959	605	761
50-54 years	7,193	3,475	2,375	1,382	615	480	454
55-59 years	6,089	5,399	1,565	755	330	227	177
60-64 years	5,263	2,304	1,135	528	178	219	82
65-69 years	4,315	1,601	750	249	89	33	28
70-74 years	3,115	1,025	410	108	33	18	7
75 and over	3,275	786	235	61	14	11	5
Not reported	—	—	—	—	60	25	28
Male, all ages	89,735	32,966	19,515	15,563	11,464	7,070	5,495
Under 5 years	9,159	2,725	1,135	499	351	169	88
5-9 years	8,207	2,521	575	469	266	149	57
10-14 years	7,713	2,118	795	480	155	120	47
15-19 years	7,622	1,009	665	555	271	209	98
20-24 years	7,633	1,707	1,145	562	886	711	419
25-29 years	7,998	2,327	1,705	1,222	1,893	1,129	684
30-34 years	8,474	2,752	1,570	1,808	2,148	1,006	823
35-39 years	6,908	2,592	1,900	2,726	1,840	1,137	888
40-44 years	5,343	2,219	2,035	2,578	1,519	883	894
45-49 years	4,713	2,324	2,335	1,802	905	580	739
50-54 years	3,736	2,500	2,070	1,283	574	466	448
55-59 years	3,137	3,466	1,410	705	315	217	172
60-64 years	2,929	1,877	1,000	492	168	213	78
65-69 years	2,582	1,317	640	229	78	32	25
70-74 years	1,792	852	350	102	31	15	7
75 and over	1,789	660	185	51	13	10	3
Not reported	—	—	—	—	51	24	25
Female, all ages	88,171	23,667	8,510	3,487	1,899	1,048	517
Under 5 years	8,745	2,992	1,310	465	312	151	68
5-9 years	7,758	2,424	470	469	272	116	66
10-14 years	7,386	2,065	635	360	138	104	36
15-19 years	7,581	1,048	560	297	122	83	48
20-24 years	9,362	1,841	1,135	308	185	137	52
25-29 years	9,402	2,420	1,195	363	255	129	78
30-34 years	8,043	2,608	865	352	220	123	59
35-39 years	6,514	1,886	695	290	150	82	41
40-44 years	5,762	1,379	460	229	102	62	24
45-49 years	4,333	1,086	370	133	54	25	22
50-54 years	3,457	975	305	99	41	14	6
55-59 years	2,952	1,933	155	50	15	10	5
60-64 years	2,334	427	135	36	10	6	4
65-69 years	1,733	284	110	20	11	1	3
70-74 years	1,323	173	60	6	2	3	—
75 and over	1,486	126	50	10	1	1	2
Not reported	—	—	—	—	9	1	3

*Based on 25 percent sample.   †Based on 20 percent sample.

TABLE B-2
Age and Sex of White Population by Nativity and Parentage, New York City, 1910-60

Age, parentage, sex	1960*	1950†	1940	1930	1920	191
Native of native parentage						
Total, all ages	3,018,894	2,660,435	2,162,660‡	1,505,311	1,164,834	921,
Under 5 years	1,202,286	464,555	248,620	195,742	156,797	126,8
5-9 years		344,025	213,480	177,234	129,354	107,9
10-14 years		235,425	205,800	150,168	115,844	103,
15-19 years	531,326	202,830	190,340	132,674	106,744	99,
20-24 years		221,835	196,440	150,381	122,602	97,
25-29 years	406,919	217,030	203,800	147,196	119,374	85,
30-34 years		186,070	190,700	129,506	97,335	68,
35-39 years	293,628	163,015	168,380	112,760	81,519	57,
40-44 years		147,945	145,500	86,510	61,897	43,
45-49 years	243,687	126,070	114,400	66,525	49,604	33,
50-54 years		109,980	92,520	51,812	39,367	28,
55-59 years	192,149	81,500	67,920	35,973	26,037	20,
60-64 years		61,620	50,020	26,283	21,256	16,
65-69 years	104,546	44,175	34,280	17,155	13,636	12,
70-74 years		27,410	21,040	11,725	9,685	8,
75 and over	44,353	26,950	19,420	11,175	10,282	7,
Not reported	—	—	—	2,492	3,501	4,
Male, all ages	1,462,713	1,292,180	1,049,220	750,482	575,847	456,
Under 5 years	612,455	237,860	127,520	99,715	79,250	63,
5-9 years		174,440	108,380	89,584	64,876	53,
10-14 years		119,895	102,380	75,924	58,042	51,
15-19 years	252,716	98,795	92,760	65,500	52,118	48,
20-24 years		102,580	90,380	73,493	58,569	46,
25-29 years	202,991	103,780	94,760	73,150	57,966	41
30-34 years		85,405	92,420	64,623	47,927	33
35-39 years	137,821	77,670	81,640	56,384	40,767	29
40-44 years		70,195	71,240	43,552	31,003	22
45-49 years	111,947	60,440	55,980	33,485	25,505	17
50-54 years		52,265	44,580	25,787	19,850	14
55-59 years	86,629	39,295	32,700	17,781	12,839	9,
60-64 years		28,945	23,340	12,699	10,374	7
65-69 years	42,546	19,275	15,680	8,003	6,332	5
70-74 years		11,430	8,140	5,192	4,147	3
75 and over	15,608	9,910	7,320	4,330	3,937	3
Not reported	—	—	—	1,280	2,345	4
Female, all ages	1,556,181	1,368,255	1,113,440	754,829	588,987	465
Under 5 years	589,831	226,695	121,100	96,027	77,547	62
5-9 years		169,585	105,100	87,650	64,478	54
10-14 years		115,530	103,420	74,244	57,802	51
15-19 years	278,610	104,035	97,580	67,174	54,626	51
20-24 years		119,255	106,060	76,888	64,033	51
25-29 years	203,928	113,250	109,040	74,046	61,408	43
30-34 years		100,665	98,280	64,883	49,408	34
35-39 years	155,807	85,345	86,740	56,376	40,752	28
40-44 years		77,750	74,260	42,958	30,894	21
45-49 years	131,740	65,630	58,420	33,040	24,099	16
50-54 years		57,715	47,940	26,025	19,517	14
55-59 years	105,520	42,205	35,220	18,192	13,198	10
60-64 years		32,675	26,680	13,584	10,882	8
65-69 years	62,000	24,900	18,600	9,152	7,304	6
70-74 years		15,980	12,900	6,533	5,538	4
75 and over	28,745	17,040	12,100	6,845	6,345	4
Not reported	—	—	—	1,212	1,156	

Age and Sex of White Population by Nativity and Parentage, New York City, 1910-60

Age, parentage, sex	1960*	1950†	1940	1930	1920	1910
Native of foreign or mixed parentage						
Total, all ages	2,159,108	2,661,215	2,751,560‡	2,788,625§	2,303,082	1,820,141
Under 5 years	258,081	115,345	160,600	306,569	388,658	358,733
5-9 years		130,600	221,160	353,201	378,973	267,353
10-14 years		150,310	301,540	380,849	323,469	237,156
15-19 years	225,268	199,060	346,180	377,662	241,670	209,324
20-24 years		263,925	371,040	334,674	221,440	164,367
25-29 years	348,320	297,050	340,700	246,300	179,635	126,325
30-34 years		322,095	273,580	200,082	128,166	111,937
35-39 years	456,316	309,920	201,040	160,163	106,032	103,521
40-44 years		255,290	158,100	112,865	90,635	80,751
45-49 years	449,629	180,940	114,200	85,317	78,756	62,577
50-54 years		149,145	83,940	74,281	64,524	47,470
55-59 years	263,444	105,430	55,920	57,284	42,802	24,668
60-64 years		69,945	47,040	43,161	31,285	12,884
65-69 years	119,429	48,235	35,980	27,992	15,074	6,899
70-74 years		31,705	21,740	17,128	6,581	3,465
75 and over	38,621	32,220	18,800	9,743	4,357	2,200
Not reported	—	—	—	1,354	1,025	511
Male, all ages	1,025,851	1,276,915	1,351,900	1,372,959	1,127,280	890,781
Under 5 years	132,026	58,220	81,660	156,057	197,021	181,079
5-9 years		67,170	112,760	178,952	190,614	133,745
10-14 years		76,370	149,940	192,407	162,591	118,491
15-19 years	109,743	97,970	172,440	187,400	117,647	101,913
20-24 years		127,725	178,320	161,583	103,970	76,268
25-29 years	172,978	141,705	164,080	118,845	86,069	60,724
30-34 years		149,260	136,540	97,802	61,445	53,570
35-39 years	211,931	147,990	100,920	79,153	50,514	49,491
40-44 years		124,515	78,540	55,304	43,024	38,739
45-49 years	210,939	87,390	56,960	40,546	38,024	30,150
50-54 years		71,240	41,540	35,342	30,290	22,997
55-59 years	123,772	50,385	26,360	26,677	20,115	11,940
60-64 years		32,490	21,540	19,187	14,304	5,943
65-69 years	50,948	20,260	14,700	12,128	6,633	3,115
70-74 years		12,725	8,760	7,209	2,787	1,527
75 and over	13,514	11,500	6,840	3,779	1,717	844
Not reported	—	—	—	588	515	245
Female, all ages	1,133,257	1,384,300	1,399,660	1,415,666	1,175,802	929,360
Under 5 years	126,055	57,125	78,940	150,512	191,637	177,654
5-9 years		63,430	108,400	174,249	188,359	133,608
10-14 years		73,940	151,600	188,442	160,878	118,665
15-19 years	115,525	101,090	173,740	190,262	124,023	107,411
20-24 years		136,200	192,720	173,091	117,470	88,099
25-29 years	175,835	155,345	176,620	127,455	93,566	65,601
30-34 years		172,835	137,040	102,280	66,721	58,367
35-39 years	244,385	161,930	100,120	81,010	55,518	54,030
40-44 years		130,775	79,560	57,561	47,611	42,012
45-49 years	238,690	93,550	57,240	44,771	40,732	32,427
50-54 years		77,905	42,400	38,939	34,234	24,473
55-59 years	139,672	55,045	29,560	30,607	22,687	12,728
60-64 years		37,455	25,500	23,974	16,981	6,941
65-69 years	64,481	27,975	21,280	15,864	8,441	3,784
70-74 years		18,980	12,980	9,919	3,794	1,938
75 and over	25,107	20,720	11,960	5,964	2,640	1,356
Not reported	—	—	—	766	510	266

Age and Sex of White Population by Nativity and Parentage, New York City, 1910-60

Age, parentage, sex	1960*	1950†	1940	1930	1920	191
Foreign born						
Total, all ages	1,463,817	1,788,625	2,080,020	2,295,181	1,991,547	1,927,
Under 5 years	5,541	8,690	2,583	5,573	3,947	14,
5-9 years	13,913	6,815	6,101	21,884	19;065	57,
10-14 years	27,292	10,910	13,642	25,309	47,369	77,
15-19 years	22,518	17,320	34,486	67,431	95,460	141,
20-24 years	40,137	36,600	41,165	162,618	181,271	257,
25-29 years	49,773	60,250	96,917	251,671	252,778	271,
30-34 years	62,328	58,735	173,415	277,079	267,272	229,
35-39 years	75,579	107,240	251,438	309,408	266,705	210,
40-44 years	65,651	174,000	281,569	292,075	213,442	178,
45-49 years	109,478	228,025	284,754	250,204	180,939	144,
50-54 years	155,105	253,990	270,272	202,176	156,830	111,
55-59 years	196,915	239,430	210,936	146,325	107,315	75,
60-64 years	197,466	214,820	162,750	117,138	82,088	63,
65-69 years	178,963	171,345	114,028	79,787	50,886	42,
70-74 years	136,822	105,030	73,558	47,205	33,241	27,
75 and over	126,336	95,425	62,406	37,703	30,004	23,
Not reported	—	—	—	1,595	2,935	1,
Male, all ages	700,744	883,385	1,057,839	1,180,947	1,020,090	987
Under 5 years	2,765	4,290	1,310	2,817	1,967	7
5-9 years	6,870	3,370	3,038	11,051	9,541	28
10-14 years	13,833	5,570	6,832	12,780	23,934	38
15-19 years	10,419	8,605	17,163	31,397	45,269	62
20-24 years	16,972	15,710	18,615	75,099	78,084	123
25-29 years	23,226	27,985	41,380	124,777	124,561	143
30-34 years	29,774	26,445	81,972	142,987	143,414	125
35-39 years	36,042	47,930	126,448	163,942	145,529	112
40-44 years	30,395	82,845	145,301	159,583	114,431	96
45-49 years	49,837	113,730	150,517	135,056	98,067	77
50-54 years	73,423	129,630	147,338	107,610	82,601	59
55-59 years	97,896	123,990	113,428	75,200	55,674	38
60-64 years	95,804	112,595	84,260	58,732	42,077	30
65-69 years	86,864	85,630	56,461	39,351	24,882	20
70-74 years	67,318	51,410	35,194	22,986	15,468	12
75 and over	59,306	43,650	28,582	16,721	12,985	9
Not reported	—	—	—	858	1,606	
Female, all ages	763,073	905,240	1,022,181	1,114,234	971,457	939
Under 5 years	2,776	4,400	1,273	2,756	1,980	7
5-9 years	7,043	3,445	3,063	10,833	9,524	28
10-14 years	13,459	5,340	6,810	12,529	23,435	38
15-19 years	12,099	8,715	17,323	36,034	50,191	79
20-24 years	23,165	20,890	22,550	87,519	103,187	134
25-29 years	26,547	32,265	55,537	126,894	128,217	127
30-34 years	32,554	32,290	91,443	134,092	123,858	103
35-39 years	39,537	59,310	124,990	145,466	121,176	98
40-44 years	35,256	91,155	136,268	132,492	99,011	81
45-49 years	59,641	114,295	134,237	115,148	82,872	67
50-54 years	81,682	124,360	122,934	94,566	74,229	52
55-59 years	99,019	115,440	97,508	71,125	51,641	37
60-64 years	101,662	102,225	78,490	58,406	40,011	32
65-69 years	92,099	85,715	57,567	40,436	26,004	22
70-74 years	69,504	53,620	38,364	24,219	17,773	14
75 and over	67,030	51,775	33,824	20,982	17,019	13
Not reported	—	—	—	737	1,329	

*Based on 25 percent sample.   †Based on 20 percent sample.   ‡Based on 5 percent sample
§Excludes 260 persons classified as Mexicans in 1930.

Age of Foreign White Stock by Nativity for Selected Countries of Origin, New York City, 1930, 1940, and 1960

Nativity, census year, and age	Total	Austria	Canada	Czecho-slovakia	Germany	Hungary	Ireland*	Italy	Poland	Scandi-navia†	United Kingdom	U.S.S.R.	All other‡
Foreign born §													
1960‖ Total, all ages	1,463,821#	84,389	29,034	27,767	152,502	45,602	101,944	281,033	168,960	30,237	73,618	204,821	263,914
Under 15 years	46,746	1,570	1,267	690	10,089	1,717	1,184	8,994	1,122	591	2,856	353	16,313
15-24 years	62,655	909	1,387	685	7,349	2,215	5,749	12,913	2,384	1,018	3,329	1,438	23,279
25-34 years	112,101	2,456	3,625	2,874	14,504	3,285	9,276	18,204	7,249	1,820	6,470	2,153	40,185
35-44 years	141,230	4,855	5,232	5,129	15,544	4,249	7,888	23,740	20,476	2,415	7,773	7,684	36,245
45-54 years	264,587	12,282	7,073	5,385	31,075	7,726	23,927	41,675	40,814	5,148	14,460	32,043	42,979
55-64 years	394,381	26,646	6,002	6,407	39,436	11,776	26,976	76,254	46,147	9,209	20,743	69,603	55,182
65-74 years	315,785	25,948	3,004	4,516	21,276	10,114	17,095	69,838	39,116	6,438	11,565	69,156	37,719
75 and over	126,336	9,723	1,444	2,081	13,229	4,520	9,849	29,415	11,652	3,598	6,422	22,391	12,012
1940 Total, all ages	2,070,500	138,500	23,880	24,560	217,760	62,500	162,840	400,880	189,500	64,480	100,660	406,220	278,720
Under 15 years	22,940	1,240	320	460	5,420	660	1,320	4,800	1,920	560	1,060	1,080	4,100
15-24 years	75,760	3,480	1,740	1,620	11,900	2,040	3,760	15,560	9,160	2,200	5,360	7,420	11,520
25-34 years	271,460	12,900	4,960	2,520	36,140	7,100	29,120	42,080	30,240	7,460	14,120	44,080	40,740
35-44 years	527,440	32,920	6,420	5,820	53,340	15,320	38,460	101,520	46,540	16,240	25,220	104,340	81,300
45-54 years	553,600	43,580	4,240	6,220	37,740	17,200	33,880	120,900	53,520	16,720	20,960	122,440	76,200
55-64 years	370,080	28,280	3,480	4,940	34,360	12,740	29,560	74,280	30,860	11,900	17,860	80,820	41,000
65-74 years	187,020	13,080	2,080	2,300	25,820	5,900	19,740	30,720	13,480	6,900	11,540	37,020	18,440
75 and over	62,200	3,020	640	680	13,040	1,540	7,000	11,020	3,780	2,500	4,540	9,020	5,420
1930 Total, all ages	2,295,181	127,169	39,622	35,318	237,588	59,883	192,810	440,250	238,339	86,493	146,262	442,431	249,016
Under 15 years	52,766	1,121	3,248	736	7,257	1,080	2,591	10,932	4,963	2,266	6,404	4,085	8,083
15-24 years	230,049	8,687	7,261	2,258	26,893	4,729	23,574	34,931	28,771	8,020	17,457	38,850	28,618
25-34 years	528,750	27,341	9,726	7,161	52,022	12,452	40,969	99,943	50,846	22,552	34,302	101,609	69,827
35-44 years	601,483	38,047	6,885	9,906	39,327	16,302	39,639	130,938	70,835	20,744	29,566	128,878	70,416
45-54 years	452,380	28,942	6,002	7,938	39,977	13,961	39,008	92,239	46,568	16,423	27,041	93,004	41,277
55-64 years	263,463	15,549	3,758	4,513	37,808	7,375	28,041	44,042	23,925	10,184	17,989	50,644	19,635
65-74 years	126,992	6,176	2,019	2,171	24,303	3,177	14,122	20,656	10,268	4,947	9,869	20,754	8,530
75 and over	37,703	1,245	679	619	9,812	782	4,658	6,305	2,049	1,290	3,524	4,386	2,354
Not reported	1,595	61	44	16	189	25	208	264	114	67	110	221	276

TABLE B-3 (Continued)
Age of Foreign White Stock by Nativity for Selected Countries of Origin, New York City, 1930, 1940, and 1960

Nativity, census year, and age	Total	Austria	Canada	Czecho-slovakia	Germany	Hungary	Ireland*	Italy	Poland	Scandi-navia†	United Kingdom	U.S.S.R.	All other‡
Native: foreign or mixed parentage													
1960‖ Total, all ages	2,159,108††	135,185	36,952	30,631	171,729	51,213	209,694	577,568	220,393	34,107	101,406	359,122	231,108
Under 15 years	258,081	8,034	9,323	7,610	23,513	6,203	21,470	55,415	34,454	3,833	15,306	14,710	58,210
15-24 years	225,268	9,203	6,384	2,422	14,698	4,314	28,189	56,078	27,337	3,907	13,907	29,440	29,389
25-34 years	348,320	18,396	5,587	3,308	11,882	6,832	28,280	119,694	35,458	4,645	14,310	58,981	40,947
35-44 years	456,316	31,456	3,605	5,872	13,080	10,105	27,179	158,503	55,489	5,309	11,646	91,430	42,642
45-54 years	449,629	36,427	4,575	6,058	26,169	12,713	36,701	129,345	44,800	7,120	15,592	96,874	33,255
55-64 years	263,444	23,213	4,565	3,344	37,832	7,188	36,681	45,943	16,033	6,109	15,476	49,802	17,258
65-74 years	119,429	7,337	2,149	1,557	29,882	3,285	21,856	11,190	5,586	2,695	10,658	16,222	7,012
75 and over	38,621	1,119	764	460	14,673	573	9,338	1,400	1,236	489	4,511	1,663	2,395
1940** Total, all ages	2,751,560	177,480	34,940	30,740	273,540	60,600	304,340	685,880	218,380	58,040	151,260	530,820	225,540
Under 15 years	683,300	37,520	9,920	5,320	36,280	13,600	61,940	207,760	60,040	14,520	34,300	121,600	80,500
15-24 years	717,220	56,180	4,780	8,640	25,560	16,540	45,680	227,420	75,600	12,460	22,780	157,480	64,100
25-34 years	614,280	46,180	6,520	7,880	39,060	16,040	50,300	166,780	54,500	13,160	25,020	148,060	40,780
35-44 years	359,140	23,980	6,240	5,060	55,940	9,280	52,100	61,580	18,180	9,720	24,260	71,900	20,900
45-54 years	198,140	9,640	3,820	2,440	52,400	3,500	41,040	17,820	6,640	5,440	20,080	24,800	10,520
55-64 years	102,960	2,860	2,440	1,060	35,020	1,320	29,440	3,380	2,420	1,820	13,300	5,100	4,800
65-74 years	57,720	900	1,060	280	21,480	260	18,880	860	760	620	8,180	1,520	2,920
75 and over	18,800	220	160	60	7,800	60	4,960	280	240	300	3,340	360	1,020
1930 Total, all ages	2,788,885	161,809	37,875	36,964	362,496	55,215	342,224	630,105	220,042	63,600	186,600	502,641	189,314
Under 5 years	306,569	16,319	3,494	3,584	12,926	5,672	21,237	99,741	30,103	7,277	14,506	60,331	31,379
5-14 years	734,050	46,516	4,879	9,783	25,844	14,481	45,642	241,891	85,294	13,864	25,194	160,251	60,411
15-24 years	712,336	50,725	7,335	11,524	47,151	17,722	57,780	193,843	70,626	16,060	30,477	162,865	46,228
25-44 years	719,410	43,879	15,401	10,070	152,509	15,664	123,079	89,626	30,289	22,377	67,229	112,392	36,895
45-64 years	260,043	3,951	5,828	1,884	101,014	1,563	77,690	4,528	3,349	3,619	38,750	6,296	11,571
65 and over	54,863	326	900	106	22,827	83	16,576	258	302	373	10,336	318	2,458
Not reported	1,614	93	38	13	225	30	220	218	79	30	108	188	372

*Excludes Northern Ireland.   †Excludes Denmark in 1960.   ‡Includes "not reported."

§Classified by own country of birth in 1930 and 1960 and by country of birth of parents in 1940.   ‖Based on 25 percent sample.

#Age was not cross-classified by race for specific countries of birth. A total of 2,530 foreign-born nonwhites are included in the figures for the individual countries shown. Conversely, the "all other" column, derived by subtraction, excludes 2,530 persons.   **Based on 5 percent sample.

††Age was not cross-classified by race for specific countries of origin. A total of 4,537 nonwhites are included in the figures for the individual countries

Age by Color and Sex of Puerto Ricans
(Persons of Puerto Rican Birth and Parentage), New York City, 1950 and 1960

Age and color	Total		Male		Female	
	1960	1950	1960	1950	1960	1950
All classes						
All ages	612,574	245,880	296,697	114,300	315,877	131,580
Under 5 years	93,152	29,480	46,960	15,165	46,192	14,315
5-9 years	73,589	22,850	37,359	11,325	36,230	11,525
10-14 years	62,193	20,995	30,949	10,275	31,244	10,720
15-19 years	54,296	22,515	25,580	9,835	28,716	12,680
20-24 years	60,820	30,340	28,663	13,260	32,157	17,080
25-29 years	62,946 }	50,080	30,000 }	22,790	32,946 }	27,290
30-34 years	54,057 }		26,025 }		28,032 }	
35-39 years	42,974 }	36,650	21,321 }	17,350	21,653 }	19,300
40-44 years	30,588 }		14,681 }		15,907 }	
45-49 years	25,279 }	19,715	12,076 }	9,615	13,203 }	10,100
50-54 years	17,272 }		8,367 }		8,905 }	
55-59 years	13,529 }	8,125	6,139 }	3,305	7,390 }	4,820
60-64 years	9,250 }		4,058 }		5,192 }	
65-69 years	5,726	2,760	2,240	790	3,486	1,970
70-74 years	3,573	1,245	1,289	340	2,284	905
75 and over	3,330	1,125	990	250	2,340	875
White, all ages	587,703	226,380	284,965	105,180	302,738	121,200
Under 5 years	89,375	27,115	45,149	13,995	44,226	13,120
5-9 years	70,500	20,735	35,722	10,225	34,778	10,510
10-14 years	59,693	19,275	29,679	9,540	30,014	9,735
15-19 years	52,167	20,820	24,589	9,020	27,578	11,800
20-24 years	58,726	28,055	27,695	12,250	31,031	15,805
25-29 years	60,501 }	46,290	28,850 }	20,995	31,651 }	25,295
30-34 years	52,061 }		25,140 }		26,921 }	
35-39 years	41,083 }	34,035	20,482 }	16,125	20,601 }	17,910
40-44 years	29,302 }		14,041 }		15,261 }	
45-49 years	24,235 }	18,065	11,591 }	8,815	12,644 }	9,250
50-54 years	16,477 }		8,015 }		8,462 }	
55-59 years	12,846 }	7,335	5,836 }	2,955	7,010 }	4,380
60-64 years	8,756 }		3,850 }		4,906 }	
65-69 years	5,409	2,540	2,146	755	3,263	1,785
70-74 years	3,414	1,125	1,211	295	2,203	830
75 and over	3,158	990	969	210	2,189	780
Nonwhite, all ages	24,871	19,500	11,732	9,120	13,139	10,380
Under 5 years	3,777	2,365	1,811	1,170	1,966	1,195
5-9 years	3,089	2,115	1,637	1,100	1,452	1,015
10-14 years	2,500	1,720	1,270	735	1,230	985
15-19 years	2,129	1,695	991	815	1,138	880
20-24 years	2,094	2,285	968	1,010	1,126	1,275
25-29 years	2,445 }	3,790	1,150 }	1,795	1,295 }	1,995
30-34 years	1,996 }		885 }		1,111 }	
35-39 years	1,891 }	2,615	839 }	1,225	1,052 }	1,390
40-44 years	1,286 }		640 }		646 }	
45-49 years	1,044 }	1,650	485 }	800	559 }	850
50-54 years	795 }		352 }		443 }	
55-59 years	683 }	790	303 }	350	380 }	440
60-64 years	494 }		208 }		286 }	
65-69 years	317	220	94	35	223	185
70-74 years	159	120	78	45	81	75
75 and over	172	135	21	40	151	95

TABLE B-5

Age and Sex of Puerto Ricans (Persons of Puerto
Rican Birth and Parentage), New York City, 1970

Age	Total	Male	Female
All ages	811,843	385,379	426,464
Under 5 years	105,216	53,495	51,721
5 to 9 years	107,468	54,551	52,917
10 to 14 years	98,014	49,658	48,356
15 to 19 years	80,621	39,697	40,924
20 to 24 years	75,396	32,548	42,848
25 to 29 years	70,708	32,073	38,635
30 to 34 years	62,422	28,737	33,685
35 to 39 years	54,098	24,463	29,635
40 to 44 years	43,327	19,644	23,683
45 to 49 years	34,403	15,608	18,795
50 to 54 years	24,805	11,369	13,436
55 to 59 years	19,444	8,880	10,564
60 to 64 years	14,239	6,140	8,099
65 to 69 years	9,398	3,804	5,594
70 to 74 years	5,491	2,300	3,191
75 and over	6,793	2,412	4,381

Age and Sex of White Population Exclusive of Puerto Ricans, New York City, 1950 and 1960

Age and sex	1960	1950
Total, all ages	6,054,116	6,883,895
Under 5 years	456,370	561,475
5-9 years	407,692	460,705
10-14 years	423,483	377,370
15-19 years	367,099	398,390
20-24 years	341,257	494,305
25-29 years	363,148 ⎫	1,094,940
30-34 years	391,630 ⎭	
35-39 years	407,827 ⎫	1,123,375
40-44 years	412,962 ⎭	
45-49 years	454,154 ⎫	1,030,085
50-54 years	463,033 ⎭	
55-59 years	444,655 ⎫	765,410
60-64 years	383,717 ⎭	
65-69 years	312,739	261,215
70-74 years	218,198	163,020
75 and over	206,152	153,605
Male, all ages	2,904,343	3,347,300
Under 5 years	233,653	286,375
5-9 years	208,329	234,755
10-14 years	215,417	192,295
15-19 years	178,041	196,350
20-24 years	159,525	233,765
25-29 years	182,079 ⎫	513,585
30-34 years	192,900 ⎭	
35-39 years	193,482 ⎫	535,020
40-44 years	188,184 ⎭	
45-49 years	208,729 ⎫	505,880
50-54 years	217,811 ⎭	
55-59 years	213,937 ⎫	384,745
60-64 years	180,478 ⎭	
65-69 years	144,148	124,410
70-74 years	100,171	75,270
75 and over	87,459	64,850
Female, all ages	3,149,773	3,536,595
Under 5 years	222,717	275,100
5-9 years	199,363	225,950
10-14 years	208,066	185,075
15-19 years	189,058	202,040
20-24 years	181,732	260,540
25-29 years	181,069 ⎫	581,355
30-34 years	198,730 ⎭	
35-39 years	214,345 ⎫	588,355
40-44 years	224,778 ⎭	
45-49 years	245,425 ⎫	524,205
50-54 years	245,222 ⎭	
55-59 years	230,718 ⎫	380,665
60-64 years	203,239 ⎭	
65-69 years	168,591	136,805
70-74 years	118,027	87,750
75 and over	118,693	88,755

Appendix C

Tables C-1, C-2, and C-4 have been compiled from data published by the U.S. Bureau of the Census. Table C-3 also contains unpublished census material made available by the New York City Planning Commission. Data for native population of foreign or mixed parentage were based on a 5 percent sample in 1940 and a 20 percent sample in 1950. All foreign stock data were based on a 25 percent sample in 1960 and a 15 percent sample in 1970.

APPENDIX C

TABLE C-1
White Population of Foreign or Mixed Parentage by County of Origin, New York City, 1890 and 1900

Country of origin	Total foreign or mixed parentage	Foreign parentage			Mixed parentage		
		Total	Both parents born in same foreign country	Mixed foreign parentage*	Total	Father foreign	Mother foreign
Total: 1890†	1,786,925	1,601,082	1,527,877	73,205	185,843	127,442	58,401
Bohemia	12,535	12,355	12,038	317	180	111	69
Canada	19,384	12,460	9,672	2,788	6,924	4,040	2,884
Denmark	5,495	4,879	3,751	1,128	616	522	94
France	24,568	20,936	16,705	4,231	3,632	2,655	977
Germany	650,443	588,331	573,753	14,578	62,112	49,351	12,761
Great Britain	163,401	126,530	105,394	21,136	36,871	23,526	13,345
Hungary	16,857	16,509	15,796	713	348	260	88
Ireland	624,883	560,269	547,375	12,894	64,614	38,978	25,636
Italy	68,736	67,492	66,421	1,071	1,244	1,094	150
Norway	8,645	8,311	7,402	909	334	263	71
Russia	77,647	76,460	72,552	3,908	1,187	976	211
Sweden	23,418	22,526	21,035	1,491	892	632	260
All other	90,913	84,024	75,983	8,041	6,889	5,034	1,855
Total: 1900	2,632,142‡	2,329,907‡	2,202,255	127,652‡	302,235	198,822	103,413
Austria	133,689	110,597	103,496	7,101	3,092	2,419	673
Bohemia	28,910	27,839	26,809	1,030	1,071	705	366
Canada	33,457	21,533	16,062	4,545	12,850	7,379	5,471
Denmark	10,456	9,233	7,219	2,014	1,223	1,004	219
France	30,369	25,278	19,574	5,704	5,091	3,608	1,483
Germany	784,882	682,050	658,861	23,189	102,832	77,091	25,741
Great Britain	210,439	153,442	121,416	32,026	56,997	35,279	21,718
Hungary	54,363	52,383	46,891	5,492	1,980	1,781	199
Ireland	710,235	612,897	595,210	17,687	97,338	54,069	43,269
Italy	220,394	216,776	214,794	1,982	3,618	3,118	500
Norway	18,903	18,072	16,118	1,954	831	628	203
Poland	55,497	54,517	50,771	3,746	980	849	131
Russia	251,027	247,625	237,870	9,755	3,402	2,933	469
Sweden	44,883	40,606	39,801	2,844	2,238	1,433	805
Switzerland	15,691	13,579	10,587	2,992	2,112	1,543	569
All other	49,132	42,552	36,776	5,776	6,580	4,983	1,597

*Country of birth of father.　　†New York City and Brooklyn as then constituted.

‡Sum of individual countries adds to 185 more than total because 185 nonwhite persons of mixed foreign parentage who could not be assigned a country of birth are included.

TABLE C-2
Nativity and Parentage of Foreign White Stock by Country of Origin, New York City, 1910-40

Country of origin	1910 Census		Native of foreign or mixed parentage			1920 Census		Native of foreign or mixed parentage		
	Total	Foreign born	Total	Foreign	Mixed	Total	Foreign born*	Total	Foreign	Mixed
Total	3,747,844	1,927,703	1,820,141	1,445,465	374,676	4,294,629	1,991,547	2,303,082	1,873,013	430,069
Austria	299,029	190,237	108,792	99,292	9,500	431,397	236,838	194,559	173,652	20,907
Canada†	50,639	26,931	23,708	6,848	16,860	43,810	18,459	25,351	7,222	18,129
Denmark	12,444	7,989	4,455	2,695	1,760	14,914	9,293	5,621	3,316	2,305
Finland	9,845	7,409	2,436	2,254	182	14,542	10,263	4,279	3,822	457
France	30,579	18,265	12,314	6,465	5,849	33,957	18,883	15,074	7,688	7,386
Germany	724,704	278,114	446,590	328,059	118,531	584,838	206,645	378,193	268,665	109,528
Great Britain	214,394	103,028	111,366	46,758	64,608	187,485	80,416	107,069	43,339	63,730
Greece	8,925	8,038	887	661	226	23,204	18,220	4,984	4,417	567
Hungary	112,584	76,625	35,959	32,776	3,183	123,175	72,440	50,735	45,014	5,721
Ireland	676,420	252,662	423,758	309,804	113,954	616,627	211,789	404,838	292,464	112,374
Italy	544,449	340,765	203,684	191,545	12,139	802,946	392,225	410,721	375,284	35,437
Netherlands	7,625	4,191	3,434	1,887	1,547	9,552	5,309	4,243	2,304	1,939
Norway	33,179	22,280	10,899	9,272	1,627	40,544	24,291	16,253	13,431	2,822
Romania	45,995	33,584	12,411	11,930	481	56,702	34,738	21,964	19,867	2,097
Russia	733,924	484,189	249,735	237,280	12,455	985,702	559,225	426,477	395,845	30,632
Spain	4,922	3,331	1,591	643	948	14,659	11,274	3,385	1,995	1,390
Sweden	55,278	34,950	20,328	16,811	3,517	57,750	34,211	23,539	18,721	4,818
Switzerland	16,691	10,450	6,241	3,215	3,026	16,063	9,050	7,013	3,444	3,569
Turkey	11,579	9,855	1,724	1,546	178	22,112	15,890	6,222	5,823	399
All other	21,087	14,810	6,277	2,172	4,105	31,768	22,088	9,680	3,818	5,862
Mixed foreign parentage	133,552	—	133,552	133,552	—	182,882	—	182,882	182,882	—

TABLE C-2 (Continued)
Nativity and Parentage of Foreign White Stock by Country of Origin, New York City, 1910-40

Country of origin	1930 Census		Native of foreign or mixed parentage			1940 Census		Native of foreign or mixed parentage		
	Total	Foreign born	Total	Foreign	Mixed	Total	Foreign born	Total	Foreign	Mixed
Total	5,084,066	2,295,181	2,788,885	2,211,974	576,911	4,831,580	2,080,020	2,751,560	2,115,320	636,240
Austria	288,978	127,169	161,809	137,805	24,004	322,586	145,106	177,480	144,400	33,080
Canada†	85,899	44,926	40,973	17,088	23,885	79,725	40,345	39,380	16,480	22,900
Czechoslovakia	72,282	35,318	36,964	30,933	6,031	57,624	26,884	30,740	24,160	6,580
Denmark	20,200	11,096	9,104	6,442	2,662	16,825	8,845	7,980	5,140	2,840
Finland	20,043	13,224	6,819	5,950	869	17,525	11,245	6,280	5,160	1,120
France	47,981	23,288	24,693	15,264	9,429	38,816	19,696	19,120	11,420	7,700
Germany	600,084	237,588	362,496	257,765	104,731	498,289	224,749	273,540	194,720	78,820
Great Britain	254,890	118,441	136,449	69,697	66,752	216,663	97,703	118,960	59,340	59,620
Greece	43,833	27,182	16,651	15,036	1,615	53,253	28,593	24,660	21,120	3,540
Hungary	115,098	59,883	55,215	46,839	8,376	123,188	62,588	60,600	49,120	11,480
Ireland‡	613,006	220,631	392,375	280,216	112,159	518,466	181,826	336,640	241,780	94,860
Italy	1,070,355	440,250	630,105	537,059	93,046	1,095,369	409,489	685,880	551,320	134,560
Lithuania	31,173	15,005	16,168	14,730	1,438	33,169	15,089	18,080	15,140	2,940
Netherlands	11,620	5,335	6,285	4,073	2,212	11,288	5,608	5,680	3,240	2,440
Norway	62,915	38,130	24,785	20,123	4,662	54,530	30,750	23,780	18,360	5,420
Palestine-Syria	15,893	8,696	7,197	6,470	727	17,558	8,598	8,960	7,480	1,480
Poland	458,381	238,339	220,042	199,269	20,773	412,543	194,163	218,380	185,860	32,520
Romania	93,479	46,750	46,729	40,416	6,313	84,675	40,655	44,020	35,320	8,700
Spain	22,509	14,000	8,509	5,900	2,609	25,283	13,583	11,700	7,520	4,180
Sweden	66,978	37,267	29,711	23,488	6,223	55,161	28,881	26,280	20,040	6,240
Switzerland	19,595	9,895	9,700	6,141	3,559	15,251	8,551	6,700	3,960	2,740
Turkey	24,678	15,115	9,563	8,952	611	31,283	17,663	13,620	12,220	1,400
USSR	945,072	442,431	502,641	439,146	63,495	926,516	395,696	530,820	443,960	86,860
Yugoslavia	10,634	6,450	4,184	3,692	492	11,355	6,475	4,880	3,780	1,100
All other§	88,490	58,772	29,718	19,480	10,238	114,639	57,239	57,400	34,280	23,120

* According to birthplace of father. † Including Newfoundland. ‡ Includes Irish Free State and Northern Ireland.
§ Includes "not reported."

TABLE C-3
Nativity and Parentage of Foreign White Stock by Country of Origin, New York City, 1950 and 1960

Country of origin	1950 Census			1960 Census		
	Total	Foreign born	Native of foreign or mixed parentage	Total	Foreign born	Native of foreign or mixed parentage
Total	4,444,141	1,784,206	2,659,935	3,622,929	1,463,821	2,159,108
Austria	293,516	124,256	169,260	219,291	84,301	134,990
Canada	77,950	35,860	42,090	64,049	28,150	35,899
Cuba	*	*	*	35,687	25,959	9,728
Czechoslovakia	64,510	30,130	34,380	58,355	27,755	30,600
Denmark	14,552	6,707	7,845	10,229	4,611	5,618
Dominican Republic	*	*	*	11,065	8,182	2,883
Finland	14,696	8,891	5,805	10,278	6,094	4,184
France	40,506	20,461	20,045	34,703	18,877	15,826
Germany	427,927	185,467	242,460	323,468	152,192	171,276
Great Britain	191,754	80,019	111,735	142,446	61,018	81,428
Greece	56,925	29,815	27,110	55,584	28,845	26,739
Hungary	114,423	51,968	62,455	96,712	45,567	51,145
Ireland†	456,408	114,808	311,600	342,381	114,008	228,373
Israel	*	*	*	10,426	7,110	3,316
Italy	1,028,980	344,115	684,865	857,659	280,786	576,873
Latvia	*	*	*	12,746	6,898	5,848
Lithuania	33,069	13,599	19,470	30,936	11,347	19,589
Netherlands	11,381	5,571	5,810	9,142	4,635	4,507
Norway	50,262	25,552	24,710	36,754	18,521	18,233
Poland	403,588	179,878	223,710	389,009	168,824	220,185
Romania	71,094	29,409	41,685	62,328	24,754	37,574
Spain	24,838	12,183	12,655	22,469	10,455	12,014
Sweden	43,774	20,424	23,350	27,473	11,677	15,796
Switzerland	14,626	7,151	7,475	11,313	5,819	5,494
Turkey	*	*	*	22,342	11,779	10,563
USSR	808,163	314,603	493,560	563,243	204,578	358,665
Yugoslavia	12,236	6,736	5,500	19,916	12,390	7,526
All other	188,963	106,603	82,360	121,314	72,077	49,237
Not specified				21,611	6,612	14,999

*Included with "all other."   †Includes Irish Republic and Northern Ireland.

TABLE C-4
Nativity and Parentage of Foreign Stock
by Country of Origin, New York City, 1970

Country of origin	Total	Foreign born	Native of foreign or mixed parentage
Total	3,306,012	1,437,058*	1,868,954†
Austria	145,981	48,024	97,957
Canada	50,564	20,545	30,019
China	56,217	37,348	18,869
Cuba	84,179	63,043	21,136
Czechoslovakia	45,960	21,523	24,437
Denmark	6,640	2,760	3,880
France	29,902	15,514	14,388
Germany	210,040	98,336	111,704
Greece	63,854	35,000	28,854
Hungary	72,071	31,717	40,354
Ireland	220,622	68,778	151,844
Italy	682,613	212,160	470,453
Japan	11,007	7,843	3,164
Lithuania	21,536	6,584	14,952
Mexico	7,893	3,541	4,352
Netherlands	7,259	3,693	3,566
Norway	23,217	10,229	12,988
Poland	292,319	119,604	172,715
Sweden	16,148	6,140	10,008
Switzerland	8,201	3,930	4,271
USSR	393,918	117,363	276,555
United Kingdom	116,342	48,798	67,544
Yugoslavia	26,077	16,491	9,586
Other America	367,247	258,356	108,891
Other Asia	93,496	59,745	33,751
Other Europe	122,631	56,205	66,426
All other	27,592	17,351	10,241
Not reported	102,486	46,437	56,049

*Includes 159,066 Negro (largely from "Other America") and an estimated 75,000 other nonwhite persons (largely from China, Japan, and other Asia).

†Includes an estimated 85,000 Negro and 30,000 other nonwhite persons.

Bibliography

NEW YORK HISTORY

The history of New York City is far too panoramic to be adequately encompassed within a single volume. Excellent references, however, are available for specific periods of the city's history. The following representative works were found to be most useful and are suggested for those who wish to obtain more detail about the city's complex past.

For the Dutch colonial period: J. Franklin Jameson, *Narratives of New Netherland 1609-1664* (1909, reissued New York: Barnes & Noble, 1959).

For the English colonial period: Arthur E. Peterson, *New York as an Eighteenth Century Municipality: Prior to 1731* and George W. Edwards, *New York as an Eighteenth Century Municipality: 1731-1776* (New York: Studies in History, Economics and Public Law, vol. 75, Columbia University, 1917).

For the Revolutionary War period: Oscar T. Barck, Jr., *New York City during the War for Independence* (New York: Columbia University Press, 1931).

For the early federal period: Sidney I. Pomerantz, *New York: An American City 1783-1803* (New York: Columbia University Press, 1938).

For the twentieth century: Committee on Regional Plan of New York and its Environs, *Regional Survey of New York and its Environs*, 8 vols. (New York, 1927-31); Edgar M. Hoover and Raymond Vernon, *Anatomy of a Metropolis* (Cambridge: Harvard University Press, 1959).

Particularly good secondary sources covering many eras of the city's life are: Bayrd Still, *Mirror for Gotham* (New York: New York University Press, 1956); James Ford (and associates), *Slums and Housing*, 2 vols. (Cambridge: Harvard University Press, 1936).

For detailed accounts of living conditions in the late nineteenth century, particularly among the immigrant communities, useful sources are Kate H. Claghorn, "The Foreign Immigrant in New York City," U.S. Industrial Commission, *Reports on Immigration* (Washington: Government Printing Office, 1901), vol. XV; Jacob A. Riis, *How the Other Half Lives: Studies among the Tenements of New York* (New York: Charles Scribner's Sons, 1917).

New York Ethnic Group History and Sociology

The diversity of New York's population has led to a vast and continuing literature concerned with the different ethnic groups that comprise sub-communities within the metropolis. The following brief list points out some of the more outstanding works particular to New York.

On Italians: John H. Mariano, *The Second Generation of Italians in New York City* (Boston: The Christopher Publishing House, 1921).

On Jews: Hyman B. Grinstein, *The Rise of the Jewish Community of New York 1654-1860,* (Philadelphia: The Jewish Publication Society of America, 1945); Moses Rischin, *The Promised City: New York's Jews, 1870-1914,* (Cambridge: Harvard University Press, 1962).

On Negroes: Gilbert Osofsky, *Harlem: The Making of a Ghetto,* (New York: Harper and Row, 1963); Seth M. Scheiner, *Negro Mecca: A History of the Negro in New York City, 1865-1920* (New York: New York University Press, 1965).

On Puerto Ricans: Lawrence R. Chenault, *The Puerto Rican Migrant in New York City (New York: Columbia University Press, 1938).*

Particularly noteworthy general references are: Oscar Handlin, *The Newcomers: Negroes and Puerto Ricans in a Changing Metropolis* (Cambridge: Harvard University Press, 1959); Nathan Glazer and Daniel P. Moynihan, *Beyond the Melting Pot: The Negroes, Puerto Ricans, Jews, Italians, and Irish of New York City* (Cambridge, Mass.: MIT Press, 1963).

Government Statistical Sources

Census

Since this book is largely a statistical monograph, the principal primary sources consulted were statistical volumes of federal, state, and city government that provide either census data based on enumerations of the population or vital statistics based on birth and death registration.

A federal census, required by the Constitution of the United States, has been taken decennially from 1790 to 1970. The returns comprise the principal documentation for population change in New York City, as elsewhere. State censuses were conducted decennially in New York State from 1825 to 1875; these are also quite valuable for the student of population growth in New York City. Although state censuses also were taken in 1892 and at three subsequent times until finally discontinued, relatively little useful material was made available from these later counts. The state and federal censuses consulted are shown under "Census Sources."

Vital Statistics

The history of the development of vital statistics in New York City is a long and interesting one. Some background information summarizing the early establishment of birth and death registration appears in Charles F. Bolduan, "Over a Century of Health Administration in New York City," *New York Department of Health Monograph Series,* No. 13 (March 1916). The primary source of pre-1866 statistics are the annual reports of the City Inspector's Office. These are variously titled: "Annual Report of the City Inspector of the City of New York for the Year Ending . . . ," and "Annual Report of Deaths in the City and County of New York for the Year."

Since 1866 the Department of Health has had responsibility for the collection of vital records and the publication of vital statistics. *The First Annual Report of the Board of Health of the Health Department of the City of New York—April 11, 1870 to April 10, 1871* appeared in 1871 and contained detailed data for the years 1866 to 1870. Annual (or periodic) statistics have appeared in the reports of the Health Department up to the present time. In recent years reports covering a series of years have replaced annual volumes. The two latest are *Vital Statistics: 1949 to 1955* and *Vital Statistics: 1956 to 1963* issued by the Bureau of Records and Statistics, Department of Health of the City of New York. In addition, a brief statistical review has recently appeared annually entitled *Summary of Vital Statistics.*

The reports issued by New York City's Department of Health, unfortunately, contain data only on place of occurrence of the vital event. Statistics based on place of residence can be obtained from Annual Reports issued by the Office of Biostatistics (previously the Division of Vital Statistics), New York State Department of Health, for the years 1930 through 1967.

The U.S. Bureau of the Census (and its predecessor, the U.S. Census Office) also published mortality statistics for American cities, including New York, in extensive detail at selected times. Outstanding volumes include *Vital Statistics of New York City and Brooklyn Covering a Period of Six Years Ending May 31, 1890* (Washington, 1894) and *Mortality Rates, 1910-1920* (Washington, 1923).

BOOKS

Abelow, Samuel P. *History of Brooklyn Jewry.* New York: Scheba Publishing Co., 1937.

Adams, Hannah, *The History of the Jews from the Destruction of Jerusalem to the Nineteenth Century.* Boston: J. Eliot, Jr., 1812.

The American Almanac 1830. Boston: David H. Williams, 1833.

The American Annual Cyclopaedia and Register of Important Events of the Year 1861. New York: D. Appleton Co., 1862.

Barck, Oscar T., Jr. *New York City during the War for Independence.* New York: Columbia University Press, 1931.

Bebout, John E., and Ronald J. Grele, *Where Cities Meet: The Urbanization of New Jersey.* New York: Van Nostrand, 1964.

Board of Delegates of American Israelites and the Union of American Hebrew Congregations, *Statistics of the Jews in the United States.* Philadelphia: Union of American Hebrew Congregations, 1880.

Bridenbaugh, Carl, *Cities in Revolt.* New York: Alfred A. Knopf, 1955.

————, *Cities in the Wilderness.* New York: Alfred A. Knopf, 1955.

Bureau of Jewish Social Research, *Jewish Communal Survey of Greater New York.* New York: Bureau of Jewish Social Research, 1928.

Carpenter, Niles, *Immigrants and their Children,* Census Monograph VII. Washington, D.C.: U.S. Government Printing Office, 1927.

Cassedy, James H. *Demography in Early America.* Cambridge, Mass.: Harvard University Press, 1969.

Coale, Ansley J., and Melvin Zelnik, *New Estimates of Fertility and Population in the United States.* Princeton: Princeton University Press, 1963.

Committee on Regional Plan of New York and its Environs, *Regional Survey of New York and its Environs, Vol. II, Population, Land Values and Government.* New York: Regional Plan of New York and its Environs, 1929.

Committee for the Special Research Project in the Health Insurance Plan of Greater New York, *Health and Medical Care in New York City.* Cambridge, Mass.: Harvard University Press, 1957.

Cooper, James Fenimore, *Notions of the Americans: Picked up by a Travelling Bachelor.* Philadelphia: Carey, Lea, and Carey, 1828.

Daly, Charles P. *The Settlement of the Jews in North America.* New York: P. Cowen, 1893.

Dawson, Henry B. *New York City during the American Revolution.* New York: Mercantile Library Association, 1861.

De Bow, J. D. B. *Statistical View of the United States...A Compendium of the Seventh Census.* Washington, D.C.: A. O. P. Nicholson, 1854.

Duffy, John, *A History of Public Health in New York City; 1625-1866.* New York: Russell Sage Foundation, 1968.

Dwight, Timothy, *Travels in New-England and New-York.* London: W. Baynes and Son, 1823.

Elinson, Jack, Paul W. Haberman, and Cyrille Gell, *Ethnic and Educational Data on Adults in New York City 1963-1964.* New York: School of Public Health and Administrative Medicine, Columbia University, 1967.

Ernst, Robert, *Immigrant Life in New York City, 1825-1863.* New York: Columbia University Press, 1949.

Faust, Albert B. *The German Element in the United States.* New York: Riverside Press, 1909.

Flick, Alexander C. *History of the State of New York*. New York: Columbia University Press, 1934.

Ford, James, *Slums and Housing*. Cambridge, Mass.: Harvard University Press, 1936.

Gerard, James W. *The Impress of Nationalities upon the City of New York*. New York: Columbia Spectator Publishing Co., 1883.

Glass, D. V., and D. E. C. Eversley, *Population in History*. Chicago: Aldine Publishing Co., 1965.

Glazer, Nathan, and Daniel P. Moynihan, *Beyond the Melting Pot*. Boston: MIT Press, 1963.

Greene, Evarts B., and Virginia D. Harrington, *American Population before the Federal Census of 1790*. New York: Columbia University Press, 1932.

Greenleaf, Jonathan, *A History of the Churches of All Denominations in the City of New York from the First Settlement to the Year 1846*. New York: E. French, 1846.

Grinstein, Hyman B. *The Rise of the Jewish Community of New York 1654-1860*. Philadelphia: The Jewish Publication Society of America, 1945.

Hall, Edward H. *A Volume Commemorating the Creation of the Second City of the World*. New York: New York Republic Press, 1898.

Handlin, Oscar, *The Newcomers*. Cambridge, Mass.: Harvard University Press, 1959.

Hardie, James, *The Description of the City of New-York*. New York: S. Marks, 1827.

Hoover, Edgar M., and Raymond Vernon, *Anatomy of a Metropolis*. Cambridge, Mass.: Harvard University Press, 1959.

Jaffe, A. J. *Handbook of Statistical Methods for Demographers*. Washington, D.C.: U.S. Government Printing Office, 1951.

Jameson, J. Franklin, *Narratives of New Netherland 1609-1664*. New York: Barnes and Noble, 1959.

Lee, Everett S., Ann R. Miller, Carol P. Brainerd, and Richard Easterlin, *Population Redistribution and Economic Growth: United States 1870-1950*. Philadelphia: American Philosophical Society, 1957.

Levasseur, A. *Lafayette in America in 1824 and 1825; Or, Journal of a Voyage to the United States*. Philadelphia: Carey and Lea, 1829.

Mackay, Charles, *Life and Liberty in America: Or Sketches of a Tour in the United States and Canada in 1857-58*. London: Harper and Brothers, 1859.

Maguire, John Francis, *The Irish in America*. New York: D. & J. Sadlier and Co., 1869.

Massarik, Fred, *A Report on the Jewish Population of Los Angeles 1959*. Los Angeles: Research Service Bureau, Jewish Federation Council of Greater Los Angeles, 1959.

McGill, Nettie P., and Ellen N. Matthews, *The Youth of New York City.* New York: Macmillan, 1940.

Miller, John, *New York Considered and Improved . . . 1695.* London: Thomas Rodd, 1843.

O'Callaghan, Edmund B. *The Documentary History of the State of New-York.* Albany: Weed, Parsons, 1849.

Osofsky, Gilbert, *Harlem: The Making of a Ghetto.* New York: Harper and Row, 1963.

Pomerantz, Sidney I. *New York: An American City 1783-1803.* New York: Columbia University Press, 1938.

Reports of the Industrial Commission on Immigration, Vol. XV. Washington, D.C.: U.S. Government Printing Office, 1901.

Research Bureau, Welfare and Health Council of New York City, *Population of Puerto Rican Birth or Parentage: New York City: 1950.* New York: 1952.

Rischin, Moses, *The Promised City: New York's Jews,* 1870-1914. Cambridge, Mass.: Harvard University Press, 1962.

Roberts, Kenneth, and Anna M. Roberts, *Moreau de St. Mery's American Journey.* New York: Doubleday, 1947.

Scheiner, Seth M. *Negro Mecca: A History of the Negro in New York City, 1865-1920.* New York: New York University Press, 1965.

Shea, John Gilmary, *The Catholic Churches of New York City.* New York: L. G. Goulding, 1878.

Shore, William B. *A Report on the Second Regional Plan.* New York: Regional Plan Association, 1967.

Sklare, Marshall, *The Jews. Social Patterns of an American Group.* Glencoe, Ill.: The Free Press, 1958.

Smyth, J. F. D. *A Tour in the United States of America.* London, 1784; reissued New York: Arno Press, 1968.

Stiles, Henry R. *History of the City of Brooklyn.* Brooklyn: Privately Printed, 1870.

Still, Bayrd, *Mirror for Gotham.* New York: New York University Press, 1956.

Syrett, Harold C. *The City of Brooklyn, 1865-1898.* New York: Columbia University Press, 1944.

Tryon, Warner S. *A Mirror for Americans.* Chicago: University of Chicago Press, 1952.

United Nations Department of Economic and Social Affairs, *Methods for Population Projections by Sex and Age,* Population Studies No. 25. New York: United Nations Publications, 1956.

United States Department of Justice, *Annual Report of the Immigration and Naturalization Service.* Washington, D.C.: U.S. Government Printing Office, 1970.

Weber, Adna F. *The Growth of Cities in the Nineteenth Century.* Ithaca, N.Y.: Cornell University Press, 1963.

Weld, Ralph Foster, *Brooklyn Village,* New York State Historical Association Series. New York: Columbia University Press, 1938.

Yasuba, Yasukichi, *Birth Rate of the White Population in the United States, 1800-1860; An Economic Study.* The Johns Hopkins University Studies in Historical and Political Science, Series 79, No. 2. Baltimore: The Johns Hopkins Press, 1962.

ARTICLES

Albion, Robert G. "Yankee Domination of New York Port, 1820-1865," *The New England Quarterly,* V (October 1932).

Barker, Howard F. "National Stocks in the Population of the United States as Indicated by Surnames in the Census of 1790," *Annual Report of the American Historical Association for the Year 1931,* I.

Chalmers, Henry, "The Number of Jews in New York City," Publications of the American Statistical Association, XIV, 1914-15 (1916).

Collections of the Massachusetts Historical Society, I, second series (1838).

Deardorff, Neva R. "The Religio-Cultural Background of New York City's Population, *Milbank Memorial Fund Quarterly,* XXXIII, 2 (April 1955).

Dublin, Louis I. "Factors in American Mortality, A Study of Death Rates in the Race Stocks of New York State, 1910," *American Economic Review,* VI, 3 (September 1916).

The Federation of Churches and Christian Workers of New York City, *Federation,* II, 3 (December 1902).

Freedman, Ronald, Pascal K. Whelpton, and John W. Smit, "Socio-Economic Factors in Religious Differences in Fertility," *American Sociological Review,* XXVI (August 1961).

Goldberg, Nathan, "The Jewish Population in America, 1917-1947: Population Growth and Birth Rate," *The Jewish Review,* V (January-December 1948).

Hansen, Marcus L. "The Minor Stocks in the American Population of 1790," *Annual Report of the American Historical Association for the Year 1931,* I.

Hutchinson, E. P. "Notes on Immigration Statistics of the United States," *Journal of the American Statistical Association,* LIII (December 1958).

Keely, Charles B. "Effects of the Immigration Act of 1965 on Selected Population Characteristics of Immigrants to the United States," *Demography,* VIII, 2 (May 1971).

Liberson, David M. "Causes of Death among Jews in New York City in 1953," *Jewish Social Studies,* XVIII, 2 (April 1956).

MacMahon, Brian, and Ernest K. Koller, "Ethnic Differences in the Incidence of Leukemia," *Blood*, XII, 1 (January 1957).

Newill, Vaun A. "Distribution of Cancer Mortality Among Ethnic Subgroups of the White Population of New York City, 1953-58," *Journal of the National Cancer Institute*, XXVI (1961).

Report of Committee on Linguistic and National Stocks in the Population of the United States, *Annual Report of the American Historical Association for the Year 1931*, I

Rosenwaike, Ira, "A Critical Examination of the Designation of Standard Metropolitan Statistical Areas," *Social Forces*, XLVIII, 3 (March 1970).

Seidman, Herbert, Lawrence Garfinkel, and Leonard Craig, "Death Rates in New York City by Socio-Economic Class and Religious Group and by Country of Birth, 1949-1951," *Jewish Journal of Sociology*, IV, 2 (December 1962).

Stander, Golda G. "Jesuit Educational Institutions in the City of New York," United States Catholic Historical Society, *Historical Records and Studies*, XXIV (1934).

Taueber, Karl E., and Alma F. Taueber, "The Changing Character of Negro Migration," *American Jorunal of Sociology*, LXX (January 1965).

Wheatley, Richard, "The Jews in New York," *The Century Magazine*, XLIII, 3 (1892).

Yuan, D. Y. "Chinatown and Beyond: The Chinese Population in Metropolitan New York," *Phylon*, XXVII, 4 (Winter 1966).

Census Sources

New York Secretary of State

Census of the State of New York for 1845. Albany, 1846.

Census of the State of New York for 1855 . . . Prepared from the original returns by F. B. Hough. Albany, 1857.

Census of the State of New York for 1865 . . . Prepared from the original returns by F. B. Hough. Albany, 1867.

Census of the State of New York for 1875. Compiled from the original returns by C. W. Seaton. Albany, 1877.

U. S. Department of State

Second Census or Enumeration of the Inhabitants of the United States. Washington, 1801.

Census for 1820. Washington, 1821.

Fifth Census, or Enumeration of the United States, 1830. Washington, 1832.

Sixth Census or Enumeration of the Inhabitants of the United States.
Washington, 1841.
Statistical View of the United States ... being a Compendium of the
Seventh Census ... by J. D. B. De Bow, Supt. of the U.S. Census.
Washington, 1854.

U.S. Census Office (all volumes published by U.S.
Government Printing Office)

Population of the United States in 1860; Compiled from the Original
Returns of the Eighth Census. Washington, 1864.
Ninth Census, Vol. I: The Statistics of the Population of the United States
... Compiled from the Original Returns of the Ninth Census.
Washington, 1872.
Statistics of the Population of the United States at the Tenth Census.
Washington, 1883.
Report on the Mortality and Vital Statistics of the United States, Tenth
Census, Part 2. Washington, 1886.
Population of the United States at the Eleventh Census, Part I, Washing-
ton, 1895; Part 2, Washington, 1897.
Twelfth Census of the United States, Taken in the Year 1900. Population,
Vol. I, Parts 1 and 2, and Vol. II, Part 2. Washington, 1902.

U.S. Bureau of the Census (all volumes published by
U.S. Government Printing Office)

A Century of Population Growth. Washington, 1909.
Thirteenth Census of the United States Taken in the Year 1910. Popula-
tion, Vol. I. Washington, 1913.
Fourteenth Census of the United States Taken in the Year 1920, Popula-
tion, Vols. II and III. Washington, 1921-22.
Fifteenth Census of the United States: 1930. Washington, 1932-33.
Population
> Vol. II, *General Report—Statistics by Subject*
> Vol. III, Part 2, *Reports by States*
> Vol. VI, *Families*
> *Age of the Foreign-born White Population by Country of Birth*
> *Special Report on Foreign-born White Families by Country of*
> *Birth of Head*
Sixteenth Census of the United States: 1940. Washington, 1943-46.
Population
> Vol. IV, Part 3, *Characteristics by Age*
> *Characteristics of the Nonwhite Population by Race*
> *Internal Migration 1935 to 1940. Age of Migrants*
> *Internal Migration 1935 to 1940. Color and Sex of Migrants*

Internal Migration 1935 to 1940. Social Characteristics of Migrants

Nativity and Parentage of the White Population. Country of Origin of the Foreign Stock

Nativity and Parentage of the White Population. General Characteristics

State of Birth of the Native Population

U.S. *Census of Population: 1950.* Washington, 1953-54.

Vol. II, *Characteristics of the Population,* Parts 1, 30, 32

Nativity and Parentage

Nonwhite Population by Race

State of Birth

U.S. *Census of Population: 1960.* Washington, 1963-65.

Vol. I, *Characteristics of the Population,* Parts 1, 32, 34

Journey to Work

Mobility for Metropolitan Areas

Mobility for States and State Economic Areas

Nativity and Parentage

Nonwhite Population by Race

Puerto Ricans in the United States

State of Birth

U.S. *Census of Population: 1970.* Washington, 1971-72.

General Population Characteristics. Final Report PC (1)-B 32; PC (1)-B 34.

General Social and Economic Characteristics. Final Report PC (1)-C 34.

Index

Abyssinian Baptist Church (Negro), 27-28
Africa, 21
African Methodist Church (Negro), 27
Age: unpublished (1870), 61n; and parentage, 75, **101**, 116, **120**, **162**; and mortality, 150
Age-adjusted death rate: defined, xiii
Age distribution: of foreign stock by origin, 80-81, 163, **195-96**; by religion, **155**; by race and sex, **188-91**; by sex, nativity, and parentage, **192-94**; of Puerto Ricans, by sex, **197-98**; of non-Puerto Rican whites, by sex, **199**
Age-specific birth rates: defined, xiii
Agriculture, 48
Alabama, **148**
Alaska, **102-103**
Albany, N.Y., 1-2, 7, 17
Albany Co., N.Y., 64, **65-66**
Albion, Robert G., 33
Aliens: in 1816, 19; at 1830 census, 35; at state censuses, 38-39
Allerton, Issac, 21
American Council of Learned Societies, 20-21
Anabaptists: 4, 9, 11; in Brooklyn, **29-30**. *See also* Mennonites
Andros, Gov. Edmund, 9, 11
Assimilation. *See* Intermarriage
Astoria (Queens), 60
Austria (Austrians): 163, **166**; number of, **67**, 69, **115**, **118**, **202-206**; in Brooklyn, **70**; migration, **94**, 97, **98**; census problems, 97, 163; family heads, **113**; religion, 122, **123**, **125-26**, 154, **156**; Jews, 127-28, 158, **159**; births, **183**; mortality, **184-85**; age, **195-96**
Austria-Hungary: **79**, 92, **95**, 96, 111, **182**; mortality, **80**, 107. *See also* Austria; Hungary

Baden (Germany), 43
Baltimore, 91, 172
Baptists: 10, 28, **86**; early churches, 25-26; in Brooklyn, 30
Barbados, 140
Barck, Oscar T., 14

Barker, Howard F., 20, 21
Bavaria, 43
Bayonne, N.J., 170
Bedford-Stuyvesant (Brooklyn), 141
Belgians. *See* Walloons
Bellomont, Gov., 7, 8
Bergen Co., N.J.: **66**, 169, 171; 20th-century growth, **134**, 170; net migration, **137**, 172-73; excluded from New York SMSA, 170n
Billings, Dr. John S., 80-81
Birth cohort: defined, xiii, 61; analysis of ethnic groups, 164-66; analysis of migration, 99-101, 166; analysis of intermarriage, 116, 120
Birth rate: 55, 104n; defined, xiii; birth ratios, 47-48; methods of estimating, 61-62; U.S. and New York (1880-1900), **62**; trends, 103-105, 150; by ethnic group (1950-60), 105-106, 111, **152-53**; by year, **178**. *See also* Fertility; Natural increase
Births: census statistics, 37-38; by race, annually, **179-80**; by birthplace of mother, annually, **182-83**; Puerto Ricans (1950-69), **185**
Bohemia (Bohemians): **67**, **70**, **73-74**, **123**; census classification, 69; location, 84
Boroughs: creation of, 57-58
Boston: 7, 109, 172; aliens, 35
Bridgeport, Conn., 171
Britain (British): 7, 21-23, 34, 57, 73, **166**; colony ceded to, 3-4; early settlers, 3, 6-7, 9-10, 12; in Brooklyn, 12, 30, 50, **51**, 70; and Revolutionary War, 14-15; and War of 1812, 18; majority of population, 19; number of, 40, **42**, **67**, **73-74**, **76**, **115**, **118**, **202-206**; mortality, 41, 80, 107-108, **184-85**; and Negroes, 45; intermarriage, 75, 115; family heads, **79**, 113; migration, 93, **94-95**, **97-98**; religion, 122-26 *passim*, **156**, **158-59**; census error, 163; age, 163, **195-96**; births, **182-83**
Brockholls, Anthony, 11
Bronx, the: borough formed, 57, **58**;

217

Bronx, cont'd.
20th-century growth, 131-32, **133;**
Negroes, **133,** 141-42; net migration,
137; Puerto Ricans, 138, **139;** Italians,
167
Brooklyn: town and village, 6, 12, 29-31;
religion, 6, 29-30, 54, 87; city growth,
37, 47, 49-50, 55, 59; population by
birthplace, **51, 63,** 69-71, 75-76; borough
formed, 57-58; intrastate migrants,
64-66; Negroes, 76-78, **133,** 141-42;
Irish, **81,** 83; Germans, **81,** 83, 85;
mortality, 81-82, 87; 20th century,
131-32, **133;** net migration, **137;** Puerto
Ricans, 138, **139;** Italians, 167; death
rates, by year, **176-77.** *See also* Kings Co.
Brooklyn Bridge, 59
Burial statistics: Catholic, 53; by denomination of cemetery, 124-29, 154-55; by
country of birth and cemetery, **156;**
by nativity, age, and cemetery, **157;** of
Jews, by age and birthplace, **158**
Bushwick (Brooklyn), 12, **31,** 50, 83
Byrd, William, 9

California: migrants from, **148;** migrants
to, 149, 173
Calvinists. *See* Dutch Reformed Church;
German Reformed Church
Canada (Canadians), **67, 70, 73-74, 79, 95, 97,**
118, 202-206; migrants to, 15; British
North America, **42, 51;** foreign-stock
classification, 109; intermarriage, 115-16;
age, 163, **195-96**
Carroll, Bishop John, 27
Catholics (Roman): 9, 25, 28, 52; in
colony, 4-5, 11; Irish, 14, 21, 27, 52-53;
pre-Civil War growth, 27, 52-53; in
Brooklyn, 30, **53,** 54, 87; German, 53;
mortality, 86-87; population estimates,
86, 88, 122-27 *passim,* 130, 152; by
ethnic group, 123-24, **125;** deaths by
origin, **126,** 154, **156-57;** by color (1952),
153; by age (1950), **155**
Censuses: colonial, 7-8; by city, 16-17, 19;
underenumeration, 55-56, 88-89
Censuses, New York State: to 1825, 16,
18; broadens scope, 36, 59, 85-86;
foreign born in 1845, 40; of 1865,
55-56
Censuses, U.S.: required by constitution,
16; expansion in 1850, 36; inaccuracies,
45-48, 139*n,* 160, 163-64; religion query,
87-88; immigration query, 89; previous
residence query, 98, 143, 145-46,
148-49; parentage classification, 109;
mother tongue query, 110-11; state of
birth statistics, 143
Chalmers, Henry, 111
Charles II, king of England, 3

Chicago, 57, 172
China (Chinese): 78*n,* 138, 167-68, **206;**
growth, 78, **141,** 142-43
Churches: number of, 11, 24-25, 27-28,
53; in Brooklyn, 29-30; census statistics,
52-54. *See also* specific religious
Church of England. *See* Episcopalians
Cincinnati, Ohio, 110
Civil War, 55-56
Cleveland, Ohio, 172
Clinton, Gov. George, 24
Coale, Ansley J., 61, 104
Cohort. *See* Birth cohort
Common Council, 16, 19
Commuters: first statistics (1865), 59; in
suburban labor force, 169-70, 171
Congregationalists, **86**
Connecticut; migrants from, 22, **42,** 46,
51, 67, 70, 102-104, 148; suburbanization,
135, **149,** 169, 171
Connolly, Bishop John, 27
Cooper, James Fenimore, 31, 34, 44-45
Cork, Ireland, 43
Cornbury, Gov. Edward, 7
Country of birth statistics. *See* Foreign-
born population; Foreign stock
Cowen, Philip, 87
Craig, Leonard, 154
Cuba (Cubans), 164, **168, 205-206**
Czechoslovakia (Czechoslovakians): **97,**
115, 125, 202, 204-206; census problems,
97, 163; age, 163, **195-96.** *See also*
Bohemia

Dade Co., Fla., 172
Death rate: defined, xiii. *See also* Mortality
De Bow, J.D.B., 36, 47
Denmark (Danes), 23, **67,** 70, **202-206.**
See also Scandinavia
Detroit, Mich., 91, 172
District of Columbia: Negroes from, **104,**
117, **148**
Dominican Republic, 164, **168, 205**
Dongan, Gov. Thomas, 7, 9, 10, 11
Dublin, Louis I., 106-107
Dutch, *See* Holland
Dutch East India Company, 1
Dutchess Co., N.Y., 64, **65, 66**
Dutch Reformed Church: 24, 28, **86;** in
colony, 4, 6, 9-11; after Revolution, 25
Dutch West India Company: 1, 3-5, 20;
incorporated, 2; encouraged settlement,
5-6
Dwight, Timothy, 21-23

Eastchester (Bronx), 57
East River, 30, 49
Elizabeth, N.J., 171
Embargo Act, 18
Embury, Rev. Philip, 26

England. *See* Britain
Epidemics: smallpox, 8, 10; yellow fever, 8, 17; and Irish, 21: cholera, 37
Episcopalians: 24, 27-28, **86;** in colony, 9-11; disestablished, 30-31; in Brooklyn, 29-30
Erie Canal, 33, 35
Ernst, Robert, 43
Essex Co., N.J., 65, **66, 170,** 171
Ethnic groups: in 1900, 78-79; location, 82-85; concentration in New York, 92; census classification of nonwhites, 138-39; importance, 162; relative out-migration, 166. *See also* Foreign stock; Race distribution

Fairfield Co., Conn., **170,** 171
Families: U.S., by parentage of head (1900), **79, 90;** by race, nativity, and parentage of head (1930), **113**
Farmer, Father Ferdinand, 27
Federation, 122
Fertility: fertility ratios, **62,** 105-106; by nativity, 82, 105-106; by ethnic group, 105-106, 111-12, 150-51, **152;** measured by children under 10 years, 112, **113.** *See also* Birth rate
Finland, **203-205**
Fire of 1776, 15
Flatbush (Brooklyn): 12, **31,** 51, 59; early settlement, 6
Flatlands (Brooklyn): 12, **31,** 51, 59; early settlement, 6
Fletcher, Gov., 11
Florida: migrants from, **102-103, 148;** Negroes from, **103-104,** 117, 140, **148;** migrants to, 149, 172-73, 174
Flushing (Queens): 51, 57, **60;** early settlement, 6
Fordham (Bronx), 56
Foreign-born population: 19th century, 39-44, 63, 67-71; death rates by origin, 41, 107; country of birth (19th century), **42, 51, 67, 70;** and year of immigration, 92-93, **94,** 110; net migration, 93-97, **98,** 137; reporting errors (1940), 97; migrants (1935-40), 98; fertility of, 105-106, 112, **113;** family heads by origin, **113;** Negroes, 117-18, **121,** 168; deaths by cemetery denomination, 124-27, 154, **156;** Jews, **159.** *See also* Foreign stock; Immigration; specific countries
Foreign stock: defined, 71-72, 109, 159; by origin, 72-73, **74,** 79, **195-96, 202-206;** by nativity and parentage, 72-73, 79, 115-16, **118, 119, 120,** 159-61; nonwhites by origin, **72,** 167, **168;** origin of family heads, **79;** mortality of, 79-82, 106-108; in major cities, 90-91; religion by origin, **123, 125;** census inaccuracies, 160,

163-64; decline of natives, 161-62; by age, 163, **192-96;** outmigration, 166. *See also* Foreign-born population; Native-born population
France (French): 21, 23, 34, 115; religion, 4, 9-11, **123;** in colony, 6-7, 9; in 1790s, 22; number of, 40, **42, 67, 73-74, 115, 118, 202-206;** mortality, **41;** in Brooklyn, **51, 70**
Frederycks, Kryn, 2
French Church, 9-11
French Revolution, 22
Friendly Sons of St. Patrick, 21

Galicia, 69
Gano, Rev. John, 26
Garfinkel, Lawrence, 154
Georgia: migrants from **102-103;** Negroes from, **103-104,** 117, 146, **148**
German Reformed Church (Calvinist), 25*n,* 26, 28
Germany (Germans): 23, 35, 56; early settlement, 20; estimate based on names, 20*n;* number of, 20, **42,** 43, **67,** 73, **74, 76, 115, 118,** 163, **202-206;** religion, 25*n,* 26, 122-26 *passim,* **156;** migration, 39-40, 68, 92-98 *passim;* Jews, 40, 122-124, 130, **158-59;** mortality, **41,** 79-81, 107-108, **184-85;** location, 43-44, 83-85; intermarriage, 75, 115; in Brooklyn, 50, **51,** 70; family heads, 79, 109-10, **113;** share of U.S. in New York, 92; births, rates, 112, **182-83;** age, 163, **195-96;** outmigration, 166
Gravesend (Brooklyn): 12, **31,** 51, 59; early settlement, 6
Greater New York: creation of, 57-58
Greece (Greeks), **115,** 164, **203-206**
Green, Andrew H., 57
Greenwich, Conn., **170,** 171
Greenwich Village (Manhattan), 25
Griesinger, Karl, 43
Grinstein, Hyman B., 44, 54
Gutwasser, Rev. Johann, 4

Haiti, 140, **168**
Half Moon, 1
Hall, Thomas, 3
Hamilton, Alexander, 24
Hamilton, Dr. Alexander, 10
Handlin, Oscar, 83
Hansen, Marcus L., 10, 19-20
Harby, Isaac, 54
Harlem (Manhattan), 25, 85, 140
Hawaii, **102-103**
Health Insurance Plan of Greater New York (HIP): survey by, 151-52
Hempstead (Long Island): 57-58; early settlement, 6
Hesse (Germany), 43

HIP. *See* Health Insurance Plan of
Greater New York
Hoboken, N.J., 170
Holland (Dutch): 22-23; 34; explorations,
1-2; in colony, 3-4, 6-7, 9, 12; religion,
4, 9-11; language, 4, 11, 26; population
trends, 10-11, 19-20; in Brooklyn, 12,
28-30
Holmes, George, 3
Hong Kong, 142
Hudson Co., N.J.: 65, **66**, 169; 20th-
century change, **134**, 170; net migration,
137, 172-73; excluded from New York
SMSA, 170*n*
Hudson River, 1-2, 49
Huguenots. *See* French Church
Hungary (Hungarians): 84, 163, **166**;
number of, **67, 73-74, 115, 118, 202-206**;
in Brooklyn, **70**; migration, 97, **98**;
family heads, **113**; religion, 123-26
passim, 154, **156, 158-59**; census problem,
163; births, **183**; mortality, **185**; age,
195-96. *See also* Austria-Hungary
Hunter, Gov. Robert, 8
Hunter's Point (Queens), 60

Illinois: migrants from, **102-104, 148**;
migrants to, **149**
Immigration: 56; 17th century, 7; of
indentured workers, 11; prior to Civil
War, 35-36, 39-40; net movement,
63, 67-68, 93-96; U.S. total, 89;
relative attraction to New York, 92-93,
98; laws, 96, 135, 142; Negroes, 117-19,
121, 168. *See also* Foreign-born
population
Independents, 28. *See also* Puritans
Indians (American): 1, 7, 36, 78*n*, 139;
sold Manhattan, 2; wars, 3, 6
Industries, 35
Intermarriage: of native and foreign born,
73-75; among immigrants, 75, 115-16
Internal migration. *See* Migration, internal
Ireland (Irish): 7, 14, 21, 23, 34-35, 56
166; early settlement, 5, 20-21; "Rebellion of 1798," 21; number of, 21,
40-41, **42, 67**, 68, 72-73, **74, 76, 115**,
118, 163, **202-206**; estimate based on
names, 21*n*; religion, 26-27, 52-53,
122-26 *passim*, 154, **156**; in Brooklyn,
30, 50, **51**, 69, **70**; migration, 39-40,
68, 79, 93-98 *passim*; occupations,
41-43; mortality, **41**, 68, 79-82, 107-108,
112, **184-85**; location, 44, 83-85; and
Negroes, 45; intermarriage, 75, 115;
family heads, **79**, 109-10, **113**; share of
U.S. in New York, 92; births, rates,
112, **182-83**; census error (1950), 163;
age, 163, **195-96**
Israel, **205**

Italy (Italians): 23, 73, 83, 91; migration,
57, 68, 93-98 *passim;* 110-11, 162-63;
number of, **67, 73-74**, 111, **115, 118,
202-206**; occupations, 68; in Brooklyn,
70; family heads, **79, 113**; mortality,
80, 107-108, 111, 124-25, 127, **184-85**;
location, 83-85, 167; share of U.S. in
New York, 92; fertility,. 105-106, 111-
12; intermarriage, 116; religion, 124-25,
127, 154, **156**; measurement of population change, 164-66; age, **165, 195-96**;
births, **182-83**

Jaffe, A.J., 97
Jamaica, 140
Jamaica (Queens), 51, 57, **60**
Japan (Japanese), 78*n*, 138, **141, 168, 206**
Jay, John, 24
Jersey City, N.J., 170-71
Jesuits, 3, 5
Jewish Board of Deputies, 54
Jews: 25, 27-28, 52, 57, **86**, 87, 91,
162; in colony, 1, 4, 9-11, 26; 19th-
century growth, 26, 40, **53**, 54, 87;
44, 83-85; in Brooklyn, **53**, 54, 70; by
national origin, 69, 93, 123-24, **125**,
127, 163;· mortality, 82, 108, 111-12;
population estimates, 110-11, 127-30,
152-59 *passim;* fertility, 111, 151;
deaths by origin, **126**, 154-158; foreign-
born by origin, 127-28, 156, 158-59;
foreign-born by age (1940), **128**; natives
by age, (1940), **129**; in HIP survey (1952),
152-56 *passim;* by age (1950), **155**;
outmigration, 166
Jogues, Father Isaac, 3-5

Kingsbridge (Bronx), 56, *63*
Kings Co.: formed in 1683, 7; race
distribution, **8**, 28-31, **32**, **77**; in colonial
period, 12, 19-20; slavery, 31; population
by town, **31, 59**; immigrants, **39**; 19th
century, 50-51, 59, 64, **65-66**; becomes
borough of Brooklyn, 57, 58; marriages,
86. *See also* Brooklyn
Knickerbockers, 34-35
Koller, Ernest K., 154

Labor force, 169-71
Lafayette, Marquis de, 35
Laidlaw, Rev. Walter, 122-25 *passim*, 130
Lambert, John, 27-28
Latvia, **97, 205**
Leisler, Jacob, 20
Le Moyne, Father Simon, 5
Levasseur, A., 35
Liberson, David M., 154
Lithuania (Lithuanians), 69, **97**, 110,
115, 204-206
"Little Italy," 84-85

Lodwich, Charles, 10
Long Island: early settlement, 5-6; counties of, 7; emigration from, 7, 23. *See also* specific areas
Long Island City (Queens), 57, 59-60
Los Angeles, Calif.: 172, 174; Jews in, 159*n*
Lower East Side (Manhattan), 82, 84, 131
Lower West Side (Manhattan), 131
Lutherans: 28, **86**; Dutch, 4-5, 9-11; German, 24-25*n*; early churches, 26

Mackay, Charles, 49
MacMahon, Brian, 154
M'Robert, Patrick, 11
Maine, 22, **42, 51, 104**
Manhattan: becomes New York Co., 7; 19th century, 48-49; borough formed, 57, **58;** 20th century, 131-32, **133;** Negroes, **133,** 140-42; net migration, **137;** Puerto Ricans, 138, **139;** Italians, 167. *See also* New Amsterdam
Manumission Society, 24
Marriages: by religion (1865), 85-86
Married population: in 1875, 74, 76; percent of women (1920), **106**
Maryland: Negroes from, **45, 78, 103-104, 148;** migrants from, **102-103, 148;** migrants to, **149**
Massachusetts: migrants from, 22, **42, 51, 67, 70,** 101, **102-104, 148;** migrants to, **149**
Mennonites, 4, 6. *See also* Anabaptists
Methodists: 11, 28, **86;** first church, 25-26; Negro, 27-28; in Brooklyn, 29-30
Metropolitan area, New York: expands beyond Manhattan, 37, 49, 55; migration to suburbs, 131-32, **147,** 149; population by county (1900-70), **134;** net migration by county and color (1950-70), **137;** Negroes, 140; internal migration, 143-49; problems defining, 169-70. *See also* New York Standard Metropolitan Statistical Area
Mexico (Mexicans), 40, **113, 206**
Mexico City, 33
Miami, Fla., 172
Michielse, Rev. Jonas, 4-5
Middlesex Co., N.J., 135, **170,** 171
Migrant: defined, xiii
Migration: outmigration of New Yorkers, 10, 19-20, 63-66, 166, 171-74; 19th century, 18, 22, 55; intrastate, 47, 63-65, **66;** status, **146-47**
Migration, internal: trends (1900-40), 99-103, **104;** Negro, 117; trends after 1940, 143-49; by state (1940, 60), **148;** outmigrants by destination (1940, 60), **149;** effect of metropolitan area defini-tion, 169*n*. *See also* Net migration;

State of birth
Miller, Rev. John, 10, 12
Milwaukee, Wisc., 91, 110
Minuit, Peter: 20; purchased Manhattan, 2
Monmouth Co., N.J., **170,** 171
Moravians, 11, 25, 26, 28
Moreau de St. Méry, M. L. E., 24, 30
Morrisania (Bronx), 52, 56, **63**
Morris Co., N.J., 135, **170,** 171
Mortality: 111; early statistics, 10, 17; and immigration, 37, 40-41; census statistics, 38; Negroes, 44, 77; trends, 60, 103, 150; by ethnic group, 79-82, 106-108, 111; Catholics, 86-87; and census underenumeration, 89*n*, 110; standardized rates, 106-108; 19th century, by year, **176;** death rates by year, **176, 178;** by race, annually, **179, 181;** by birthplace, annually, **181, 184-85;** Puerto Ricans (1950-69), **185.** *See also* Burial statistics; Natural increase
Mount Vernon, N.Y., 170
Mover: defined, *xi*

Nassau (Germany), 43
Nassau Co., N.Y.: 137, 169; formation, 57-58; growth, 132, **134,** 170; net migration by color (1950-70), **137;** Italians, 167
Native-born population: foreign stock by origin, **74, 76, 115, 118,** 166, third generation, 79, 84, 91-92, 110, 112-15, 159, 162; early American stock, 92, 109; net migration, 98-102, **136;** "generation;; movement, 100-101, 112-15; percent of foreign stock, **101, 162;** fertility of (1920), **106,** 112-13; of mixed parentage, 115-16, **118-20;** defined, 119; by area of birth and color, **144;** Puerto Rican classifica-tion, 161. *See also* State of birth statistics
Native stock. *See* Native-born population
Nativity: population by, **63, 141;** of family heads (1900), **79;** by parentage, **110, 192-94;** in metropolitan counties, **133-34;** of foreign stock by origin, **203-205.** *See also* Native-born population; Foreign-born population
Natural increase: defined, xiv, 17-18; 19th century, 18, 60-63; and Negroes, 77; 20th century, 103-108, 150-51
Negroes: in colony, 5, 11, 12; mortality, 8, 44, 77, 108; in Brooklyn, 12, 50; in early republic, 23-24; churches, 27-28, 30; in Richmond Co., 32; occupations, 44-45; 19th century, 44, **45,** 76-78; fertility, **106,** 150; 20th-century growth, 116-19, 140-42, 174; foreign-born, 117-19,

Negroes, cont'd.
121; Puerto Rican, 119; religion, 123, 130; migration to New York, 132, 135; percent of nonwhites, 138-39; location, 140-42; census deficiency, 145; foreign stock, 167-68. *See also* Nonwhite population; Race distribution; Slaves
Netherlands, 4, 203-206
Net migration: defined, xiv, 93; methods of estimating, 93-96, 97, 99, 135*n*; by country of birth, 95, 97-98; by parentage and age, 99-101, 120-21; after 1940, 131; by race and nativity (1940-70), 135-37; in metropolitan counties (1950-70), 137; of Negroes, 140; measured by previous residence query, 145-46, 172-74. *See also* Immigration; Migration; Native-born population; Foreign-born population
New Amsterdam: population, 2-3; granted municipal government, 3
Newark, N.J., 81, 171
Newark Standard Metropolitan Statistical Area, 171
New England: 3; migrants from, 22-23, 33-35, 42, 50, 51
New England Society, 34-35
New Hampshire, 42, 51
New Haven, Conn., 171
New Jersey: 5, 55; Dutch growth, 19; migrants from, 23, 42, 46, 51, 67, 70, 101, 102-104, 146, 148; Negroes from, 45, 78, 103, 148; early commuting, 49, 59; migrants to, 65-66, 149, 173; suburbanization, 135, 149, 169, 170-71; excluded from New York SMSA, 170*n*; problems of migration statistics, 172-73. *See also* specific counties
New Lots (Brooklyn), 31, 51, 59
New Netherland: 6; early colonists, 2-3; ceded to England, 3
New Netherland, 2
New Rochelle (Westchester Co.), 170
Newtown (Queens): 51, 57, 59, 60; early settlement, 6
New Utrecht (Brooklyn), 12, 31, 51, 59
New York, colony of: counties formed, 7; population growth, 9, 13
New York Co.: formed in 1683, 7; 18th-century population, 7-8; compared with Kings Co., 12; consolidation, 57, 58. *See also* Manhattan
New York Metropolitan Region, 169
New York Standard Metropolitan Statistical Area (SMSA): population by area of birth (1960), 144; migration status (1960), 147; Italians in, 167; defined, 169, 170*n*. *See also* Metropolitan area, New York
New York State: early growth, 16; natives in New York City, 42, 50, 51, 67, 70,

102-103, 144; nonwhite natives in city, 45, 78, 103, 144; population by county of birth and residence, 65-66; intrastate migrants, 149; Cubans, 164; immigrant Negroes, 168; natives outside state, 173-74
Nicholls, Richard, 3
Nonintercourse Act, 18
Nonwhite population: by state of birth, 45, 78, 103-104, 144; by nativity, parentage, 72, 78, 110, 141; net migration, 135-37; percent Negro, 138-39; census error (1970), 139*n*; internal migration (1940, 60), 148; birth rates, 152-53; by religion (1952), 153; foreign stock, 168, 206. *See also* Race distribution; specific races
North Carolina: Negroes from, 77, 78, 103-104, 117, 146, 148; migrants from, 102-103; migrants to, 149
Northern Ireland, 163
North Hempstead (Long Island), 57
Norwalk, Conn., 171
Norway (Norwegians), 67, 70, 202-206. *See also* Scandinavia

Oakland, Calif., 172
Odessa Pogrom, 69
Ohio: migrants from, 102-104, 148; migrants to, 149
Orange Co., N.Y., 64, 65-66
Oyster Bay (Long Island), 57

Palatines, 20
Palestine, 204
Panama, 168
Parentage. *See* Foreign stock
Passaic Co., N.J., 66, 170, 172-73
Paterson, N.J., 171
Pelham (Bronx), 57
Pennsylvania: population comparison, 16; Germans, 20; Negroes from, 45, 78, 103, 148; migrants from, 42, 46, 51, 67, 70, 101, 102-104, 146, 148; migrants to, 149
Philadelphia: 1, 7, 33, 57, 91, 172; population comparison, 16; Germans, 20; aliens, 35
Philippines (Filipinos), 102-103, 139, 168
Pintard, John, 17
Pittsburgh, 172
Poland (Polish): 166; number of, 67, 69, 115, 118, 202, 204-206; census classification, 69, 96-97, 163; in Brooklyn, 70; family heads, 79, 113; mortality, 82, 184-85; Jews, 84, 93, 127-28, 158, 159; migration, 93-98 *passim;* age, 163, 195-96; births, 182-83
Portugal (Portuguese), 5, 23
Poverty: among immigrants, 21; and mortality, 82

Presbyterians: 11, 27-28, **86;** in colony, 6, 9-10; early churches, 24-25; in Brooklyn, 29-30

Protestants: **53,** 62; French, 25; in Brooklyn, **53,** 54, 87; population estimates, 86, 122-27 *passim,* 130, 152, 154; by ethnic group, 123-24, **125;** deaths by origin, **126,** 154-55, **156-57;** by color (1952), **153;** by age (1950), **155.** *See also* specific denominations

Providence, R.I., 109

Prussia, 43, 69

Puerto Rico (Puerto Ricans): growth, 102, 174; by color, **103,** 119, **197;** census classification, 119, 135, 139-40, 161; migration to U.S., 120-21; settlement in New York, 132, 135, 138; net migration (1940-60), **136;** by borough, 138, **139;** fertility, 150-51, **152-53;** religion, **157;** deaths, **157,** 185; births, **183, 185;** by age and sex, **197-98**

Puritans: in Dutch settlements, 4, 6; in colony, 9-10. *See also* Independents

Putnam Co., N.Y., **170,** 171

Quakers: 11, 24, 28; in colony, 9-10; freed slaves, 24; early churches, 26; decline, 27

Queens Co.: colonial period, 7, 12; 19th-century growth, 51, **58,** 59-60, **65-66;** becomes borough, 57-58; 20th-century growth, 131, 132, **133;** Negroes, **133,** 142; net migration, **137;** Puerto Ricans, **139;** Italians, 167

Race: fertility by (1920), **106;** mortality by (1920), **108;** children per family by (1930), **113;** net migration by (1950-70), **137**

Race distribution: in colonial censuses, **8;** 19th-century censuses, 18, **36,** 77; in Kings, Richmond Cos., **32,** 77; of family heads (1900), **79;** by nativity and parentage (1890-1900), **110;** by religion (1935), **125;** in metropolitan counties (1900-70), **133,** 134; by nativity (1900-70), **141;** by migration status (1940), **146,** 147; of outmigrants, **149;** by age and sex (1910-70), **188-91.** *See also* Non-white population

Race relations, 12

Ravenswood (Queens), 60

Religious groups: marriages (1865), **86;** estimates by Laidlaw, 122-23; Welfare Council Survey, 123-24; by country of origin, **123, 125;** estimates from death statistics, 124-29; by color, **125, 153;** deaths by, **126, 156-57;** distribution (1952), 151-52; by age (1950), **155.** *See also* Churches; specific denominations

Revolutionary War: 1, 20; effect on New York, 14-15

Rhode Island, 22, **42, 51, 104**

Richmond Co.: in colonial period, 6-7, 12; slavery in, 32; 19th century, 32, 51, 59-60, 64, **65-66, 77;** becomes borough, 57, **58;** 20th century, 131-32, **133;** net migration, **137;** Puerto Ricans, 139; Italians, **167.** *See also* Staten Island

Rockland Co., N.Y.: **65, 167;** commuters, 59, 169-70; growth, **134,** 170; net migration, **137**

Romania: **95, 97, 115, 203-205;** Jews from, 111, **123,** 124, **125**

Russia (Russians): **166;** number of, 67, **73-74, 76, 115, 118, 202-206;** migration, 68-69, 73, 94-98 *passim;* in Brooklyn, 70; family heads, **79, 113;** mortality, **80,** 82, 107, **184-85;** Jews, 84, 111, 127-28, 158, **159,** 163; share of U.S. in New York, 92; census problems, 96-97, 163; religion, 122-26 *passim,* 154, **156;** births, **182-83;** age, **195-96**

Sabbatarians, 9

St. Christopher (St. Kitts), 7

St. Louis, Mo., 172

St. Méry, Moreau de. *See* Moreau de St. Méry

St. Nicholas Society, 35

San Francisco, Calif., 142, 172

San Juan, Puerto Rico, 138

Santo Domingo, 22

Saxe-Weimar-Eisenach, Karl Bernhard, duke of, 19

Scandinavia (Scandinavians), **73-74, 79-80,** 95, 97, **113,** 115, 118, **125-26,** 137, 154, **156, 184-85, 195-96.** *See also* Denmark; Norway; Sweden

Scotland (Scottish): 7, 21, 23, 34, 41, **42, 123, 182;** in Brooklyn, 30, **51**

Seidman, Herbert, 154, 155

Selyns, Rev. Henricus, 5-6

Sex distribution: by race and age, **188-91;** by age, nativity, and parentage, **192-94;** of Puerto Ricans, by age, **197-98;** of non-Puerto Rican whites, by age, **199**

Shearith Israel (Jewish congregation), 26

Slaves (slavery): brought into colony, 5, 11; number of, 9, 18; in Kings County, 12, 29, 31; number of families owning, 23; gradual emancipation, 23-24, 29; in Richmond Co., 32

Slovaks, 110

SMSA. *See* New York Standard Metropolitan Statistical Area

Smyth, J. F. D., 29

Somerset Co., N.J., *170*

South America, 40

South Carolina: Negroes from, 77, **78, 103-104,** 117, 146, **148;** migrants from,

South Carolina, cont'd.
  102-103
Spain (Spaniards), 23, **203-205**
Stamford, Conn., 171
Staten Island: early settlement, 6; becomes
  Richmond Co., 7
State of birth statistics: **42, 67, 102;** for
  nonwhites, **45, 78;** use of, 46, 143; for
  Brooklyn, **51, 70;** race distribution,
  103-104. *See also* Native-born population;
  Nativity
Stiles, Ezra, 26
Stuyvesant, Peter, 3-5
Suburbanization: in 20th century, 131-32,
  145, 152, 168-71, 174; net migration,
  135. *See also* Commuters; Metropolitan
  area
Suffolk Co., N.Y.: **59, 65-66,** 137, 169;
  formation, 7; growth, 132, **134,** 170; net
  migration, **137;** Italians, **167**
Sweden (Swedes), 23, **67, 70, 123,** 164
  203-206. *See also* Scandinavia
Switzerland, **67, 70, 118, 202-206**
Syria, **204**

Texas, **149**
Trade: colonial importance, 6-7; setbacks,
  18; growth of, 19; and New Englanders,
  33-34
Treaty of Ghent, 18
Trinidad and Tobago, 140
Turkey, **203-205**

Ulster (Ireland), 11
Union Co., N.J., **66, 170,** 171
Unitarians, 28, **86**
United Kingdom, *See* Britain
United States: fertility, **62, 153;** percent of
  foreign groups in New York, **79, 93-94;**
  family heads by parentage (1900), **90;**
  Puerto Rican born, **121;** Negro immi-
  grants, **121,** 168

Universalists, 28, **86**

van Wassenaer, Nicolaes, 2
Vermont, **42, 51**
Virginia: migrants from, 3, **67, 70, 102-103,**
  148; Negroes from, **45,** 77, 78, **103-104,**
  117, 140, 146, **148;** migrants to, **149**
Virgin Islands, **102,** 119-20

Wakefield (Bronx), 57
Wales, 41
Walloons, 2, 4
War of 1812, 14, 18
Washington, D.C., 172, 174
Waterbury, Conn., 171
Westchester Co., N.Y.: colonial period,
  6-7, 12; prior to Civil War, 52; cedes
  territory, 56-57, **58;** commuters, 59,
  169-70; intrastate migration, 64, **65-66;**
  20th-century growth, **134;** net migration,
  137; Italians, **167**
West Farms (Bronx), 52, 56, **63**
West Indies (West Indians): 7, 21, 23;
  Negroes, **45,** 117-19, 140, 167, **168**
Williamsbridge (Bronx), 57
Williamsburg (Brooklyn): **31,** 37, 83;
  annexed by Brooklyn, 50
Wurttemberg, Germany, 43

Yankees, 22, 33
Yasuba, Yasukichi, 61
Yiddish mother tongue: 110-11; compared
  with Jews, by age, 128-30
Yonkers (Westchester Co.), 170
York, James, duke of, 3
Yorkville (Manhattan), 84
Yugoslavia, 163, 164, **204-206**

Zelnik, Melvin, 61, 104
Zenger, John Peter, 20